MW00833937

Palgrave Macmillan's
Content and Context in Theological Ethics

Content and Context in Theological Ethics offers ethics done from theological and religious perspectives rooted in the particular contexts and lived experience of real people in history, in the present, and looking with hope toward the future. The series raises the contexts or cultures out of which an increasing number of scholars do their thinking and research regarding the influence of those contexts on the content of ethics and how that content has been applied historically, traditionally, and/or subversively by members of the context or community or culture under scrutiny or raised as paradigmatic or as a novel or passing fad. The series explores normative claims about right and wrong, human flourishing or failing, virtues and vices—the fundamental bases and questions of ethics—within the context, culture, or community identified and in correlation with norms inherited from or imposed by colonizing/dominant forces or ideologies while recognizing new voices and/or new understandings of theologically and/or religiously inspired concerns in response to knowledge uncovered by other disciplines that impact ethical reflection on the content explored.

Series Editor:

MARY JO IOZZIO, active in the American Academy of Religion, Catholic Theological Society of America, Catholic Theological Ethicists in the World Church, Pax Christi USA, and the Society of Christian Ethics, is Professor of Moral Theology at Boston College School of Theology and Ministry, USA, and co-editor of the *Journal of the Society of Christian Ethics*.

Justice and Peace in a Renewed Caribbean: Contemporary Catholic Reflections
Edited by Anna Kasafi Perkins, Donald Chambers, and Jacqueline Porter

Theology in the Age of Global AIDS and HIV: Complicity and Possibility
By Cassie J. E. H. Trentaz

Constructing Solidarity for a Liberative Ethic: Anti-Racism, Action, and Justice
By Tammerie Day

Religious Ethics in a Time of Globalism: Shaping a Third Wave of Comparative Analysis
Edited by Elizabeth M. Bucar and Aaron Stalnaker

The Scandal of White Complicity and U.S. Incarceration: A Nonviolent Spirituality of White Resistance
By Alex Mikulich, Laurie Cassidy, and Margaret Pfeil with a foreword written by S. Helen Prejean CSJ

Spirituality in Dark Places: The Ethics of Solitary Confinement
By Derek S. Jeffreys

TOWARD A THEOLOGY OF MIGRATION
SOCIAL JUSTICE AND RELIGIOUS EXPERIENCE

Gemma Tulud Cruz

First published in 2014 by
PALGRAVE MACMILLAN®
in the United States—a division of St. Martin's Press LLC,
175 Fifth Avenue, New York, NY 10010.

Where this book is distributed in the UK, Europe and the rest of the
World, this is by Palgrave Macmillan, a division of Macmillan Publishers
Limited, registered in England, company number 785998, of
Houndmills, Basingstoke, Hampshire RG21 6XS.

Palgrave Macmillan is the global academic imprint of the above
companies and has companies and representatives throughout the world.

Palgrave® and Macmillan® are registered trademarks in the United
States, the United Kingdom, Europe and other countries.

ISBN: 978–1–137–40076–5

Library of Congress Cataloging-in-Publication Data

Cruz, Gemma Tulud, 1970–
    Toward a theology of migration : social justice and religious
    experience / Gemma Tulud Cruz.
        pages   cm. — (Content and context in theological ethics)
    Includes bibliographical references.
    ISBN 978–1–137–40076–5 (hardback : alk. paper)
    1. Emigration and immigration—Religious aspects—Christianity.
    2. Social justice—Religious aspects—Christianity.
    3. Globalization—Religious aspects—Christianity.
    4. Catholic Church—Doctrines.   I. Title.
    BV639.I4C78 2014
    261.8′36—dc23   2013038316

A catalogue record of the book is available from the British Library.

Design by Integra Software Services

First edition: March 2014

10 9 8 7 6 5 4 3 2 1

To my husband,
Edmund Kee Fook Chia

CONTENTS

FOREWORD

One of the most striking signs of contemporary globalization is worldwide migration. Proponents of globalization describe it as the free flow of capital, goods, and knowledge. They typically mention the flow of people as well, but often do not note that this flow is not like the others. The flow of people in migration—now estimated to be 1 out of every 35 people on the planet—faces all kinds of restrictions. Migrants do not enter other countries freely. Once in the new country, their rights are often not acknowledged or protected. Only a small number of sending countries engage in any kind of advocacy for their citizens who are migrants.

A great deal is being written about migration. An important segment of the literature grapples with national and international policy regarding migrants, regarding their status and treatment in host countries, the impact of remittances migrants make back to their families in their home countries, and judging the economic and social impact of their labor on national economies. Another segment has been concerned with the migration of elite professional and academic personnel, and the need to provide easy movement of these people for the sake of utilizing their specialized knowledge in areas of science and of research and development. A smaller portion of the literature addresses the plight of the unskilled or semi-skilled migrant in the midst of the larger macro-forces of globalization.

This book by Gemma Tulud Cruz is an important contribution to understanding this latter group, who constitute the majority of today's migrants. She addresses the experience of these migrants as they leave their home countries, struggle to make a living in their home countries, and find themselves caught between two lands. Within that experience she focuses upon their religious experience. Religion is a component of migrant experience that is often overlooked in migration studies, due to secular bias in the academic settings of the investigators. Such a bias views religion as a private matter that should not impinge upon public discourse. If religion does so, it becomes a nuisance or a genuine problem. But it is the religious sensibilities of migrants that often sustain them in their travails as migrants. Common religious practices also form an important social glue that helps migrants build a sense of community and belonging in the midst of an environment too often hostile to them.

Findings from the Pew Research Center indicate that the majority of today's migrants are Christian and women. Religion is often not taken into consideration in the literature; the gender question often also gets passed over. Cruz does us a double favor by focusing on the religious experience of Christian migrants and on the experience of women. Her religious focus is on Christians in general, and Roman Catholics (who make up slightly more than half of all Christians) in particular. And her focus on the female face of migration is perhaps the very first book to do so from a global perspective.

At another level, this book combines insights into the personal experience of migrants and questions of religion and gender into what is the first book on the theological significance of worldwide migration. Studies have been done on specific groups or areas of the world, but this book reaches beyond those confines. In doing so, Cruz not only explores the lives of individual migrants, and the role that religion plays in sustaining them in the arduous life of a migrant, but also questions what these experiences mean for a worldwide institution such as the Roman Catholic Church. What does the experience of such massive migration mean for this Church's understanding of itself and its mission in the world? This has been an understudied area in the extensive body of Catholic Social Teaching, and Cruz's book makes a significant contribution to the necessary next steps that need to be taken to include this important matter into the teaching and ministry of the Church. A more comprehensive vision of the phenomenon of migration with these insights will aid developing and enforcing clearer policies on the rights of immigrants and the responsibilities of both the host and sending countries. It will also provide elements of the groundwork for a more adequate understanding of a multicultural society.

Although there is a certain ebb and flow in migration that matches expansion and contraction of economic cycles, migration on a significant scale will continue to be a phenomenon with which we must grapple in the coming decades. So long as there is poverty and income inequality, so long as some countries cannot provide adequate and secure standards of living for their citizens, and so long as demographic patterns shift and reshuffle in different parts of the world, migration will be with us. The relative ease of travel not present in earlier times ensures the continuing movement of peoples. Added to all the economic push-and-all factors currently experienced in migration, the looming consequences of climate change are also already being felt in migratory patterns. Extreme weather conditions and rising sea levels will likely ignite stronger waves of migration than we have seen to this point. Gemma Tulud Cruz's important book will stand as a landmark in an important region of this map of human movement and dislocation: it probes the deeply spiritual dimensions of the migration experience, and especially that of women, who make up a majority of the world's migrants. These two dimensions will be important for understanding the needs and aspirations of migrants today, and also the challenges of those institutions who try to support them in their quest for a more humane standard of living for themselves and their families.

Robert Schreiter
Catholic Theological Union, Chicago

Introduction: Migration as a Locus for Theological Reflection

Mobility is as old as the human species. In fact, it is regarded as an engine of human history. Borders have been redrawn; people's stories have been rewritten; and identities and subjectivities have been transformed because individuals, groups, or masses of people took the risk to cross borders by either land, sea, or air. But mobility, particularly in its contemporary phases and faces, comes with considerable challenges. There is, for instance, the matter of density. At no other point in history has the number of people on the move been at such a large scale that the current period is being referred to as the age of migration.[1] To be sure, this claim is not without merit. The International Organization for Migration's (IOM) World Migration Report, for instance, says that the number of people living outside their country of origin dramatically increased from 150 million in 2000—when IOM published its first World Migration Report—to more than 214 million in 2010. That's an increase of 64 million in a matter of ten years. Moreover, the IOM reports that the figure could rise to as much as 405 million by 2050.[2] Today, about 3 percent of the world's population comprises of migrants. While the percentage may seem miniscule, it actually represents a lot of people. In fact, if all migrants in the world were to come together to constitute a country, theirs would be the world's fifth most populous.

But who are these people who are on the move across borders? Where do they come from? What are their motivations, what are their reasons? What forces compel them to leave their homeland and move to foreign lands? Perhaps it would be best to begin with some kind of definition or description of different types of international migrants to have a kind of framework to stand on.

The United Nations (UN) defines *migrants*—the term generally used in this book[3]—as persons residing outside their country of origin.[4] Migrants are generally classified in two ways. First, they are categorized as either *sojourners/ temporary migrants*, those who move briefly to visit, study, or work in another country, for example, international students, scholars, and contract workers,[5] or *emigrants/ immigrants* or *permanent migrants*,[6] those who leave one's country or region permanently to relocate or settle in another. Second, they are labeled as either *forced migrants*, those who have been driven from home by wars, persecutions, and natural calamities, or *voluntary migrants*, those who move independently or on their own accord, for example, migrant workers and brides or family members of immigrants. It must be noted here, however, that the terms "forced" and "voluntary" reflect more of a continuum in motivations rather than clear distinctions.

Moreover, there are specific types of migrants under the forced and voluntary migrants category. Under forced migrants, for instance, are the *refugees*. Refugees are defined by the 1951 UN Convention Relating to the Status of Refugees as persons who have had to flee across an international border because of well-founded fear of being persecuted for reasons of race, religion, nationality, membership in a particular social group, or political opinion. This definition was then expanded in the convention's 1967 Protocol to include persons who had fled war or other violence in their home country. Refugees are also often called *displaced persons*.[7] Until a request for refuge has been accepted, displaced persons who move across international borders are referred to as *asylum seekers*. It is only after the recognition of their need for protection that they are officially referred to as refugees and enjoy refugee status, which carries certain rights and obligations according to the laws of the receiving country.[8] In recent times due to severe environmental problems and hardships brought in large part by global warming, a new group of refugees, *environmental refugees*, has also emerged in the global migration landscape. New Zealand, for example, is now home to a number of people who have fled their homes in the small island country of Kiribati, which is slowly being swallowed by rising sea levels attributed to global warming. The UN even warns that rising sea levels, desertification, and shrinking freshwater supplies will create up to 50 million environmental refugees by the end of the decade.[9] Then there are the 800,000 to 2 million people who are victims of human trafficking each year, a phenomenon that activists consider as the most pernicious human rights scourge created by globalization.[10] *Trafficked persons* could also be seen as forced migrants, particularly those who fall prey to or become victims in the illegal human trade that coerces people into commercial sexual exploitation, drug trafficking, forced marriage, domestic work, and other forms of forced labor,[11] making this contemporary illegal trade in human beings a modern-day form of slavery.

The majority of modern-day migrants, however, fall under the voluntary migrants category. Moreover, these people who move on their own under less problematic conditions are either *cultural migrants*, for example, international students or scholars on cultural exchange; *family (re)unification migrants*, for example, spouses and family members petitioned by their loved ones; or *economic migrants*, who constitute the vast majority of migrants globally. Understandably, migrant workers are the most dominant face of economic migrants. In migration history, particularly in the West, there have been various types of migrant workers. There is the *guest worker*, who comes under a temporary permit system aimed at the importation of temporary contract laborers. France and Germany ran such programs in the 1960s and 1970s importing laborers largely from Algeria and Turkey, respectively.[12] The *bracero* program, which ran in the 1940s–1960s and involved Mexican workers, is the American equivalent of the guest worker system. Visas were renewable, but the workers were not given permanent residence rights.[13] In the United States the guest worker has made a comeback, albeit mostly in agricultural work and on a shorter visa, through the H2A visa or the agricultural worker visa. This visa allows American employers to hire foreign workers for temporary or seasonal jobs, specifically for no longer than one year. Technically, these guest workers fall under the category of unskilled workers together with the army of domestic workers, construction workers, factory workers, hospitality workers, and workers in the garment, agriculture, and fishing industry who make up the bulk of unskilled migrant workers today. Then there are the *skilled workers* or *STEP OUT migrants*, as Michelle R. Pistone and John J. Hoeffner prefer to call them in *Stepping Out of the Brain Drain: Applying Catholic Social Teaching in a New Era of Migration*.[14] These are highly educated professionals, for example, nurses, doctors, engineers, scientists, and communication technology experts who are highly sought for their expertise (and, in certain cases, for their willingness to take a lower pay compared to their local counterparts) and are usually given permanent residence rights as well as possibilities for citizenship and family reunification. Last but not the least are the businesswo/men or rich *entrepreneurs* whose considerable financial resources make it much easier and quicker for them to get not just a visa but also permanent residency and, eventually, citizenship.

THE PROMISE AND PERILS OF CONTEMPORARY MOBILITY: MIGRATION AS A LOCUS FOR THEOLOGICAL REFLECTION

Clearly migrants are people in search of a better life for themselves and their families. This liberative quest is the enduring theme of wave after wave, generation after generation of migrants worldwide. And because it is the world's poor that is mainly on the move, or at least desperate to move, in many cases migration is actually rooted in the search for the bare necessities of life: food on the table,[15] a decent roof over one's head, education for the children or the siblings (sometimes even nephews and nieces), and, if they are lucky, a house or a more comfortable life for the migrant's aging parents. Not surprisingly, there are many ways in which contemporary migration offers both hope and promise not just for migrants themselves but also for the millions whose lives are touched by migration. A brief look at some of these ways, most of which will be elaborated in the chapters of the book, should be useful here.

First, migrants are increasingly becoming a form of social capital. Take the case of remittances. Though they are not a cure-all, recent studies on migrants' remittances have pointed out that it helps ease poverty in countries of origin. In fact, a special report on migration in *The Economist* argues that for many poor countries, remittances provide more than aid and foreign direct investment combined. Close to 50 percent of Guinea-Bissau's GDP, for example, comes from remittances. Eritrea and Haiti, in the meantime, relies on remittances for 38 percent and 21 percent of their GDP, respectively.[16] A study commissioned by the World Bank is more explicit on the difference remittances make:

Remittances raise the incomes of migrant households and increase the recipient country's foreign exchange reserves. At the household level, the literature suggests that remittance income helps meet a variety of family needs, such as increased consumption—of food, housing, and durable items—and increased investment—in business, microenterprise, education, and financial enterprises. Through these means remittances support a wide variety of development purposes: improving family welfare, reducing economic vulnerability, and boosting the local economy, while increasing the use of formal banking services by the poor. If remittances are invested in productive activities such as local business and the education of young children, they can contribute to output growth and generate positive multiplier effects.[17]

Contemporary migrants also offer hope in the way they revitalize and enrich the cultural and religious landscapes of countries of destination as they bring and continue to observe their rich cultural and religious traditions. Away from their home country and in search of company, familiarity, acceptance, and intimacy, religion becomes, for migrants, a deep and enduring source not only in expressing and holding on to their cultural identity but also in making sense of and dealing with the (dis)continuities and (dis)empowerment that are brought by migration. Consequently, the rich religio-cultural gifts they offer, the economic and political challenges they encounter, as well as the way their social and religious transnational networks play a vital role in their struggle provide a way of re-imagining Christian identity and mission.

And yet contemporary migration also constitutes a wound of our time. To be sure, many migrants are victims of injustice before, during, and after migration. First and foremost, the majority of the world's migrants and would-be-migrants come from developing countries that suffer not just from the uneven distribution of the world's wealth and resources but also from regional and global economic policies that burden or further disadvantage these countries. An example related to this, in the case of the United States, is the North American Free Trade Agreement (NAFTA), which has displaced and disillusioned small Mexican farmers forcing them to either make their way into Mexico City, where they do bit jobs, or cross illegally into the United States to find work.[18] Migrants are victims, as well, of the injustice not just between and across countries but also within their own countries, particularly in the hands of their governments who not only cannot provide them with jobs but, as seen in the case of Mexico, cannot protect their livelihood either. When they migrate, migrants also experience exploitation not just in the hands of their governments, who create a migration industry that turns migrants into primary exports and commodities or cash cows for their remittances, but also in the hands of various local and transnational vultures from exploitative recruiters, *coyotes*,[19] and abusive employers to multinational companies, banks, and agencies who prey on their (migrants') vulnerability. Worst, border crossing has become not only difficult but downright dangerous. This is particularly true in the case of the southern border of the United States, where the combination of a militarized border, the harshness of the desert, abandonment by human traffickers or smugglers, and the threat of running into vigilante groups has exacerbated the perils of border-crossing resulting into numerous tragic deaths.

Those who actually get into the United States without proper documentation, in the meantime, still has the threat of deportation constantly hanging over their head, especially since the Obama administration—under political pressure to keep out undocumented immigrants—has toughened its position on deportation. In 2012 alone the Obama administration deported at least 400,000 irregular immigrants, which is a new record.[20] The condition in detention centers, where undocumented migrants usually spend some time, also ought to be mentioned here, especially in view of detention centers that do not provide good conditions for women and/or for their babies or children.[21]

Even when migrants do get inside the country legally, there are still a host of problems that they face disproportionately. They could suffer, for instance, from inequities in the educational or health care system. Health care providers unfamiliar with the migrants' languages and cultures and the pressures migrants face may minimize or misunderstand their symptoms. For women there could be an added gender dimension to these inequities, especially for those who may be dependent on male family members for access to health care.

Unfortunately, migrants experience unfair treatment not only at the level of governments or in schools, hospitals, streets, and other public places but also to a certain extent even in churches or places of worship. In some cases they encounter resistance, especially if they do not share in the country's (or community's) dominant religion. John Allen writes, for instance, how retired Cardinal Biffi of Italy issued a pastoral letter that suggested that the Italian government should give preferential treatment to immigrants from traditionally Catholic nations in order to defend Italy's Catholic identity, calling the increases in immigration from non-Catholic cultures "one of the most serious and biggest assaults on Christianity that history remembers."[22] Aside from this problem that stems from differences *across* religious traditions, there is also the problem rooted in differences *within* religious traditions. Within Christian communities, for instance, immigrant and local congregations experience conflicts because of racial and ethnic differences in religious practice as well as differences due to socioeconomic class.

It is precisely this double-edged face of contemporary migration that makes it an important locus for theological reflection. Migration's current density, velocity, multidirectionality, and most especially, complexity offer us insights not just into human geography but also into the human condition. To be sure, its roots and tentacles of misery and injustice make it in the words of the Vatican II document *Gaudium et Spes*,[23] a "grief and anguish of people of our time" (GS, no. 1).[24] Moreover, immigration itself, according to sociologist Timothy Smith, is a "theologizing experience"[25] since immigrants often make sense of the alienation that is inherent in migration in religious terms. This makes migration not only a sociological fact but also a theological event.

Migrants are, first and foremost, human beings. This fundamental idea, in itself, carves out a space for theological reflections on the plight of people on the move. This is particularly true for theologies whose primary purpose is to deal with historical reality. "To do theology means, in part, to face reality and raise it to a theological concept. In this task theology should be honest with the real."[26] Anselm Min drives this home in the context of migration by drawing attention to the fact that theology is a reflection on the transcendent significance of all aspects of human experience, but especially of those aspects in which human dignity and solidarity are at stake.[27]

In reality migration has only recently engaged the attention of theology.[28] It is clear, however, that it needs more serious theological attention and consideration.[29] This is because migration is not only rearranging human geography and redefining cultures and religions, but also reshaping identities and subjectivities. It is not only bringing new forms of oppression, but also creating other paths to human survival and liberation. This dialectic between oppression and survival toward liberation provides gifts and challenges for theology on many fronts, making migration a valuable place in articulating contemporary forms of understanding and forging relationship with the sacred.

* * *

ABOUT THIS BOOK

This book offers a theological reflection on global migration and hopes to serve as a contribution to the growing, yet still very sparse, literature on theology and migration. While the book is generally from a Christian perspective the Catholic tradition significantly informs it. It is global in terms of the context it engages, albeit with a generous dose of the American experience. The book relies on interdisciplinary document research conducted over a period of years in the United States, where the author has lived and worked for several years, and other countries. To a certain extent, the book also draws from observations and notes from encounters and informal interviews with migrants from the author's travels to more than 20 countries as well as from attendance in private and public events organized by different types of migrants and groups working for/with migrants in various parts of the world from Tamil Indian refugees in Sri Lanka to Filipina brides in Australia, Indonesian women domestic workers in Hong Kong, Caribbean migrants in the Netherlands and immigrants in the US. Most importantly, this book is based on analyses of documents, especially books, journals, conference proceedings, as well as websites, newspaper and newsmagazines, documentaries, case files, pamphlets, newsletters, flyers and other documents on migrants and migration.

The book offers a theology of migration by exploring key aspects of the human and religious experience of migrants. Accordingly, this book is divided into two parts, each of which includes three chapters. The first part, Migration and Social Justice, includes chapters 1, 2, and 3 and engages the human dimension, particularly the social justice question, of contemporary migration in relation to the experience of unskilled migrant workers, migrant women, and the ensuing challenge for reform of migration policies. Chapter 1 sets the stage by bringing into focus the historical and multi-faceted entanglements between migration and globalization. It puts the spotlight on the inequities of global migration, particularly as seen from the experience of unskilled workers, as well as its positive aspects. It submits that, theologically, such conditions highlight migration's linkages with humanity's (and, for that matter, Christianity's) quest and evolution into a better version of itself. Thus, the chapter draws attention to the links between migration and salvation, the challenges that the stranger and the border pose to theology, and the need for a globalization with a human face.

Chapter 2 gives a face to another group who deeply experiences migration as both promise and peril. More specifically, the chapter tackles the plight of migrant women by interrogating the gendered aspects of migration. The chapter shows how such gendering could be seen in migrant women's experiences of gendered migration, gendered transitions, and gendered violence which, the chapter argues, has roots in a global political economy of gender that marginalizes women. The chapter then discusses how a woman-friendly global economy and re-imagining the nature of women and the family constitutes a primary challenge for a theology of migration.

In view of what has been laid out in chapters 1 and 2, Chapter 3 proposes an ethical roadmap for reform of migration policies and approaches. More specifically, this chapter explores the possible contribution of modern Catholic Social Teaching or CST toward a more appropriate or ethical treatment of people on the move, by examining key themes in the CST that could address critical issues in the current debate on migration reform. At the same time the chapter points to the need for a more adequate consideration and integration of women's experience and perspective as a weakness of CST. The chapter then concludes that an ethic of risk which, the author submits, runs through the key themes of CST could serve as an approach in articulating how Christian discipleship could foreground citizenship in the context of migration policy reform.

The second part, Migration and Religious Experience, includes chapters 4, 5, and 6 and scrutinizes the key aspects of the religious experience of migrants. Chapter 4 puts the spotlight on the role and characteristics of religion (especially Christianity) and mission in the context of migration. The chapter contends that, while beset with challenges, migrant religion and religious practice are also a source of much hope not just for migrants but also for the faith communities in their destination countries. The chapter then reflects on Christian theology's need to articulate a broader theology of religions, a Church that is home for the stranger, and an understanding as well as practice of mission that is rooted in incarnational evangelization.

Chapter 5, meanwhile, builds and expands on the previous chapter by examining more deeply the role of culture(s) not only in the (dis)continuities and transformations in the religious practices of migrants but also in the revitalization of religious faith in churches in destination countries. More specifically, the chapter scrutinizes inculturation in the context of migration by mapping out the ways in which migrants' faith is expressed or integrated in migrant congregations or churches, particularly in the liturgy and in popular piety. At the same time, it discusses issues that pose problems and prospects for doing inculturation in the context of migration, hence need further attention or consideration. The chapter then ends with the conclusion that inculturation in the context of migration not only bring some kind of *ecclesiogenesis* to faith communities in destination countries but also pathways toward building an intercultural church.

Last but not the least, Chapter 6 delves into the area of spirituality as it plays out in the lives of migrants. It examines migrants' sources of inspiration or orientations in life, especially the practices, deepest values, and meanings with Christian undertones or underpinnings that migrants cultivate as they navigate the challenges that contemporary migration entails. In particular, the chapter probes how courageous hope, creative resistance, steadfast faith, and festive community spirit is lived by migrants, and reflects on what these values and practices could teach us about Christian spirituality. The book then ends with a brief conclusion.

PART I

MIGRATION AND SOCIAL JUSTICE

CHAPTER 1

Living on the Edge: Migration, Globalization, and the Unskilled Worker

As a social phenomenon, globalization has primarily been associated with the flexibility and extension of the forms of production; the denationalizing and rapid mobility of capital, information, and goods; the deterritorialization of culture; the interpenetration of local communities by global media networks; and the dispersal of socioeconomic power. One can deduce from such a description that the shrinking of spaces is a distinguishing feature of globalization, especially given the fact that, as a concept, it has to do with both the compression of the world and the intensification of the consciousness of the world as a whole.

While globalization as a term emerged fairly recently when the world economy rapidly evolved new forms of integration and independence, globalization structures are not new. Roland Robertson, for instance, maintains that patterns that connect the world have appeared from time to time throughout history and that these patterns have almost always resulted from or resulted to a wide-scale movement of people.[1] In fact, I submit that nowhere is globalization's strongest impetus and effects most illustrated than in the ability of a huge number of people today to move from place to place at an increasingly faster pace.

Migration and Globalization: Historical Perspectives

Migration's relationship with globalization goes way back in history. It dates back to the 1500s, when Europe expanded by colonizing and causing large intercontinental movements of people.[2] These movements involved peoples of three continents and existed in two separate circuits, namely the tropical and nontropical circuit. Up to 61 million Europeans moved to the settlement colonies to search for better living conditions and to enable some parts of Europe to avoid serious overpopulation. This group then fueled migration by going back and forth between the colonies and their countries of origin. Moreover, this period involved the movement not only of millions of European colonizers but also of the colonized peoples.[3] About 11 million Africans were forcibly removed from Africa in order to work in overseas plantations and mines. Roughly 1.3 million Indians and Chinese, also known as Asian "coolies," in the meantime, were placed on indentured labor in plantations in Asia, Africa, and the Caribbean.

European colonization also triggered the mass migration of another group of colonizers, that is, those who colonized the soul of the natives. To be sure, European culture and religion was subtly, if not forcibly, imposed on the colonies. Among Filipinos, as was the case among Latin Americans colonized by Spain, sixteenth-century Spanish Catholicism is the icon of this means of colonial subjugation. As such, one cannot discount here the Christian missionaries who also came in waves with the merchant and battle ships. These missionaries played a crucial role not just in the religious conversion but also in the political pacification and, consequently, easier subjugation of the natives.

This combination of voluntary and involuntary migration went on for more than four centuries. As a result, over 1 million people a year, or about 10 percent of the world's population, moved or were transported to the "new world" by the turn of the twentieth century. What is also clear is that, as with the current process of globalization, international trade significantly expanded in this period.[4] In fact, the migratory paths and patterns followed throughout this period established well-worn routes still traveled today by peoples and goods.

After the collapse of the European colonial empires and the creation of the nation-states, lesser transport costs relative to wages, lower travel risk, and in particular, existing ties between European colonizing countries and their former colonies facilitated the movements of people. While formal and regulated system of passports and visas has been developed at this time to control the flow of people across national borders, people continued to move considerably. In search of a better life and reunification with their loved ones, who have been brought as slaves or recruited as workers by their former colonizers, colonized peoples noticeably moved again in this period. Indonesians moved to the Netherlands; Indians and Pakistanis moved to England;

while Vietnamese, Cambodians, Algerians, Tunisians, Moroccans, and other French-speaking Africans moved to France. The effects of this phase of international migration could still be seen in the diverse ethnic make-up of many countries in the Western Hemisphere today.

The social upheavals brought by the two world wars also led to a significant wave of migration of a new breed of people on the move, that is, refugees and asylum seekers. A large number of people also moved as the colonizers used or recruited many of their former subjects to be foot soldiers then lured more by opening their doors to immigrants to help rebuild their war-devastated economies. While there were definitely positive aspects, tragedy litters the stories of many immigrants in this period. The earlier waves of immigrants, especially in the Western Hemisphere, were confined in ghettoes, blamed for crime, disease, and the persistence of poverty. Europe and the United States had to learn how to cope with multicultural societies, resorting to restrictive policies in the process. Asian immigrants in the United States, for example, suffered from outright racism, particularly through various restrictive legislations.[5]

Migration Today

Today migration continues to define humankind's story and remains embedded in global patterns of integration. What makes contemporary migration different is that it is intensified by changes and processes rooted in or related to globalization as we are experiencing it today, such as growing demographic disparities, the effects of environmental change, new global political and economic dynamics, technological revolutions, and social networks. Moreover, some of these processes that serve as "push and pull factors" are new if not different. The combination of graying population and falling fertility rates in developed countries, for instance, has not only fueled the demand for immigrants to bolster the decreasing pool of workers; it has also created a lucrative job market for health professionals, who are sorely needed for taking care of the exploding elderly population.[6] The recent political turmoil in various countries in North Africa and the Middle East, in the meantime, has dramatically increased and put the spotlight again on people displaced by civil wars and conflicts.[7] The irresponsible use of the world's natural resources for survival and profit, meanwhile, has created a different type of refugees, that is, environmental refugees. Last but not the least, global patterns of integration have also created a different breed of economic migrants. These are the "skilled transients" (the corporate managers, consultants, and technicians who hop or get transferred from one international branch of the transnational company to another) and the "transnational migrants" (the elite group of rich entrepreneurs who can "buy" citizenship and shuttle or split their time in two or more countries).[8] All these have led to a switch in the nature of migrants and destination countries from migrants as citizens of colonial powers entering new lands to migrants as displaced persons, refugees, and laborers entering industrialized nations. These have also led to the evolution of migrant rights from essentially a recognition of the rights of the individual's country of origin to a recognition of the rights of the individual himself or herself.[9]

What makes contemporary migration also different is that it is far more complex than it used to be. It is noteworthy to mention, for example, how the statistical breakdown of a report by the United Nations on international migrants somehow challenges traditional assumptions that the West is the only destination of all migrants. The specific intake of migrants (in millions) by continent (Europe: 50.5, Asia: 42.0, North America: 39.3, Africa: 13.0, Latin America: 4.9, and Oceania: 4.3) actually shows Asia receiving more migrants than North America.[10] The distribution also shows that continents stereotyped as migrant-sending such as Latin America and Africa also received a significant number of migrants. Speaking literally and figuratively, Dennis Müller correctly points out that "the cards have been shuffled and that it is no longer so easy to distinguish between the host countries and countries through which migrants travel" as "the supposedly clear distinction between countries of arrival and countries of departure is equally tending to become blurred."[11] The density and velocity of contemporary mobility also contribute to this complex blurring of boundaries.

Of course all these changes are largely made more possible by the advances in communication, transport, and technology as well as the forging of alliances between nation-states (e.g., European Union's Schengen treaty) and economic integration brought by globalization. And while there are certainly positive developments, migration conditions and patterns in the context of contemporary globalization show, in many ways, the worsening of existing problems and the emergence of new forms of oppression. First, because global economic integration has increased the economic divide between rich and poor countries,[12] more and more people see international migration as the only way out of poverty. In fact, the UN points out that the most notable root of the phenomenon is the underlying disparities in livelihood and safety opportunities. While migrants are arguably not the poorest of the poor, survival still impels countless people to risk their life and limb as high levels of unemployment plague Third World countries. Impoverished nation-states, whose political and economic powers are diminished by transnational companies and institutions,[13] then capitalize on and exploit their citizens by legitimizing and promoting migration.[14] Today, migrants are the primary "exports" of many poor countries saddled by debt, consequently making migrants contemporary globalization's flexible, expendable, and disposable capital.[15]

Ironically, while there is a considerable increase in terms of volume in contemporary migration, there is also a growing restriction on people's ability to move, particularly for those who move for economic reasons. Despite the relative movement of capital and information, economic migrants are more and more subjected to restrictions on entry and settlement. Under pressure from their citizens, destination countries are particularly making it difficult for unskilled workers to enter. This is lamentable in the face of the reality that it is the unskilled workers who make up the bulk of the millions of people who are desperate to move,[16] and the ones destination countries need the most, since many of the unfilled or available jobs are the so-called SALEP (shunned by all citizens except the poor) jobs or 3D (dirty, dangerous, and demeaned) jobs. In the United States, for example, the job areas that grew the most in the past few decades are the low-wage areas, which are oftentimes the SALEP and 3D jobs.

The threat and fear of terrorism among destination countries, especially in the West, is also putting people's mobility in jeopardy as borders are now policed with the full array of military surveillance and pursuit techniques. When one factors in citizens' growing negative perception of immigrants, particularly for irregular migrants,[17] on top of the passage of local or state legislations curtailing political, economic, and cultural opportunities for migrants, one can say that the migration process is becoming more daunting, even life threatening, for migrants. This is particularly true for (irregular) unskilled workers whose plight arguably constitutes the heart of the justice question as far as migration in the context of globalization is concerned. The next section explores the risks and difficulties faced by this group.

The Challenge of the (Irregular) Unskilled Migrant Worker

The majority of people on the move are undeniably those who are poor and are looking for work, particularly unskilled work. On the surface, poor and unskilled migrant workers stand a good chance for migration because, in keeping with the current processes of economic globalization and the trajectories of international labor migration, the majority of jobs available on the global job market are in areas considered as unskilled.[18] The problem is the trend on unskilled work for foreigners in the global job market is that of declining wages. Oftentimes, there are also terms and conditions of employment such as wage discrimination, which apply only to foreign workers,[19] hence are less fair.

For poor migrant workers, economic globalization's relentless pursuit for profit, combined with xenophobic sentiments in destination countries that are inflamed by politics or anti-immigrant political parties, leads to various forms of discrimination, abuse, and exploitation before, during, and after migration. There are a number of ways in which poor migrant workers experience such difficulties. First of all, unskilled migrant labor is usually not integrated into the global economy. Second, it is undervalued by national economies. Hence, unskilled migrant workers become easy target, on the one hand, in identifying scapegoats for economic hardships. On the other hand, they become convenient solutions to economic downturns as employers (even governments) turn to migrant jobs or wages for cost-cutting measures.[20] Third, unskilled migrant workers have to live with national laws and foreign policies that disadvantage migrant workers, in general, and unskilled migrant workers, in particular.[21] In its desire to propagate the myth of "Japan as one ethnic nation," for example, Japan, despite its acute labor shortage, does not grant visas to unskilled workers except to the *nikkeijin* (of Japanese ancestry) who are mostly from Brazil and Peru. The combination of the glut of contractors, small and large enterprises desperate for workers, and enticing Japanese wages then creates clandestine migration flows. Fourth, unskilled migrant workers' jobs are unfairly regarded as "needed but not wanted," cheap, and exploitative labor. In most cases this is because their jobs, for example, fishing and agriculture, construction, trade, and service sectors are the SALEP or 3D jobs, which are often mired in deplorable working conditions.[22] Thus, in some cases they are at the receiving end of problematic labels such as "disposable people."[23] Photographer Philippe Chancel even describes migrant construction workers in the United Arab Emirates as "the new slaves" of the Gulf.[24] Last but not the least, while skilled workers or "skilled transients" are wanted and lured and can more freely circulate in the global job market, unskilled workers are restricted.[25]

This overall restriction and marginalization of unskilled migrant labor has serious repercussions as it renders unskilled work invisible or excluded altogether from fair labor laws. Taiwan, for example, has a law that mandates employers to pay migrant workers the minimum wage for a full-time local worker, which is about NT$500 per month. On the surface the policy looks just. The problem is that the wage requirement was instituted not for the sake of the migrant workers but in order to protect the wage scale of local workers. As Lou Aldrich, S.J. comments:

The Taiwan wage scale was just, but for the wrong reasons, hence, as long as the official salary of NT$16,000 was paid to protect the local worker, how much of that was stolen by illegal broker fees was not a great concern of either Taiwan or the sending nations. This manifests a grave failure to see the migrant worker as a person offering and receiving mutual benefits in a spirit of solidarity; rather the migrant is regarded primarily as a commodity, perhaps even a dangerous commodity.[26]

Indeed, certain destination countries' migrant labor policies aggravate the situation of unskilled migrant workers such that some are pushed to become irregular migrants. For example, in the Middle East, migrant workers are able to enter only through sponsorship by *khafels*[27] and are required to surrender their passports to the *khafel* as soon as they enter the country. The *khafel* must give clearance before the worker can leave the country. In addition, workers are prohibited from changing employers and, therefore, are literally at the mercy of the sponsors. Turning to irregular employment then often becomes a means of escaping from a situation of bondage,[28] thereby creating an underclass within the underclass, that is, the irregular unskilled worker. The International Labor Organization (ILO) reports that there are between 30 million and 40 million irregular migrant workers worldwide who occupy the "bargain basement of globalization."[29] The ILO also contends that the exploited condition of irregular migrant workers in host states is the result of the integration of the global markets.

What makes life more difficult, sometimes downright dangerous, for irregular unskilled migrant workers is the fact that they are most vulnerable to negative and potentially vicious stereotypes. Aviva Chomsky and Patricia Fernandez-Kelly write that irregular migrants are often unfairly characterized as competing with low-skilled workers or taking away jobs and driving down wages. Moreover, they are labeled as people who do not pay taxes; burdens on public services, for example, schools and hospitals; and, consequently, a drain on the economy. Last but not the least, they are blamed for criminal activities.[30] Not surprisingly, Hispanic (and especially Mexican) immigrants who have borne the greater burden of these stereotypes in the United States have been subjected to racial slurs, for example, "wetback"[31] and other forms of discriminatory treatment,[32] but also actual physical violence.[33]

THE BENEFITS OF MIGRATION

While migration in the context of globalization obviously presents serious challenges or forms of injustice, it cannot be denied that it also offers a number of gifts or benefits to those touched by it. In the case of migrant workers themselves, it means having a (better) job and, consequently, the means for securing the basic necessities in order to live. Moreover, migrants' experience and perspective of the world, in general, and other people and their cultures, in particular, is broadened. For the skilled or more affluent transients, who are usually given easier and quicker paths to permanent residency or citizenship, it means being able to avail of the social benefits and privileges, as well as better opportunities, for themselves[34] and their children in destination countries. For refugees and asylum seekers, migration offers critical or urgent relief from dire conditions. For migrants joining their loved ones in other countries, their journey means reunification with their families. And for all those who make it, for all those who find their promised land for themselves and their descendants, their sojourn or emigration leads to greater well-being in the form of not only better economic conditions but also a deeper sense of self-worth and a higher level of self-development. In the case of immigrant Latino youth, Catherine R. Cooper and Rebecca Burciaga say migration often serves as a "pathway to college, to the professoriate, and to a green card."[35]

For poorer migrants' immediate families it means having the much needed money or resources for necessary living expenses and, possibly, the chance of migrating overseas, especially in view of the phenomenon of chain migration.[36] For receiving developed countries, especially those with falling fertility rates, exploding elderly population, and a dwindling pool of people in their working age, migrants provide a certain sense of stability not just economically but also demographically.[37] In the United States alone, immigrant workers contributed as much as 31.7 percent to the GDP growth of the country in 2000–2007.[38] A survey of life in Qatar, in the meantime, found that an overwhelming majority of Qatari nationals value the contribution of foreigners to the development of their country because of their hard work (89 percent) and their talents (89 percent). Qataris also agree that foreigners—expatriates as well as labor migrants—make the country more receptive to new cultures. A survey by the ILO of how migrant workers were perceived in the Republic of Korea, Malaysia, Singapore, and Thailand, meanwhile, found that the majority of respondents believed that migrant workers were needed to fill labor shortages.[39] Indeed, despite the presence of fears on migrants taking up jobs or using up and straining resources or social services,[40] there is considerable recognition of the value of migration in the overall economic and cultural health of the countries of destination.

For the countries of origin, in the meantime, contemporary migration could be seen as a source of hope and development.[41] For instance, international knowledge transfer, money transfer, and technology development transfer given by skilled and educated professional migrants—whether during their migration or upon their return—play a significant role in the economies of sending countries.[42] And while, as pointed out earlier in the text, remittances do not definitively offset the long-term problems of sending developing countries, the considerable impact of money sent home by migrants is still noteworthy to mention here.[43] According to the World Bank, officially recorded remittance flows to developing countries grew by 5.3 percent to reach an estimated US$401 billion in 2012. World Bank also points out that remittances to developing countries are expected to grow by an annual average of 8.8 percent for the next three years and are forecast to reach US$515 billion in 2015. These remittances are often higher than overseas development assistance (ODA) and, in net terms, probably greater than net foreign direct investment (FDI).[44] The UN reports, as well, that when one factors in goods in kind and cash carried by travelers, perhaps one in ten people on the planet gains from remittances.[45] To be sure, money sent by migrants keep the economy of many developing countries afloat or relatively steady. Official and unofficial remittances included, the US$22 billion that Filipino migrants sent to the Philippines in 2006, for instance, even exceeded by 25 percent the country's national budget for the same year.[46]

Moreover, as Pistone and Hoeffner mention, migrants' contributions go beyond sending money or goods. There are also the so-called "political and social remittances"—the ideas, behaviors, identities, and economic resources that flow from the host to the sending country via migrants and their transnational networks—which promote entrepreneurship, community development, as well as greater political consciousness and participation in sending countries.[47] Migrants not only transfer knowledge and technology development. They also invest; help build vital infrastructures like schools, wells, and health centers; establish educational scholarships; raise money for calamity victims; etc. All these and more are actually re-casting the migrants as social capital,[48] which refers to the cumulative capacity of social groups to cooperate and work together for the common good.

THEOLOGICAL REFLECTIONS

The worldwide movement of people is as much a defining feature of globalization as the movement of goods, services, and capital. Like globalization, migration is not a new phenomenon. On the one hand, the contemporary situation of migration, in itself, is fraught with great challenges. On the other hand, it is also a source for the improvement of the quality of life for migrants, their families, as well as the countries of origin and destination. Indeed, while migration comes with great difficulties, it also brings some positive changes, making it a rich source for learning about and understanding the contemporary human condition. The theological themes arising from this double-edged character of migration in the context of globalization will be discussed in the following section.

MIGRATION AND SALVATION

A case could be made, based on the preceding discussion, on the link between migration and redemption. Indeed, one might say that migration could serve as a heuristic lens on the meaning of and quest for salvation today. Catholicism believes that after the Fall humanity did not become totally corrupt but was "wounded by sin" and stands in need of salvation from God. Salvation, in a word, is about the liberation of the human person or the human race from sin and its consequences. In Christian history a number of models or ways of understanding salvation have been expounded. These include the idea of Christ as expiation and sacrifice, Christ as defeating cosmic evil, Christ as bringing about satisfaction for evil, Christ as substitution for punishment, Christ as paradigm, and Christ as effecting anthropological change.[49] To be sure, these models do not exhaust the understanding of salvation. Many of the abovementioned models, for example, were articulated with reference to a particular context that no longer has significant credence in the contemporary world. Thus, one of the challenges for theology today is to articulate an understanding of salvation, which speaks to contemporary times.

Anselm Min contends that at the heart of Christian faith is the reality and hope of salvation in Jesus Christ and that the Christian tradition has always equated this salvation with the transcendent, eschatological fulfillment of human existence in a life freed from sin, finitude, and mortality and united with the triune God. Min submits that while this understanding of salvation is perhaps *the* nonnegotiable item of Christian faith, what has been a matter of debate is the relation between salvation and our activities in the world.[50] I posit that contemporary migration sheds light on this relation between salvation and our activities in the world in the way it provides a window into sinful conditions and, at the same time, efforts toward liberation.

As could be seen in the case of poor migrant workers, death-dealing conditions compel people to move. People move in order to survive and, in many cases, thrive despite further obstacles and unjust policies that they encounter in the migration process. In the annals of human history, borders have been redrawn; people's stories have been rewritten; and identities and subjectivities have been transformed because groups or masses of people crossed either by land, sea, or air. Indeed, time and time again people's liberation or the need for it is caused by human movements. Even Christianity's master narratives are embedded in migration stories. The Bible itself is basically "a literary tapestry woven from the stories of migrants"[51] in search of a better life. In the Old Testament the central story, in which the redemption of the chosen people themselves is rooted in, is the journey out of Egypt and into the promised land. In the New Testament, Jesus' role as an itinerant preacher is a critical part of his ministry. Then there's Paul and his followers whose multiple back-and-forth journeys across the Roman Empire gave birth to and nurtured the early Christian communities.[52] The early Christian movement itself was called the "Way" (Acts 9:2).[53] Truly, Christianity would probably not have been the global religion that it is today without the countless Christians who crossed the seas and continue to travel to uncharted territories to propagate or witness to their faith.

The combination of profound oppression in the midst of glimpses of human liberation also makes migration a lens for a contemporary understanding of redemption. As could be seen in the preceding sections, migration provides windows into human suffering and, at the same time, human well-being; it is rich with situations where death meets life and hope overcomes fear and despair. This dialectic underscores the notion that redemption's "already" aspect is as real as redemption's "not yet" aspect. It drives home the point that the divine is both present and absent and life is both horror and love. As Silvano Tomasi stresses,

[M]igration is graced even in difficult circumstances...[It can be seen as] part of the ongoing mystery of redemption, contributing to solving the great problems of the human family. [Migrants] are, thus, also part of God's plan for the growth of the human family in greater cultural unity and universal fraternity.[54]

P. Giacomo Danesi more explicitly articulates the link between migration and redemption:

Against the Gospel ideal of brotherhood, migrations, whatever form they may take, are always revealed as ways of gradually forming a new social fabric, a new body, which the Gospel message is called to animate; by virtue of the tragic aspect they often entail, they are transformed into appeals to brotherhood on a world scale; by virtue of the conflicts that accompany them, they are an aspect of the painful birth of the pilgrim Church; by virtue of the discords and disparities they disclose, they become an appeal for a juster universal order; and by virtue of the rapprochement they effect between the most diverse components of the human family, migrations are ways to—and the foundation of—a pentecostal, universalistic, catholic, and ecumenical experience of Christian brotherhood [sic].[55]

This ensemble of conditions and experiences embedded in contemporary migration is a reminder that redemption never takes place in isolation but in communion; it is not achieved in a static state but in dynamic purposeful life-changing movements. Migrants move in order to live. In the process they encounter death, but, like Jesus, dying is not the last word but the life that comes after death. Migration is, thus, a microcosm of the Christian belief in dying to live.

THE BORDER AS THEOLOGICAL FRONTIER

To migrate is to cross borders. For today's migrants, however, borders are no longer just the political membranes through which goods and people must pass, in order to be deemed acceptable or unacceptable. Today, borders have become the "thin porous membrane"[56] that people risk to pass and cross toward freedom or toward the promised land only to find spoils and end up in a no wo/man's land. Borders have become places where "people cross and sometimes remain, as if suspended, awaiting the next step in their life's journey" trapping people "in a reality that is filled with human suffering, poverty, neglect, and despair."[57] That is why Jerry Gill posits in *Borderland Theology*[58] that while the borders in question do not have to be geographical borders, these national boundaries do provide especially fertile ground for borderland reflection and witness in the twenty-first century.

Borders themselves are largely socially constructed as symbols of exclusion. First of all, the advent of borders signified the increasing domination of an "owning class" over the market, resources, and labor of a particular region, and defined the territorial limitations of rival owning classes. This exclusionary nature of borders lives on today with the idea of a border transformed from a political partition between two countries to that of a "fortress barrier" and the last line of defense of the "homeland."[59] In recent times we have seen the increase in borders and the fortification of borders. Still, migrants continue to cross the border because to them it is the gateway to the land of their dreams or, to refugees, the gateway to security.

For migrants, especially unskilled and/or irregular workers, to cross the border today is to live on the border, for the border, as Gloria Anzaldua posits, is an "open wound." As a physical fortress it is a gaping wound that serves as a testament to the violence of difference and the ever-widening gap between the haves and the have-nots. "On top of the walls at the frontiers among nations there are borders inside our cities, borders in schools, borders in health care, borders within workplaces. Borders intend to impede that the poor become our neighbors."[60] They are like bleeding wounds inflicted by discrimination and infected by a sense of loss and isolation. Cuban-American theologian Ada Maria Isasi-Diaz lays bare these wounds as she says:

I am caught between two worlds, neither of which is fully mine, both of which are partially mine....As a foreigner in an alien land I have not inherited a garden from my mother but rather a bunch of cuttings. Beautiful but rootless flowering plants—that is my inheritance. Rooting and replanting them requires extra work...it requires much believing in myself.[61]

Borders serve as indicators of the limits of existence, identity, and belonging. When one crosses the border, one traverses the yawning gap between being a citizen to being an alien or a foreigner, a visitor, a guest, in short, an outsider.[62] To cross the border is to live on the margins and be a stranger. Xenophobia—fear of the stranger—is the curse of the migrant for today's migrant is today's stranger—"the image of hatred and of the other."[63] As people left at the borders or pushed to the margins, migrants are today's marginal people.

What gets lost in all of this is that authentic borders are actually meeting points.[64] They exist not to separate but for people to meet. They are not meant to ward off or drive people away but they are places where we meet people halfway. As Justo González notes "a true border is a place of encounter [and] is by nature permeable. It is not like a medieval armor, but rather like skin. Our skin does set a limit to where our body begins and where it ends. But if we ever close up our skin, we die."[65] A true border then is a space where "we may choose to lay our bodies bare, where[in] we may choose to tell the truth of our lives."[66] Space creates presence. Space empowers presence and our bodies are the primary mediators of this presence. As such, when one is considered some-body, and not a no-body, one is made present. When one is present, one counts. This notion of space as presence is significant to theology because it is revelatory.

Migrants, while pushed to live in ghettoes or on the fringes of their destination countries, refuse to do so completely and create spaces for themselves to survive. Their strategic forms of struggle for recognition and their creative use of "imposed shrunken spaces" (e.g., using basement or abandoned shop lots and offices for their social and religious gatherings) has a revelatory quality. Their transformation of highly public and core spaces, for example, parks and community centers, into ethnic centers gives us a glimpse of how "bordered" or marginal(ized) existence can be transformed into spaces of presence. These reconfigurations of borders into "spaces" by migrants bring a new frontier into theology. For one, their collective protests, ethnic centers, transnational families, and international links challenge theology to articulate home not as a place "but a movement, a quality of relationship, a state where people seek to be 'their own,' and [be] increasingly responsible for the world."[67] This also means re-assessing the adequacy of "land" as an analytical category for identity. More concretely, this means that "land" is probably no longer enough as a category to theologize about "home" and "identity," especially in view of the increasingly vital role that transnationalism and transnational networks play in migrants' idea of belonging, community, kinship, and affinity.

In a nutshell, the border constitutes a frontier for a theology on migration today in the way it simultaneously symbolizes the human drama of exclusion and inclusion, of death and life. To be sure, the border is not only a site of the pathos of migrants but also a marker or a symbol for freedom, a new home (for refugees and asylum seekers), and a better life (for all migrants). This demarcation, that is, the border, is both a barrier and a gateway between hope and despair, dreams and nightmare. Crossing it makes a lot of difference, if not all the difference, between a life of poverty and misery and a life of promise and possibilities.

The Challenge of the Stranger

As could be seen in the plight of the irregular unskilled worker, the barriers oftentimes installed by destination countries and communities are not only physical but also political, economic, racial, etc. Such barriers result in further estrangement of migrants and challenges theology to articulate a way of understanding and dealing with strangers that is more just. The Bible provides some rich clues for such a theology. For example, being a stranger is the primary condition of the people of God (Exod. 23: 9; Deut. 24: 18) and migration is woven into this "stranger condition." "The land is mine," says the Lord, and we "are but strangers and guests of [His]..." (Lev. 25:23). As David acknowledges in prayer: "All comes from you; what we have received from your own hand, we have given to you. For we are strangers before you, settlers only, as all our ancestors were; our days on earth pass like a shadow..." (1 Chr. 29:14–15). God even commanded the Israelites to love the stranger, as they were also strangers in Egypt (Deut. 10:19). In fact, many other Old Testament laws were put in place to protect the stranger[68] (Exod. 22:20; Lev. 19:33–35; 24:22; Deut. 14: 28–29; 16:14; 24:14; 26:12–15; Num. 15:15–16; 35:15) to the point that anyone who does not respect the rights of the stranger will be cursed (Deut. 27:19). The New Testament, and Jesus himself, also have very specific exhortations to show goodness to the stranger, not only because it is a recognition of our fundamental Christian identity as strangers but, most especially, because Jesus himself, by His incarnation and by being an itinerant preacher, took on the conditions of a stranger. Moreover, Jesus advocated for the care for the stranger (Mt. 25:36).

The Christian tradition is rich, as well, with exhortations on how to treat strangers, particularly in relation to hospitality.[69] For example, in the time of the Fathers of the Church, the time of pilgrimages and huge forced migrations, hospitality to pilgrims and displaced people was a major concern. John Chrysostom's *Treatise on the Priesthood* even says that one of the main pastoral concerns for a bishop was providing the necessary funds to assure a worthy welcome to strangers and the care of the sick[70] (Treatise on the Priesthood, III, 16).[71]

As such, theological construction of the self or of ourselves as Christians cannot be separated from the acceptance of the stranger, just as the identity of the Israelites as a people of God is very much linked with the stranger. The God we believe in is a God of the stranger (Deut. 10:17–18; Ps. 146:9). In times of backlash and xenophobia, Christian theology cannot but articulate a theology of migration with the "stranger," particularly the biblical concept of the stranger, as heuristic lens. At the same time, if this theology is to be in dialogue with the experience of today's migrants as strangers, it has to integrate dimensions of contemporary migrants' experience that are unique compared to the biblical stranger. For instance, Carmen Nanko Fernandez accurately points out that contemporary strangers, particularly in formerly indigenous-dominated countries like the United States and Australia, are not only the newcomers to the land but also the inhabitant encountered by the sojourner.[72] Moreover, whereas the stranger in the Bible already has some laws put in place for his/her protection, migrants today still have to actively seek, negotiate, and fight for certain laws as existing laws either do not consider their rights or work against them.[73] Whereas there is a "preferential option" for the biblical stranger,[74] there is structural marginalization of contemporary migrants.

At the same time today's migrants have more sources and resources to draw from and these make them, to a certain extent, more empowered than strangers in biblical times.[75] Migrants today tend to be (more) organized and are more likely to demand stronger legal rights and formal recognition than migrants in biblical times or in previous waves of migration in history. They are also more open, insistent, and defensive about their religious and cultural identity. Economically, for example, most migrant workers have regular wages and even have extra jobs. Politically, they organize and have access to national and transnational organizations (either church-related or NGOs) catering to migrant workers. Socially, they are able to maintain links with their family and friends as well as ethnic or work-related transnational networks. Religiously, they are relatively free to practice their own religion.[76] As such, today's theological reflections on the stranger could benefit from a nuanced version of reflections on the stranger in biblical times.

GLOBALIZATION WITH A HUMAN FACE

Globalization has clearly facilitated and accelerated migration. Despite its positive effects, however, the plight of irregular unskilled workers illustrates that globalization has brought "globalization not of the included but of the excluded . . . not a planet-wide family-embrace but a cruel abyss between peoples."[77] Indeed, as could be seen in the millions of people who continue to move in search of better political and economic security, it cannot be denied that in the midst of the opening up of the markets, free flow of enterprises, domination of multilateral institutions, and proliferation of transnational companies is the marginalization of individuals and communities. It is not surprising, therefore, that globalization is the current context of the Church's mission.[78] The recent encyclical *Caritas in Veritate* reflects this serious concern with regard to the effects of globalization. As the encyclical points out, while "it is true that growth has taken place" or that "it has given many countries the possibility of becoming effective players in international politics . . . this same economic growth has been and continues to be weighed down by *malfunctions and dramatic problems*" (CV, 21).

To be sure, globalization's market economics is hegemonic as it cuts or disregards any ties with other institutions such as religion, family, and politics and even usurps the power of the nation-states. It is exploitative as it tends to look at everything in terms of cost, benefit, and exchange value at the expense of human dignity, especially of the vulnerable in society. Destination countries' laws and policies, for example, serve the interests of employers and the larger state apparatus.[79] They deter workers from pursuing their rights to ensure the continued availability of an affordable pool of foreign workers, particularly unskilled irregular workers who are easier prey for abuse and exploitation.[80]

In the face of such realities, Silvano Tomasi maintains that we need to have a new mentality by looking at the challenges posed by migrants and migration as a justice issue both for the Church and for society, and not only an option of charity.[81] A growing number of theologians echo such stance by relating migration's challenges to Christian social teachings (more on this in the third chapter). What they make clear is the reality that salvation history (understood as salvation in history) today is inevitably tied with the plight of the millions of migrants all over the world and the millions more who (will) continue to be forced to embrace migration in the name of survival.[82] Such a perspective takes on significance in the face of the IOM contention that predicted global mismatch between labor supply and demand may result in a further increase in irregular migration, with more people moving to find work than will be facilitated by labor mobility agreements.[83]

Given globalization's good effects it does not make sense to throw the baby with the bath water, so to speak. What is needed is a globalization with a human face. As Gustavo Gutierrez points out, "globalization as it is now being carried out exacerbates the unjust inequalities among different sectors of humanity and the social, economic, political and cultural exclusion of a good portion of the world's population."[84] What is needed, in other words, is a globalization that advances the human good such that, as we consider the reality of life in the borderlands and the cultural forces, social processes, historical contexts, and economic institutions that influence how globalization is experienced, we consider over and above everything else the human person. As the US bishops' landmark pastoral letter on the economy *Economic Justice for All* eloquently draws our attention to, the economy is made for human beings, not the other way around.[85] "For this reason," Gill argues with the American context in mind, "a just and rational immigration policy must begin with a just global economic policy, one that allows Central American and Mexican farmers to survive on their own lands, one that provides jobs that can support families everywhere, not just in the United States."[86]

The story of the Parable of the Workers in the Vineyard could be helpful in making a case for a globalization with a human face, particularly from an economic perspective. Jean Pierre Ruiz's essay titled "The Bible and People on the Move: Another Look at Matthew's Parable of the Day Laborers" is particularly instructive in this regard. Citing various interpretations by contemporary scholars, Ruiz points out that, on the one hand, this parable could be regarded as "the parable of the good employer" or "the parable of the Affirmative Action Employer."[87] On the other hand, Ruiz contends that the lesson from the parable is not about the employer's generosity or magnanimity but about his own power, about the workers' dependence on him, and about the insignificance of their own toil. It is not a matter of gifts or grace, Ruiz insists, but of a fair day's wage for a fair day's work.[88] Ruiz clearly shares the interpretation of most scholars that day laborers in biblical times are victims of poverty and injustice. What Ruiz argues for is a shift in focus from the supposedly gracious employer, who is often made as a stand-in for God, to the marginalized day laborers, whose plight and voice get drowned out in the process.

A globalization with a human face, above all else, is about "taking the crucified people down from the cross."[89] In the migration context the Church carries out this mission by providing—like Jesus—the intellectual vision and the practical inspiration to serve and to love by making herself the neighbor of all the beaten, wounded, defeated, and forcibly uprooted persons along her endless road.[90] Thus, the basic moral imperative is the globalization of what is truly human.

CONCLUSION

While it brings some benefits and advantages, migration in the context of globalization has its own share of problems. Whether it is in the past or at present, the movement of people, as accompanied by the processes of globalization, arises from or results in inequities. As could be seen in the plight of unskilled workers, especially those who are forced to turn irregular, this entanglement of migration with globalization has resulted in the creation of a global underclass of migrants. For these millions of marginal(ized) migrants, life is lived on the edge. To live on the edge is to stay on the "boundary," "verge," or "brink," and live a life of survival and liminality.

To be sure, the current process of globalization is irreversible. Thus, a theology of migration needs to articulate how globalization might work for migrants, in general, and marginal(ized) migrants in particular. Moreover, a theology of migration needs to seriously take into account life on the border or the margins as experienced by migrants. Such an approach needs to look at the plight of not only irregular migrants or irregular unskilled workers but also women who are vulnerable to more complex forms of marginalization. The gender dimension of contemporary migration and its accompanying moral concerns will be explored in the next chapter.

CHAPTER 2

OLD CHALLENGES, NEW CONTEXTS, AND STRATEGIES: THE EXPERIENCE OF MIGRANT WOMEN

The marginalization of women worldwide is common knowledge. Such marginalization is so prevalent that it has created women's movements and spawned critical concepts such as patriarchy and sexism. Today, the struggle for gender equality lives on[1] as improvements in the life and role of women in society, especially in the past few decades, continue to trickle. Globalization has paved the way, for example, for a worldwide increase in the participation of women in the labor force. In particular, the globalization of labor flows, growth of global cities, and patterns of corporate restructuring have not only increased mobility at the high and low ends of the job market for women. They have also provided women increased access to wages and salaries at both the upper and lower ends of the market as well as increased prominence as both visible power-brokers and significant consumers within the global economy. Ann Brooks points out, however, that important questions emerge, as well, for gender analysis and for patterns of inequality as a result of globalization[2] because of the gender and digital divide it brings. In particular, Brooks maintains globalization has led not only to the growing differentiation within the division of labor between and within gender frameworks but also to the growing "feminization" of job supply and of business opportunities.[3]

It cannot be denied, indeed, that the individuals and groups of people marginalized by globalization have a more discernible face: a woman's face.[4] As economist Maria Arcelia Gonzales-Butron points out, out of every 100 hours worked worldwide, 67 hours are worked by women, but they receive only 9.4 percent of the income.[5] Women's multiple roles in production, reproduction, and community management means that they have to cope with the global way of living by working more, risking more, and suffering more.

For many women throughout the world, particularly those from the Third World, coping with the global way of living oftentimes means giving up careers, leaving their families, and risking life and limb by resorting to international migration.[6] Since they often carry the heaviest burden of survival for themselves and their families, many women are also forced to move across borders in dire conditions, that is, as refugees.[7] Not surprisingly, international migration is increasingly taking on a woman's face, bringing with it some complexities, gifts, and challenges that are unique to women on the basis of their gender as it intersects with their other social identities such as class and race. It is to these distinctive aspects of women's experience of migration that the ensuing discussion focuses on.

Gender[8] as a Factor in Migration

Previously, only the men migrated (mostly for work) and the women and children were either left behind or followed as dependents. Until very recently, it was assumed that migrant workers were also mostly men and most women migrated to re-unify families. Until fairly recently, as well, documents of the International Labor Organization (ILO) described a migrant worker's family as comprising "his wife and minor children." The participation of women in international labor migration has then shattered traditional barriers and patterns. As Mirjana Morokvasic illustrates clearly in her essay,[9] women are now migrating independently in significant numbers and are taking on the role as breadwinners.[10]

In fact in certain parts of Asia, especially in the Philippines,[11] Indonesia, and Sri Lanka, women are joining the international workforce in significant numbers, creating the phenomenon of the feminization of migration. Starting in 2002 women migrants from Indonesia, for instance, have exceeded men migrants by as much as four to one.[12] As Nikos Papastergiadis contends, the modern migrant no longer conforms to the stereotypical image of the male urban peasant.[13] Women in manufacturing, electronic assembly line, and domestic work are now at the front line of global migration.

Gendered Migration

Female migration in the context of globalization is arguably gendered as many women on the move, especially from the Third World, come as fiancées or spouses, work in gender-specific, service-oriented jobs like health care, hospitality, and domestic work or, worse, trafficked into prostitution. In fact, 80 percent of the 800,000 to 2 million victims of trafficking each year are women, most of whom are involved in the sex trade. Sr. Eugenia Bonetti, a leading voice in anti-trafficking effort, says that in Europe there are an estimated 50,000 to 70,000 women on the streets, mostly from Africa, Latin America, and Eastern Europe, most of whom are victims of cross-border trafficking of human beings for purposes of sexual exploitation.[14] In Nepal alone some 10,000 to 15,000 women and girls are brought annually to India under the pretext of labor migration.[15] There is also a surge in human trafficking in Central Asia, especially from Uzbekistan, where up to 10,000 people, mainly young women, are forced into the sex trade by international crime syndicates. This multi-billion dollar industry also accounts for the illegal movement of 400 Bangladeshi women monthly to Pakistan, the undocumented entry of 300 Thai women annually to Australia, and the trafficking of Filipinas and Russian women in US military bases in Korea.[16]

The predominant face of women migration, that is, labor migration, could also be argued as gendered in a number of ways. First of all, the new global division of labor ensures that women will most likely face a gendered global job market, which confines them to low(er)-paying jobs in their destination countries. In particular, migrant women from the Third World are often confined to service and hospitality-oriented jobs, a perspective and approach that have roots in the traditional stereotyping of women in domestic and/or care work. As pointed out by Rita Monteiro, women migrant workers are concentrated as cleaners of public facilities, nannies, housekeepers, maids, and industrial and hotel workers.[17] In many cases the poverty and the ensuing lower level of educational background, as well as rural and less sophisticated background of migrant women workers, are taken advantage of by unscrupulous recruiters, traffickers, and employers. The debt bondage that plague Indonesian migrant domestic workers, for example, begins in Indonesia itself with placement agencies charging inflated and fictitious fees purportedly for training, medical checks, and travel and administrative costs for finding employers, some of which have already been paid by the employer. These unscrupulous agencies even sub-contract the women as cheap labor on the pretext that "on the job training" is needed with "real" employers.[18] Contract violations as well as unlawful treatment and terminations could also occur and persist because of the inability of poor migrant women workers to grasp the complexities of policies and their vulnerability to their employer's and destination country's wants and needs on account of their status as unskilled migrant workers. Last but not the least, the possible lack of exposure to, or familiarity with, modern lifestyle, infrastructure, technologies, and equipment could also lead to some serious difficulties for poor migrant women workers.

Secondly, the very decision of women to migrate, which is often a family strategy for upward social mobility, could also be seen as gendered. This "gendering" occurs in the way sexual division of labor, rooted in gender stereotypes, plays a major role in singling out the womenfolk to be the one to leave and work abroad. Many Asian families, for example, think it is but "natural" for the daughter, sister, or wife to apply as domestic worker because domestic work is a woman's work. For single women, families often capitalize on the imposed and popular notion of the language of care among women as nurturance in all aspects, for example, emotional and physical care, in order for the women to agree to leave and be a domestic worker. Parents especially tap into the highly ingrained sense of responsibility among women in choosing them to be the one to migrate. Such a perspective is not without merit as female migrants are not only more inclined to send remittances. As illustrated in Keiko Osaki's study, female migrants also tend to send higher proportion of their wages compared to male migrants.[19] In certain cases when women internalize these gendered roles and relations, they volunteer or agree to migrate even at their own risk. The following case sheds some light on this aspect of gendered migration:

When Consuela left her home to search for bread for her family, she hired a coyote smuggler for $2,000 to take her across the border. She tried to cross the deadly desert four times. On her first attempt she was caught by the U.S. Border Patrol. On her second attempt someone tried to rape her. On her third attempt she was robbed at gunpoint by border thugs. And on her fourth attempt, she ran out of food and water and almost died.... After she had a chance to recover she wanted to try again because she said her family at home depended on her.[20]

In the case of fiancées and spouses a number of such migrations may also be gendered, especially in cases of mail-order-brides where Western men purposely seek poorer women from largely patriarchal societies who are docile or submissive and are more than willing to take on caring for the husband, the house, and, sometimes, stepchildren as their primary duty and responsibility. As Deirdre McKay's study of Filipino women caregivers in Canada illustrates, even if marriage is strategically employed by migrant women to escape from domestic work, Canadian men see them as marriageable precisely because of their association with domestic work.[21] In fact if these women identify themselves as Filipino-Canadian, the men who approach them lose interest because they (men) prefer a newly arrived domestic worker who fits their orientalized vision of the woman/wife who will serve her husband.

While the overwhelming motivation for migration for most women is the desire to help the family, it also becomes a tool toward liberation.[22] In fact, there are studies that show that the impulse to migrate for individuals, particularly for women, may be rooted in a desire to escape from the strictures of the traditional patriarchal family. This could be seen in Indonesia, which has a highly feminized face of migration (as much as 80 percent) and where the search for greater freedom and opportunity is an important motive for women to migrate. This double-edged face of migration for women is also reflected in a study of Colombian and Dominican women migrants in Europe, many of whom claim that one of the reasons they migrate is to escape from the *machismo* culture in their home countries and some of them even choose Europe, not America, to be as far away as possible.[23] In fact, personal agendas ranging from the simple desire for travel or adventure, or the more serious need to gain financial independence, or to simply escape from filial duty or from a problematic family or marriage are often embedded into migration as a family project.[24] Some women even migrate despite family objections.

Gendered Transitions

Gender also comes into play in the course of migration primarily due to gendered demands that migrant women face or negotiate. For unmarried or unattached women, marriage or committed relationships get sidelined as work and family roles or responsibilities take center stage. Those who migrate to countries with a different dominant culture and religion, meanwhile, encounter difficulty in finding a prospective boyfriend, husband, or partner. This is especially true for women migrants from the Third World, who are either feeling the pressure to get married due to their advanced age or wanting to use their migration to find ways, for example, marriage to a citizen to become permanent residents or citizens in their country of destination or in other developed countries.[25]

Gendered transition is more pronounced, however, for migrant wives and mothers. First, there is the issue of unfaithful husbands or partners. At the same time, some migrant women are constantly

suspected or accused of marital infidelity by their husbands or partners at home. Such is the case of Nestor, who even went to the local
radio station to ask help to repatriate his migrant wife who has not
come home for six years.[26] In other cases married migrant women
do consciously resort to extra-marital affair as a way of coping with
loneliness or as a means of getting back at their unfaithful husband or
partner.

Indeed, maintenance of family relationships and responsibilities,
especially for migrant mothers, is the most prominent form of
gendered transition. In most cases migrant mothers maintain the
responsibility of nurturing their children by resorting to transnational
mothering, which is defined as the organizational reconstitution and
rearrangement of motherhood to accommodate the temporal and
spatial separations forced by migration.[27] Transnational moms, often
described as "supermoms" by their children, reconstitute mothering
not only by providing acts of care from afar but also by overcompen-
sating for their physical absence. "In sharp contrast to migrant fathers
who reduce their relationship with children to monthly remittances,
mothers personalize their ties" by making "regular communication
part of the weekly routine of transnational family life."[28] There are
the migrant mothers, for instance, who are dubbed as the "cell phone
mothers" because they literally help their children do their homework
via the cell phone. Some send not only letters and material gifts regularly but also "daily bread" for their children in the form of biblical
messages sent via short message service (SMS) to their children every
morning. One interesting case is that of a migrant mother who never
failed for more than ten years to call her three children at three o'clock
every Sunday afternoon (sometimes three times a week, especially if a
child is sick), planned the menu for the week, and gave advice on
school projects, aside from keeping abreast of what's happening to
her children inside and outside the school.[29] Such experience highlights not only the reinforcement of gendered oppression but also
the fragility of spatially fractured family relations, especially as far as
women are concerned.

Guilt because of their being "absentee mothers" is obviously one
of the heaviest burdens for migrant women who have to leave their
children in their countries or origin. At the root of their guilt is what
they perceive as a transgression of a "good" Christian woman's proper
place and role, which is at home with her husband and children. This
personal and even societal perception of their migration as a betrayal
of their primary duty and responsibility, then, becomes like a mill-
stone hanging over their neck. Such is this perception that some of

them do not even say goodbye to their children nor immediately tell the truth as to where they are going. To ease their guilt, migrant mothers find a surrogate whereby they pass on their direct nurturing responsibility to another woman, for example, their mother, a sister, female cousin, or their eldest daughter, or hire the services of a poorer woman to be their own domestic helper.[30] Indeed, whether it is the one who is away or the one who is left behind, many women remain dutiful daughters and sisters or devoted wives, aunts, mothers, and grandmothers. In fact "the reconstitution of the gendered division of labor by women's migration involves not so much an equal reciprocal exchange between men and women in the family but instead an extended kinship exchange between women."[31]

Indeed, gendered transition in the context of migration could be seen in the reinforcement of patriarchal roles and relations. The Migration Policy Institute, for instance, contends that since their economic contributions are usually essential for the survival or upward mobility of their families, many immigrant women participate in the labor market. This means that they bear the triple burden of work, family care, and sending remittances to their home countries. The traditional stereotype and expectation for women as keepers of culture and tradition also means that women immigrants are expected to integrate their families while maintaining the cultures of their countries of origin.[32] Not surprisingly, these responsibilities are difficult to reconcile in unfamiliar school, health care, and social service systems, especially when combined with limited English proficiency, unfamiliarity with the host society, poverty, and social isolation.

For some migrant women, however, gendered transition takes the form of some kind of reconstitution of patriarchal roles and relations. This reconstitution of women and gender roles, especially in the family, occurs not only in the context of temporary migration but even more so in the context of emigration, particularly to Western or developed countries where social systems and infrastructures provide more opportunities for women's growth and development. It also occurs not only in the form of the women taking on the role of breadwinners. Take the case of the Vietnamese women in Finland studied by Kathleen Valtonen. First of all, the opportunity to learn Finnish, to enter into labor market relations, and the necessity of interfacing with the wider society in many areas of public life have expanded the Vietnamese women's role and repertoire at home. For those who like to look for work, increased income means material security for the immediate and the wider family. On a more personal note, working outside the home enables them to avoid loneliness and isolation.

On top of this they value the opportunity for social interaction, the social status, and the active lifestyle that employment brings. For mothers, the availability of local child daycare is one of the decisive factors that facilitate their decision to take up salaried employment.

Because the women are now working, adjustment became necessary in the domestic division of labor in families. Since the basic culture-based collective goal, that is, priority for the welfare of the family, offsets or overcomes the potentially disruptive effects of role adjustment in the family, it has been possible for male spouses to eventually come to terms with situations in which wives are the ones to have found employment, or to be in better paid work. As a husband reveals:

Nowadays I know how to cook and clean, and can manage to do the laundry and look after the children too, when necessary. We have all ended up learning to do all these chores. It does not present any problem for us. In the family, my wife is the one who works. In the family of my older friend, he always helps his wife, but not in the presence of others.[33]

As one could imagine, migrant women's gendered transition occurs not only because of gender but in concert with other factors such as race or culture and religion. In her study of female migrants from the Middle East and the North African (MENA) region in Australia, Yaghoob Foroutan argues that the differentials in paid work between MENA migrant women and native-born as well as other female migrants are not always necessarily rooted in disadvantage or discrimination. Foroutan writes:

[D]espite migrating to a country identified by gender characteristics, including a high rate of women's waged work, female migrants from the MENA region mainly prefer to remain committed to the cultural characteristics of their own origin society, where the dominant culture associated with gender roles such as women's traditional roles in the household, patriarchy, and male breadwinner pattern result in a markedly low rate of women's paid work....although migration provides opportunities for change, this does not inevitably apply to all migrant groups like the female migrants from the MENA region who experience greater "cultural distance" and tend to retain cultural values of the origin society rather than integrating in the residing society.[34]

Religion plays an equally significant role in migrant women's gendered transitions. In their study of migrant congregations, for example, Helen Rose Ebaugh and Janet Saltzman Chafetz point out that while there are conditions under which (migrant) religious congregation promotes an improvement in the status of women, situations that legitimate their traditional subordinated status persist. For instance, they often do traditional women's work in their churches like preparing food, teaching Sunday school classes, and performing music and social services.[35]

Gendered Violence

Violence, influenced by gender, also plagues migrant women. There are various types of this gendered violence. There is the more obvious and most pernicious, that is, sexual violence. Usually, irregular migrant women and refugees are more vulnerable to this type of gendered violence. Women crossing the US-Mexico border and the border between Mexico and Guatemala without papers, for example, are vulnerable to *coyotes* who sometimes demand sex as payment or take it by force. As Olivia Ruiz Marrujo writes,

Coyotes or migrant traffickers, insofar as they almost have exclusive control over the people who have paid them to go north, often gain access to the bodies of women migrants. *Coyotes* may refuse to take a woman north, threaten to turn her over to unknown men, or abandon her midway if she refuses his advances. A woman, aware of the possibility of such a demand, and seeking to avoid a confrontation and possibly greater violence, may "agree" from the beginning of her negotiation with a *coyote* to have sex with him in exchange for his "help" or "protection."[36]

Binaifer Nowrojee describes a similar situation in the case of women refugees, particularly in Africa. Nowrojee reveals that women refugees are subjected to rape or other forms of sexual extortion in return for the granting of passage to safety, refugee status, personal documentation, or relief supplies. What is worse is that perpetrators are sometimes fellow refugees. In many refugee camps, Nowrojee writes, women are vulnerable to sexual violence on the outskirts of the camps while searching for employment and carrying out daily tasks and routine for survival, such as fetching water, collecting firewood, or gathering vegetables, which often fall on the shoulders of women and girls.[37] Even humanitarian or UN presence is often not enough to protect women refugees from sexual violence as is the case with Darfuri women refugee in Chad.[38] It is also worse for other raped women refugees to speak about it as coming out in the open becomes "a death sentence." They are left with three options: (1) marry the rapist, (2) be sent to prison for their own protection from their family, or (3) be killed by their family for dishonoring them.[39] Hence, in some cases these women say they would rather be dead than speak about it.

Indeed, women refugees are particularly vulnerable to sexual violence. A report released by the United Nations High Commissioner on Refugees states that mass rape of women and children has been documented in Bosnia, Cambodia, Liberia, Peru, Somalia, and Uganda during their respective wars.[40] In Malaysia, Tenaganita maintains that almost all women refugees who have been through arrest and detention will undergo some form of abuse. These female refugees are subjected to invasive body searches or made to strip and carry out humiliating exercises. Mya, a Myanmarese refugee, said that women refugees in detention camps who have no money to buy sanitary napkin would have to rely on visitors to give them sanitary napkins. Mya, who found the situation demeaning, said they would share with other women their sanitary napkins. Mariah's case was worse. She not only went through physical and mental torture in the hands of her guards. She was also "deported" (sold) by unscrupulous members of Malaysian immigration authorities known as RELA[41] to traffickers. Together with a few other women she was then raped by the traffickers who threatened to sell her for RM5,000 into prostitution. She was released only when her friends paid RM2,500.[42]

In the case of regular migration, the Migration Policy Institute says that the traditional problems of domestic violence are exacerbated for female immigrants when spouses control the immigration status of their family members, trapping battered immigrant women in violent homes because of fear of deportation if they complain to authorities. The institute also maintains that despite new mechanisms such as visas for battered women and victims of trafficking, legal reforms are needed to improve justice system procedures and training, as well as access to immigration relief, legal services, and public benefits.[43] For instance, the involvement of local law enforcement in immigration prosecution may dissuade battered immigrant women from reporting abuse if doing so could result in their deportation or that of a family member.

Gendered violence in the realm of economics also plagues migrant women, especially unskilled migrant women workers. Foreign domestic workers in Hong Kong, for example, have been victimized a number of times already to solve or alleviate Hong Kong's economic woes. The wage cuts that targeted only the domestic workers—an occupation the Hong Kong government knows is women dominated—was meant to ease Hong Kong's economic slowdown. With domestic workers also already the lowest paid worker in Hong Kong, singling them out for further reduction of wages is tantamount to "making the poor even poorer."[44]

The Hong Kong government further reinforced this institutionalized gendered violence with the proposal to remove maternity protection for foreign domestic helpers. Concocted as a means to offer "flexibility" to employers to terminate their foreign domestic helpers (FDH) on the basis of "mutual agreement," the proposal, according to a letter by the Asian Migrant Coordinating Body, is not only "discriminatory, as it is applicable only to those in the category of foreign domestic helpers ... racist as it seeks to exclude workers of certain nationalities from enjoying a right available to local workers and those of other nationalities ... [and] sexist as it targets women for oppression [by considering] pregnancy and maternity as a 'hindrance' to more effective and productive labor."[45] More recently migrant women domestic workers have challenged what they perceive as the discriminatory policy of the Hong Kong government of denying them permanent residency,[46] which it grants to other foreigners who have worked and lived in the city-state for at least seven years.

The scourge of foreign domestic workers in Hong Kong as women comes not only from the Hong Kong government but also from their employers and recruiters. For instance, because of the popular perception and fear in Hong Kong that foreign domestic workers will go to great lengths to snag rich or economically stable men like their male employers, the domestic workers' physical appearance is controlled mostly by women employers. Dress codes are imposed through the maid's uniform. For those who do not make the domestic worker wear a uniform, they require her to wear jeans and T-shirts or other "harmless" and gender-neutral clothes. Moreover, body control and discipline as women[47] are important adjustments the domestic worker has to make right at the start. Recruiters, upon the desires of prospective employers, "transform" the domestic worker's body and appearance by dictating her body weight, length of hair, facial appearance (no make-up), kind of shoes to wear, etc. When the external fits the prescribed ideal domestic worker's body appearance, the internal is the next one the recruiters tinker with. Aside from being subjected to the x-ray machine and the weighing scale, the domestic worker's body is exposed to numerous tests as part of the application process. These include tests for hepatitis, syphilis, herpes, and even pregnancy. When the domestic worker passes the "body quality control," she is photographed with her "signature" clothes: the standard pastel pink or blue-striped maid's uniform. This "perfect maid" look is then photographed twice: a close-up of the face and a "full body" shot. All in all, the ideal domestic worker must be neat and tidy but not so attractive.

James Tyner's study on the Web-based recruitment of female foreign domestic workers in Asia lends credence to such gendered violence. In analyzing the data collected on 25 agencies specializing exclusively or predominantly in domestic workers, Tyner contends that there is a cyber-commodification of female foreign domestic workers, particularly in the (re)presentations of both "the product" (the domestic worker) and the "expected performance" (the job requirements) of the domestic worker. To stay competitive, recruitment agencies bend over backward to prospective employers' needs.

On their websites they offer a range of services that objectify potential maids from "collection" and "delivery" of the domestic workers to creating "catalogues" (through bio-data and photos of women in a maid's uniform) of the product.[48] Worse, recruitment agencies offer services that disenfranchise migrant domestic workers by offering employers the ability to "order" and "reserve" a domestic worker on-line to being entitled to "warranties" (as much as three months) or free "replacements" (anytime during the first year) for their products.[49] Nicole Constable points out that some recruitment agencies offer as much as three free replacements if the employer is not satisfied with the "product." An agency, at one time, even put domestic workers on "sale" with a "15% discount" price tag because it is celebrating its 15th anniversary.[50] Domestic workers, then, become like goods in the store where one has the ultimate freedom to choose what to buy, and if the "goods" are "damaged," you can return them, free of charge.

Theological Reflections

Many women undeniably migrate for the sake of others, primarily their family. For migrant mothers, in particular, the children's future is usually the primary motivation for migration. Migrant mothers will do everything; they will go to great lengths out of love for their children. As could be gleaned from the abovementioned practice of transnational motherhood, however, such an admirable reason does not necessarily make the migration easier. Whether single or married, with or without children, migration for women brings experiences that are unique to them on account of their gender, especially as it intersects with their class, race, religion, civil status, and so on. So what are the theological implications of women's experience of migration, particularly as described above? How does the Christian tradition make sense of women migration in the first place? Moreover, how are we to see and understand women and the family amidst all the serious changes and challenges brought by migration? The following section tackles these questions.

A Woman-Friendly Global Economy

Women are much better today in many areas of life than women in previous generations. The fact that women can migrate and work overseas, either on their own or with their families, partly reflects this improvement in the status and treatment of women. However, while women's labor participation and mobility increased under the aegis of globalization, it would appear that the prevailing market economics still carry forms of injustice for women in the context of migration, especially those coming from the Third World and patriarchal societies.[51] For example, because the economy tends to view women as not productive or competitive, they are not considered to be entitled to a full share in or control over available social resources. This gendered economic violence starts in the economy of the household or the family, especially in patriarchal societies, where boys are prioritized, for example, in getting education, and "female" roles are ingrained, for example, domestic work and care work. These roles are then picked up in the migrant job market by assigning or leaving women with jobs that are gender specific, for example, domestic worker or caregiver. Since these jobs are marginal(ized) jobs, migrant women become vulnerable to incidents of sexual harassment and sex discrimination in the workplace, even in terms of wages and promotion. The worse of the lot falls on migrant women workers since migrant labor is not integrated into the global economy. As Monteiro points out, their vulnerability is heightened by the fact that the sectors that they are often concentrated into tend to be excluded from national labor legislation and international migration instruments.[52]

This structural denigration of migrant labor has serious repercussions, especially on women, who are doubly exploited. Because their job is segregated by the international division of labor and devalued by the global economy, the accordance of dignity is minimal, if not downright lacking. Consequently, recognition of human rights as migrant women's rights is also minimal. Domestic work, for instance, is "invisible" because it is done within the confines of "privacy" of a particular family or household. It is also not usually reflected in labor statistics and is excluded from labor laws. If it does get accorded some kind of legislation, for example, minimum wage, it is not only the lowest paid; it is also the first victim in times of economic slowdown or restructuring.

Feminist theologians believe that there is an interaction of the threefold exploitation or oppression of women, namely, gender, race, and class, in this issue. Elisabeth Schüssler-Fiorenza, for instance, asserts that there is "structural interconnections between the gendered economic system of capitalist patriarchy, its racist underpinnings, and women's global poverty" and that this "must be seen as due to the global colonialisation and systemic exploitation of women's labor in production and reproduction."[53] Shawn Copeland adds that this is very much apparent or strong for colored women, especially for the domestic workers, who have to sell their very persons as the condition of their labor.[54]

Since the global economy is forged on unjust relations between, among, and across countries and gender,[55] justice must be the primary theological category for Christian theology to respond to this reality. Usually, theological discourse in view of economic justice is drawn from classical Latin American liberation theology. Although it offers considerable theological basis to address the plight of women as victims of economic injustice, this theological discourse has limitations. First of all, the generic term "poor" is problematic as it totalizes the "subject." Lumping women with the category "poor" does not necessarily integrate the fact that there is a "woman face" to poverty[56] or to global economic injustice. This failure to integrate the gendering of economics in classic liberation theology's discourse on the politics of economics then marginalizes women's experience and perspective in general and migrant women from the Third World in particular.

As it is, migrant women from the Third World suffer not just because they are poor but also because they are women. Option for the poor as an option for poor women,[57] then, makes necessary the broad unmasking of the dichotomy between the private and the public, especially in terms of how it constructs, controls, disciplines, confines, excludes, and suppresses gender and sexual difference and, in effect, upholds patriarchal power structures.[58] Gendered justice in the global economy means shattering this persistent dichotomy because it is a critical factor in why women get crumbs when it comes to economic rights and opportunities. Elisabeth Schüssler-Fiorenza, for instance, laments how women are viewed as economic dependents. They supposedly work for pin-money until they get married and for extra money to complement the salaries of their husbands. As such, women's active economic participation is not encouraged. If they do work, discriminatory pay-scale awaits them.[59] In the context of migration, for example, the image of the typical migrant as young, male, and economically motivated persists, and this bias leads to the formulation of unrealistic and unresponsive policies.[60] One reason for this, as Anne Joh correctly points out, is the marginalization of "domestic labor" to women due to the patriarchal assumption that domestic labor is not "real" labor. Joh insists that economic calculations of domestic labor are often not included in studies of national economies despite the fact that it is, in itself, a powerful aspect of the economic system that enables the formal and global economy to function.[61] Clearly, gender-based analysis and planning is essential for the formation of immigration policies and legislation.

In the context of migration, justice as an option for the poor woman also takes on a specific face, that is, option for the poor (unauthorized) migrant woman. Obviously, there are different types of women migrants and they have different experiences and perspectives on migration based on the nature of their migration. Injustice also happens between and among migrant women. Justice with a poor migrant woman's face then necessitates covering *different* women's experience and perspective of migration, particularly in the areas of productive and reproductive work.[62]

From a theological perspective there is also a need for justice, understood here as right relations, to be construed beyond equality into that of love. Since economic injustice to women is rooted in relationships that are often in the realm of the private, equating justice with love will strike at the "emotional capital" of such injustice, that is, the patriarchal and romanticized notion of love that drives or compels women to risk their lives overseas or stay in problematic living and working conditions for the sake of the people they love. Margaret Farley, for example, argues for "just love" as a framework for Christian sexual ethics.[63] Along this line of thinking, Isabel Carter Heyward asserts that love is justice. It is not necessarily a happy feeling or a romantic attachment but a way of being in the world. Justice, Heyward insists, is the moral act of love because injustice is the doing of moral wrong, specifically of breaking the relational bond between ourselves in such a way that one, both, or many parties are dis-empowered to grow, love, and/or live.[64]

Anselm Min echoes such a position by looking at love from an explicitly political dimension. Min says we should not be content with a moralistic preaching about love. We need to learn to concretize and politicize our love and emphasize not only the change in consciousness but also the imperative of transforming the structures, policies, and laws into effective instruments of human liberation.[65] Love, in this sense, is not so much a noun but a verb. It is not simply a nice feeling but, more importantly, a way of being in the world.

Feminist theologians also point out that relationships on the basis of complementarity may not necessarily lead to just/loving relationships. Complementarity basically posits that certain realities belong together and produce a whole that neither produces alone.[66] It could be seen as quasi-justice, a token equality. Authentic just/loving relationships, feminist theologians say, are characterized by mutuality.[67] Mutual relations enable or empower others to discover and develop their capabilities to make their contributions, while simultaneously making one's own. It is about sensitivity and solidarity, affinity and facilitation.

Reimagining Women and the Family

Migration, particularly South to North migration, obviously takes place in networks based on kinship or pseudo-kinship between people localized within social fields encompassing two or several countries. Therefore, migration as a life-changing decision and process is deeply embedded, and must be understood in the context of family norms, relations, and politics,[68] especially since it often reconstitutes the family in ways that are sometimes destabilizing, sometimes affirming.

When the family is touched by international migration, it immediately becomes a geographically split household or a transnational family.[69] As could be seen in migrant women's gendered transitions, transnational families experience significant challenges. Female transnationalism arguably initiates the reconstitution of gender relations as it forces the rearrangement of household labor by distributing a portion of women's household chores, including childcare, to men.[70] It cannot be denied, however, that the reconstitution of roles still has vestiges of patriarchy. As Rhacel Salazar Parreñas argues, while the maintenance of transnational families holds tremendous promise for the transgression of gender boundaries, it also upholds gender boundaries. This gender paradox, Parreñas contends, could be seen in the fact that while the reorganization of the household into transnational structures questions the ideology of women's domesticity, women's migration has not led to a more egalitarian division of labor in the family.[71] Parreñas points out that the caring practices still maintain female domesticity,[72] most notably the transfer of immediate care-giving from the migrant mother to a female relative, for example, grandmother, aunt, or eldest daughter, or to a poorer woman who is hired as a nanny or domestic worker.

Obviously the desire to go on being a family under such conditions means that the shape and conditions that the family takes might have to be reworked.[73] The Catholic Church, for example, teaches that the Christian family must spring from Christian marriage. This raises a question as to what happens in families where kinship springs from a relationship that is not marriage, for example, the migrant women and refugees who end up having a child outside of marriage (sometimes because of rape)? This also raises a question in the case of married migrants (both men and women) who resort to extra-marital affairs[74] as a way of coping with loneliness and isolation and ending up having children out of such affairs.[75] Moreover, some of these migrant men and women either separate or divorce their spouses and leave their families, or try to maintain two families, one in the country of origin and one in the destination country. Also, what about the women who are choosing to migrate because they are running away from failed or abusive marriages?

Since migration reshapes the family for various reasons, it obviously poses a challenge[76] whether or not to recognize the diversity in which contemporary families are formed.[77] Within Catholicism, for example, Lisa Cahill notes a broad spectrum of a new generation of scholars—married, with children—who argue for a more social view of marriage, with special concern about socioeconomic pressures.[78] Cahill points out that though these scholars do not stress absolute norms, they would like to see greater attention to and support for marital and parental commitment needs rather than the justified exceptions. Cahill submits that the position of these scholars is largely influenced by current social conditions such as increased but still incomplete gender equality, more economic stress on couples and relationships, more seductive promotion of consumerism by the mass media, and a stronger hermeneutic of suspicion against North American culture as a genuine and evolutionary purveyor of "liberty and justice for all."[79] At the same time, other Catholic theologians raise concerns with such a very inclusive understanding of the family. Joseph Atkinson points out the ecclesiological problems this poses, particularly as it relates to the idea of the family as domestic church. Atkinson believes that

[t]here is a real danger that the concept of domestic church may become an empty theological tag, used without due regard for its constitutive theological nature.... This may be done out of a misplaced compassion as people seek to be inclusive. "Define family any way you are comfortable with and you

are Church." But is this legitimate? The danger is that domestic church can become a "concept" into which anyone of us can pour one's own "content": we can then have preferences as to its meaning. The non-objective approach leads inevitably to restructuring the very identity of the family (with implications for the salvific order) which no longer has any objective definition. This would be unfortunate as the concept of domestic church could then be "filled" with any content and become merely a tool to be used for whatever end one was pursuing. In effect, it would only be an empty label.[80]

Reimagining the family in the context of migration also entails interrogating the role of the family in some of the death-dealing conditions experienced by women on the move. For example, at the heart of most situations adversely affecting the social development prospects of women are strongly prevailing ideologies that lead to a gender gap in employment, education, wages, and access to services,[81] and one enduring ideology that finds its roots in the family is the ideology of domesticity. As shown in the gendered migration of women, it is an ideology that is strongly instilled and nurtured in the family. As feminist theologian Hope Antone writes:

[W]omen have been socialized early in life to do multiple responsibilities in the home—for their siblings, their parents, the elderly, and sometimes even others in the community. This ideology of domesticity is so ingrained that many Asian women feel it is their fate or destiny to sacrifice in order that those who depend on them can have a better life. Migration then becomes an option not only for mere economic reasons but also for the ideological-cultural factor of gender socialization into the ideology of domesticity and multiple responsibilities.[82]

Thus, if "just love" and mutuality are to be used as the bases for praxis, it is important for Christian theology to expose how the private realm, particularly the family, produces and re-produces the ideology of domesticity in a way that is harmful for women's well-being.

CONCLUSION

The situation of women on the move in the context of the global economy and geo-political conflicts is arguably in flux. It could be seen as a struggle between the forces of tradition and change as old contexts, particularly patriarchal systems, play out in the midst of changed environments bringing new challenges that call for new strategies to deal with these old contexts. The situation of women in contemporary migration could be seen, in other words, as a kind of bits and pieces of detraditionalization, since migrant women's experience shows that identities are reworked or that there are certain changes occurring on the locus of identity and authority from "without" to "within."[83] This does not mean, however, that traditions will vanish overnight, nor will they disappear completely. This means that what currently exist between tradition and change are permeable not invincible boundaries. Thus, one could say that what is happening is a case of "tradition *in* liberation" and I use this phrase in two interrelated senses. First, I use it to capture the reconstitution or re-appropriation of traditional norms, roles, and relations (whether positive or negative) in the context of migration. I use it, at the same time, to point to the persistence or continuation of traditional norms, roles, and relations (again whether positive or negative) in the midst of migration.

For many women, indeed, migration mirrors the story of Ruth, the Bible's quintessential female migrant. It is a complex experience of, among others, loss, invisibility, change, transformation, independence, (self)respect, (self)recognition, empowerment, self-definition, or fulfillment.[84] This double-edged effect could be seen in migrant women's dual experience of mobility and immobility, continuity and discontinuity, empowerment and, at the same time, disempowerment.

The experience of migrants in the context of globalization, in general, and the experience of irregular unskilled workers as well as migrant women, in particular, raise the question of social justice. As could be seen in Chapter 1 and in this chapter, it does not suffice to speak of justice in general terms or as simply *suum cuique* (to each what is due to him/her). What is called for is social justice, or the creation of patterns of societal organization and activity that are essential both for the protection of minimal human rights and for the creation of mutuality and participation by all in social life,[85] such that justice is about appropriate treatment not just equal treatment, or "to each according to his/her needs" not just "to each according to what is due." Such a position inevitably entails reforms in current policies toward people on the move, especially in countries of destination. It is this subject of reform that the next chapter will focus on.

CHAPTER 3

CITIZEN-DISCIPLES: AN ETHICAL ROADMAP FOR MIGRATION REFORM

Contemporary global migration, particularly as seen in the experience of unskilled workers and women, is clearly plagued with serious problems. When one factors in the plight of irregular migrants as well as that of refugees, the picture looks even bleaker. For example, the plight of African migrants trying to cross into Europe without proper documentation is tragic. This is especially true for those coming into Europe via Spain, where Red Cross estimates put the number of deaths between 2,000 and 3,000 every year.[1] There are also horrific stories about people trying to escape the recent political turmoil in the Middle East and North Africa. At the height of the conflict in Libya, for example, a ship carrying 600 migrants fleeing the violence sank after the unseaworthy vessel, which smugglers crammed with people way beyond capacity, broke apart.[2] The tragedy of it all is that it was discovered that the ship sank when numerous bodies of migrants were seen floating on the sea.

THE CASE FOR REFORM OF MIGRATION POLICIES

Anyone who maps or tracks the movements of migrants today will see that there are certain countries or regions that receive more migrants. Whether these countries or regions like it or not they naturally become destinations for people on the move not just because of their proximity to conflict-ridden or conflict-prone countries or region but, in particular, because of their greater political stability, advanced economies, and better standard of living. In most of these receiving countries the "pull" factors are such that thousands, possibly even millions, try to enter every year.

As could be seen in chapters 1 and 2 it cannot be denied that many destination countries have policies that are, at best, discriminatory toward migrants and, at worst, xenophobic. It cannot be denied, as well, that migrant and refugee deaths are exacerbated by the riskier route and longer journeys via the sea that most of them take[3] because destination countries put up more sophisticated security systems and made legal entry systems more difficult, even for refugees and asylum seekers.[4] Australia—a migration hot spot in the Asia-Pacific region—takes flak, for instance, for its policy of mandatory detention for asylum seekers while their claims are processed. Australia also gets criticized for its practice of holding the processing of immigrants at the remote Christmas Island in the Indian Ocean. With the increase in the number of poor immigrants, mainly poor Asians fleeing conflict and economic hardship like Iraqis and Afghans, the country was forced to reopen isolated centers on the country's mainland. Migrant journeys to Australia are also rife with hardships as is life in the detention centers.[5]

In the United States, which has more or less 12 million irregular migrants, the "prevention through deterrence strategy" that Border Patrol officials began to implement in 1993 along the US-Mexico border has resulted in untold tragic deaths.[6] In fact since the policy was implemented, at least 8,000 bodies of dead migrants have been recovered on the border.[7] These tragic deaths coupled with the economic and political implications of the massive number of irregular migrants have been a source of tension among Americans, particularly in relation to immigration reform. This divisive battle on immigration reform has been reignited nationally with Arizona's passing of a law—the toughest law in the country so far—which aims to identify, prosecute, and deport unauthorized immigrants.[8] More recently the US Senate passed a significant overhaul of the country's immigration laws that provide a path to citizenship to the millions of unauthorized migrants. To date, however, the bill has yet to be taken up in the Republican-dominated House of Representatives, which is focused in coming up with a much narrower legislation that does not provide a path to citizenship.[9] In the meantime, the tragic stories of border crossing continue to highlight the hardships and dangers migrants are subjected to by "coyotes" just to make it to *el norte*, the land of their dreams.

THE LIBERAL EGALITARIAN AND REALIST PERSPECTIVES ON MIGRATION REFORM

Sustained substantial immigration, particularly when it is irregular and is not wanted by a considerable segment of the population, often leads to restrictive, even deadly, policies and practices. Ultimately, however, such policies and practices do not really deter migrants from coming or entering with or without proper documentation. The search for survival and a better life, most migrants would say, is far more important. For those who are desperate to move, what potentially lies ahead is far better than what they have to leave behind. As could be seen in the previous section, the dangerous mix of desperate migrants and xenophobic policies has disastrous effects.

As things stand, there are two discernible camps or positions in the debate on migration policy reforms. The first, the liberal egalitarians, begins with how things ought to be and holds as foundational the equal moral worth of all people. This group, which advocates for a path toward citizenship, also maintains that nothing or no accidental matter such as place of birth or nationality of parents diminishes the moral worth of all people. Justice, from a liberal egalitarian perspective, requires an open border policy. In John Rawls's theory of justice, for example, "freedom of movement and free choice of occupation against a background of diverse opportunities" are part of the basic structure of society.[10]

The second camp, the political realists, begins with how things are. They argue that the current global political system, which divides the world into nation-states, does not make migration a basic human right and favor tougher enforcement of laws. Political realists also think that migrants can be admitted but solely on the basis of cost–benefit analysis.[11] Moreover, they argue that priority should not be given to the welfare of migrants but to the welfare of citizens since the first duty of the state is toward its citizens.[12]

Realists believe, indeed, that states should act in their national interest even if such actions could raise moral questions. For realists, who tend to privilege and protect national membership, a nation-state should not simply accept the economic disruption or destruction brought by migration. They also believe that a nation-state cannot simply put aside the question of the social order and historical continuity which migration could wreak havoc on. Liberal egalitarians, on the other hand, put the premium on freedom, non-aggression, and the politics of recognition on both the individual and the group level.[13] They believe that in order to maintain the highest levels of justice and freedom, people must be allowed to do whatever they want to so long as they respect the identical rights of all others.[14] Thus, they support open borders or open immigration. In the US context, the former, that is, the political realists, aim at inclusion in America's capitalist democracy while the latter, the liberal egalitarians, struggle to create a society that would be more democratic and more just.

Catholic Social Teaching as an Ethical Roadmap for Reform

As illustrated in chapters 1 and 2 and at the beginning of this chapter, the political realists' position arguably dominates migration policies and approaches, particularly in destination countries. The realist position, however, brings moral concerns that lead to questions on what constitutes appropriate treatment for migrants.

The issue, as sketched so far in this book, is clearly an ethical one and the

humanitarian principle pushes the ethical reflection beyond the realist approach, questioning the current divide among states and economies as unjust and expanding the state's and people's responsibilities beyond the confines of the national community, also because such a gap is not simply in the nature of things or the result of bad management but because of unfair relations among nations.[15]

Ethos in classical Greek is not only habit and behavior, but also a way of inhabiting the world. So how might Christianity help in the articulation of appropriate or more ethical treatment of migrants? To be sure, Christian social teachings in general provide a rich source for articulating a Christian contribution toward immigration reform. For purposes of focus, however, this book will engage the Catholic tradition, particularly Catholic Social Teaching, or CST.

CST is a body of doctrine or documents in the Catholic Church that expresses or reflects the Catholic Church's engagement and commitment to the social questions of the time.[16] I argue that CST, especially the themes that are foundational to the various documents that form part of it, contributes toward the issue at hand. Kenneth Himes himself argues that CST offers some kind of "ethical coordinates" that could help steer the ship of globalization,[17] and it is to the main themes of this ethical roadmap, especially as they address issues within the debate on immigration reform, that I now turn.

Human Dignity

The human cost and the tragic nature of contemporary migration obviously brings up questions on human dignity. Indeed, the amount of lives lost all over the world, the conditions in which these lives are lost, and the continuing struggle of migrants for rights and recognition make the idea of human dignity a cornerstone in any reform of migration policies. To be sure the dignity of the human person is the foundation for CST. From a Catholic point of view, life comes from God; the human person was created by God in the divine image (Gen. 1:27); hence, human dignity is intrinsic to being a human person. *Gaudium et Spes*, for example, locates in this dignity the foundation of its understanding of the human person (GS, 12–22) in the same way that *Dignitatis Humanae* anchors its understanding of human rights on it (DH, 2) and *Sollicitudo Rei Socialis* (SRS, 39) situates solidarity in it. As someone with dignity, the human being in the eyes of the Catholic Church is not like an animal driven and hunted down at all cost in the mountains or deserts nor like an object squeezed and abandoned to die in train-box cars. As someone with dignity, the human being is not a means to an end, not a worker seen only as means for profit such that s/he is given unfair wages and made to live in horrible living conditions. The Catholic Church condemned these labor practices (which many irregular workers are routinely subjected to) as an injustice as early as 1891 through *Rerum Novarum*:

Let the working man and the employer make free agreements, and in particular let them agree freely as to the wages; nevertheless, there underlies a dictate of natural justice more imperious and ancient than any bargain between man and man, namely, that wages ought not to be insufficient to support a frugal and well-behaved wage-earner. If through necessity or fear of a worse evil the workman accepts harder conditions because an employer or contractor will afford him no better, he is made the victim of force and injustice (sic).[18]

Gaudium et Spes puts this more succinctly in the context of migration:

Justice and equity likewise require that the mobility, which is necessary in a developing economy, be regulated in such a way as to keep the life of individuals and their families from becoming insecure and precarious. When workers come from another country or district and contribute to the economic advancement of a nation or region by their labor, all discrimination as regards wages and working conditions must be carefully avoided. All the people, moreover, above all the public authorities, must treat them not as mere tools of production but as persons, and must help them to bring their families to live with them and to provide themselves with a decent dwelling.[19]

The overt and covert denigration of the humanity of migrants to the point of driving them to their death (literally and figuratively) is undeniably characteristic of a relationship of oppression. What CST offers is an anthropological perspective that insists on the integrity of humanity without any exclusion of persons or certain aspects of the human person.

Human Rights

Undoubtedly at the center of the debate for reform is the question of human rights. As mentioned earlier, political realists do not make migration a basic human right and favor tougher enforcement of laws. As could be seen, however, in the traumatic separation of families, mass arrest and detention of irregular workers right in their place of work, for example, the Postville case in Iowa,[20] as well as summary deportations, the political realists' approach arguably lead to possible human rights violations.

CST insists that, in view of their dignity, human beings are to be regarded and treated as subjects entitled to a decent and humane life. Moreover, as far as CST is concerned, human rights is foundational to human dignity.[21] While Catholicism has not been a paragon for human rights, especially in the past, it actually has some of the most notable articulations on human rights. *Dignitatis Humanae*, which focuses on the right to religious freedom, for example, maintains that human rights are based "in the very dignity of the human person as this dignity is known through the revealed word of God and by reason itself" (DH, 2). The assertion of John XXIII in his encyclical *Pacem in Terris*, in the meantime, drives home the indispensable role of human rights toward a humane life. John XXIII maintains that "every human being is a person, that is, his nature is endowed with intelligence and free will. By virtue of this, he, he has rights and duties, flowing directly and simultaneously from his very nature. These rights are therefore universal, inviolable, and inalienable" (PT, 9). The message of John Paul II for the 1999 World Day of Peace—held on the occasion of the fiftieth anniversary of the Universal Declaration of Human Rights—goes even further by affirming the universality and indivisibility of human rights as "essential for the construction of a peaceful society and for the overall development of individuals, peoples, and nations" (cf. Art.3).[22] What is also significant in this message of John Paul II is that he went on to stress rights that are critical for immigrants, for example, right to life, right to religious freedom, rights of ethnic groups and national minorities, and right to education and work.

Other documents within CST argue for migrant-specific rights. There is the right to live with the family as affirmed in *De Pastorali Migratorum Cura* (cf. Art.7) and *Apostolicam Actuositatem*, which declares that "in policy decisions affecting migrants their right to live together should be safeguarded" (AA, 11).[23] *De Pastorali Migratorum Cura* also points to the cultural rights of migrants, which undergird the Church's primary position and concern for a specific pastoral care for migrants (DPMC, 11). Most importantly, the CST's recognition of the right to migrate itself is laid down in *Pacem in Terris*, which states: "When there are just reasons in favor of it he must be permitted to emigrate to other countries and take up residence there" (PT, 25).[24] This stance is echoed in the Catechism of the Catholic Church, which stipulates that "the more prosperous nations are obliged to the extent they are able to welcome the foreigner in search of the security and the means of livelihood which he cannot find in his country of origin" (CCC, 2241). The 2009 papal encyclical *Caritas in Veritate* also points to this right by considering migration as an integral aspect of human development (CV, no. 62).

Last but not the least, CST affirms the rights of irregular migrants. In his message on the occasion of World Migrants Day in 1995, for example, John Paul II contends that irregular migrants are not excluded from the human rights perspective of the Church and that "irregular legal status cannot allow the migrant to lose his dignity since he is endowed with inalienable rights, which can neither be violated nor ignored."[25] What Michael Blume, S.V.D., points out regarding the principles on which the social teaching of the Church operates with regard to the question on "illegal" migrants is noteworthy to mention here. Blume, who worked for the Pontifical Council for the Pastoral Care of Migrants and Itinerant People, makes it clear that as far as the social teaching of the Church is concerned, "there are no illegal migrants, for migrants are persons, and no person is illegal. Persons can engage in illegal movements but their Creator does not do illegal things . . . . The dignity of a person in an irregular situation does not expire as a visa or a passport does."[26] To be sure, the Church respects civil law, including migration law, but also advocates that it be just. In a resolution on immigration reform, for instance, the United States Conference of Catholic Bishops (USCCB) points out that it recognizes the right and acknowledges the responsibility of the US government to secure its national borders and to not condone or encourage undocumented migration into the United States. At the same time the resolution affirms the dignity of irregular persons and the need to make every effort to ensure that their human rights are respected and protected. The resolution also called on federal policymakers to revise the nation's immigration laws and policies in a manner that upholds basic dignity and human rights by including certain key elements.[27] These elements are then summed up in *Strangers No Longer: Together on the Journey of Hope*—the landmark pastoral letter issued by the USCCB together with Catholic bishops from Mexico—which called on a comprehensive immigration reform that includes global anti-poverty efforts, expanded opportunities to reunify families, temporary worker program, broad-based legalization, restoration of due process, and reforms in the system for responding to asylum seekers.[28]

Clearly, as Silvano Tomasi posits, the effectiveness of the human rights approach rests not only on its universal appeal and potential for coalition building but also on its legitimating function vis-à-vis the state.[29] And while the Catholic Church itself "profoundly experiences the need to respect justice and human rights within her own ranks,"[30] the fact that justice is at the heart of its mission[31] places it in a good position to be a voice of moral reason when it comes to human rights.

The Common Good

A good ethical framework is clearly essential for the elaboration of humane migration policies, and human rights undeniably hold a strategic place within such a framework. There is an awareness within the CST, however, of possible gaps or loopholes with a human rights approach. Hence CST raises the ethical demand by proposing the notion of the common good.[32] The Compendium of the Social Doctrine of the Church points this out:

> *Unfortunately, there is a gap between the "letter" of the law and the "spirit" of the law of human rights,* which can often be attributed to a merely formal recognition of these rights. The Church's social doctrine, in consideration of the privilege accorded by the Gospel to the poor, repeats over and over that the more fortunate should *renounce* some of their gifts so as to place their goods more generously at the service of others and that an excessive affirmation of equality "can give rise to an individualism in which each one claims his own rights without wishing to be answerable for the common good" (italics in original).[33]

The value of the notion of the common good becomes more apparent in view of how migrants have come to be relatively stereotyped, stigmatized, and treated as burden for the welfare system, as strangers and potential criminals in the local community, and more recently, as possible terrorists. Moreover, they are blamed for driving down wages, the disappearance of jobs for local people, even the poverty of communities. Ordinance 5165, a law that prohibits businesses and landlords from hiring or renting to undocumented immigrants, was recently passed by the residents of Fremont, Nebraska, partly on the basis of the belief that irregular migrants are taking away local jobs.[34] More often than not, migrants also end up being confined in ghettoes and/or in places that make them more vulnerable to environmental racism.[35]

Mater et Magistra confirms that it is the duty of the state to realize the common good in the temporary order (MM, 20). Scalabrinian priest Graziano Battistella himself acknowledges that "the state has the right to regulate migration"[36] but also points out that "the church also constantly adds that the principle of the common good must be properly understood, as it could lead to oppressive consequences for the person."[37] For instance, political realists in the migration policy debate, which wants migration controlled at a cost–benefit analysis, are also called communitarians. In a sense they actually think of the common good; the problem is it is only or primarily *their* common good or the common good of their own families, communities, or state. Thus, their position could end up being exclusive or highly restrictive as could be seen in the casualties of current policies and practices (whether sanctioned by law or not), which actually adhere to much of the political realists' or communitarians' perspective. Thus, the CST's articulation of common good as *universal* common good makes a contribution at this point.

CST certainly recognizes the important duty of the state toward its citizens. However, in view of the fact that the state apparatus is also often used to create death-dealing conditions for people on the move, CST argues that "the duty of the state towards migrants and, therefore, the limitations of the state in its migration policies derive from the larger community to which all belong, the human family." In view of this, *Pacem in Terris* insists that "the fact that he [the migrant] is a citizen of a particular state does not deprive him of his membership in the human family, nor of citizenship in that universal society, the common, world-wide fellowship of men" (PT, 25). *Pacem in Terris* goes on to affirm that the common good of the state, in other words, "cannot be divorced from the common good of the entire human family" (PT, 98).[38]

Olivia Ruiz Marrujo's articulation and analysis of immigrants *as* risk and immigrants *at* risk[39] provide some kind of theoretical framework on how common good works or does not work in contemporary migration. The former contends immigrants present a threat to society, which is falling victim to the dangers (crime, disease, for example) these displaced (or out of place) people present. By implication, immigrants are responsible for their own misfortunes, be they deaths or the loss of limbs. This approach places the discussion of immigration in the realm of national interests, security, and sovereignty. The latter argues that immigrants live at risk, as victims of dangers created, accepted, and ignored by the countries of origin, transit, and destination, thus situating the movement of people around the globe within the framework of national and international human rights. This approach maintains that the responsibility for immigrants and their misfortunes is ours.

Marrujo goes on to point out that the "immigrants *as* risk" approach is more common in the developed industrial world like the United States. Marrujo argues that this approach, in fact, brings epistemological comfort and suggests that inasmuch as this point of view presents immigration as a risk to the fabric and integrity of modern industrial nations, its roots lie in the founding of nations and the construction of their identities, and in the traditions and myths that have defined, consolidated, and justified these national ways of being.[40]

It is this arguably profound understanding and advocacy of the common good that most likely accounts for the CST's less-than-enthusiastic approach to STEP OUT migration, particularly the mass migration of professionals in critical areas of public service that put already strained developing countries in further jeopardy. The Sacred Congregation for Bishops writes:

[E]ven though they have a right of emigrating, citizens are held to remember that they have the right and the duty . . . to contribute according to their ability to the true progress of their own community. Especially in underdeveloped areas where all resources must be put to urgent use, those men gravely endanger the public good, who, particularly possessing mental powers or wealth, are enticed by greed and temptation to emigrate. They deprive their community of the material and spiritual aid it needs.[41]

The US bishops echoed the above-mentioned position in their reaction to the US immigration policies that facilitated STEP OUT migration:

The special preference afforded by the United States to highly skilled persons should be restricted. Our immigration policy should not encourage a flow of educated persons needed for development in other countries. . . . It does not make good sense to direct foreign aid to developing countries and, at the same time, receive reverse foreign aid in the form of professional persons whose talents are badly needed in the same countries.[42]

Solidarity

Ethically, CST could also contribute to reform of migration policies through its articulation of solidarity. From the perspective of the CST, "solidarity highlights in a particular way the intrinsic social nature of the human person, the equality of all in dignity and rights and the common path of individuals and peoples towards an ever more committed unity."[43] CST also sees solidarity in two complementary aspects. First—as a social principle—solidarity entails the transformation of sinful structures that dominate relationships between individuals and peoples, into structures of solidarity. Second—as an authentic moral virtue—solidarity is "not a feeling of vague compassion or shallow distress at the misfortune of so many people ... [but] a *firm and persevering determination* to commit oneself to the *common good* ... of all and of each individual because we are all responsible *for all*."[44] Christopher Llanos, S.J., echoes and elucidates on this universalist emphasis in CST. Llanos contends that CST identifies a larger universal human community in which we all share responsibility for each other and that from the perspective of the CST this universal human community is both a reality and something to be accomplished.[45] This universal human community enters the picture, Llanos writes, when political communities on the local level fail to realize their responsibility toward their members.[46]

Economically, this would mean that, as *Sollicitudo Rei Socialis* urges, "the stronger and richer nations must have a sense of moral responsibility for the other nations" (SRS, 39). This stance is significant as it addresses the problem of injustice among countries that contribute to the political and economic turmoil in Third World countries, which then drive people to migrate. The same text (SRS, 39) also contends that the exercise of solidarity within each society is valid when its members recognize one another as persons. Consequently "the 'other', the migrant, must be seen as 'our neighbor', a 'helper' (cf Gen. 2:18–20) to be made a sharer, on a par with ourselves in the banquet of life to which all are equally invited by God."[47] In fact Ada Maria Isasi Diaz speaks of solidarity as love of neighbor and as one that requires mutuality and praxis.[48] As the pastoral letter *Strangers No Longer: Together on the Journey of Hope* insists, our common faith in Jesus Christ moves us to search for ways that favor a spirit of solidarity. It is a faith that transcends borders and bids us to overcome all forms of discrimination and violence so that we may build relationships that are just and loving.

Accordingly, CST's perspectives on solidarity as "fundamental social virtue" and as a "virtue directed par excellence to the common good"[49] consider responsibility to migrants as a global humanitarian responsibility. *Caritas in Veritate*, for example, insists that international norms and legislative systems dealing with contemporary migration should be identified and implemented with a view to safeguarding the needs and rights not only of the host countries but also of individual migrants and their families (CV, 62).

The action of the Catholic community itself clearly witnesses this idea of global humanism that is derived from its faith when it comes to addressing the plight of migrants, particularly refugees. As Tomasi writes,

As an actor in the public sphere, the Church advocates new norms to overcome unequal interdependence; calls for the protection of the most vulnerable groups, like the forcibly displaced; encourages an active role for the international community; and influences the formation of public opinion. A multiplicity of Church groups are engaged in witnessing their solidarity through their presence in refugee camps and in resettlement networks; through providing medical assistance, education, food, and job placement; through preparing laws; and even through participating in the political arena.[50]

CST, indeed, drives home the point that the moral worth of a society is measured by how it treats its most vulnerable members. I reckon it is also from this sense of responsibility for the underprivileged that Catholics give primacy to hospitality, which I see as a critical component of solidarity.

While human dignity, human rights, common good, and solidarity are not new and are not exclusive to the Catholic Church, collectively they drive home the point that the classical divide between "self" and "other" should be transcended. Together these ethical principles make clear the message that when discipleship animates citizenship, meeting the "other" is, ultimately, a sacred encounter.

THE CONTRIBUTION OF CATHOLIC SOCIAL TEACHING

Having said all of the above, what then, in a nutshell, could be a CST contribution toward reform of policies toward people on the move? What possible themes run through the CST's conception of human dignity, human rights, the common good, and solidarity? I believe one could discern two themes running through these ethical norms.

The first is a liberationist ethic. From a liberationist perspective the impoverishment and victimization that characterize the lives of the poor and the underprivileged constitute serious violations of human rights and, consequently, human dignity. This situation, a Catholic liberationist ethic maintains, cries out to our sense of social responsibility and challenges us to be in solidarity with the poor in their struggle. A liberationist ethic also argues that violations of the human rights of the poor tears at the very fabric of the universal common good insofar as the poor are our very own brothers and sisters. In fact a liberationist ethical perspective insists the sacred dwells in a special way among the poor and the underprivileged by virtue of their impoverishment. In view of this, liberationist ethic argues that the primary ethical demand is an option for the poor.

Although migrants are arguably not the poorest of the poor it is undeniable that poverty or the search for a better life is at the center of the reasons for their migration. Moreover, many migrants suffer impoverishment in various ways from having to live in ghettoes or environmentally unfriendly conditions to discrimination and exclusion in American communities and legal policies. Hence as the widely acknowledged father of liberation theology (Gustavo Gutierrez) himself illustrates, one can argue that, in many ways, the contemporary immigrant is iconic of the face of the poor not just in America but in the modern globalized world.[51] In view of this it could be argued that liberationist ethical perspectives provide a more consolidated CST contribution toward the articulation of more humane reform of migration policies.

The second is an ethic of risk. Clearly "other-ing" is at the heart of the problem in current approaches to migration.[52] Hence the primary challenge is to reach out, accept, and embrace the "other." In the modern world the migrant, by virtue of being the "strange-r," has come to symbolize the marginal(ized) "other." But the reality is reaching out, accepting, and embracing the migrant as the "other" is not easy. In an open forum after my lecture at a meeting on migration in Australia, for instance, one participant blamed the Australian socialization into the notion of "stranger danger" for the difficulty of Australians to deal with immigration in a more Christian way. I submit, however, that Australians are not alone in this. Instinctively we fear the unknown. Biases in the mass media, discriminatory public and government rhetoric, as well as our own selfish interests exacerbate our difficulty to accept the immigrant as the other.

Arguably, to do so is risky. It is not easy to give up some of our rights or comforts for the sake of the other as the CST's idea of common good dictates. Neither is it easy to practice solidarity or say *mi casa su casa* to anyone or everyone especially in this day and age that is characterized by uncertainty, insecurity, and violence. But risk we must, because risk itself is an important virtue in Christian ethics.

Time and time again Christian social teachings serve as a reminder that the hallmark of discipleship lies in the ultimate risk of "commitment to the good of one's neighbor with the readiness, in the Gospel sense, to 'lose oneself' for the sake of the other instead of exploiting him, and to 'serve him' instead of oppressing him for one's own advantage (cf. Mt. 10:40–42, 20:25; Mk. 10:42–45; Lk. 22:25–27)."[53] Liberationist ethic itself exhorts Christians to "nourish the subversive memory of Jesus" effectively pointing to a crucial facet in the identity of Jesus as one who takes risks.

Risk, in effect, could serve as a heuristic lens for a CST contribution toward reform of migration policies. Risk is inherent in following the social teachings of the Church. The Catholic Church itself, although not spotless when it comes to fighting for the defenseless, also has a considerable record of taking great risks by standing on the side of the voiceless and powerless. Hence, Catholicism stands at a strategic place to understand the risk that occurs on both sides of the aisle whether it is the migrant who struggles in order to live a better life for himself/herself and his/her family or the citizen who struggles with giving up some "comforts" and "privileges" and a sense of his/her own identity.

What is at the heart of this ethic of risk finds eloquent expression, I believe, in what Sharon Welch writes about in her book *A Feminist Ethic of Risk*. Welch maintains that life is the ultimate value of an ethic of risk. A person who risks, she says, cares for as well as loves life in all its forms. Welch argues this is made possible by grounding the struggle in a redefined responsible action. This means that struggle for justice should be, first and foremost, within the limits of bounded power. It should begin with the recognition that we cannot guarantee decisive changes and the achievement of desired ends in the near future or even in our lifetime; we can only possibly create a matrix or conditions, in which further actions are possible or the possibility for desired changes are possible. Welch maintains an ethic of risk as responsible action can be seen when resistors name, find, and create other resources that evoke persistent defiance in the face of repeated defeats. For Welch, this "sheer holy boldness" is about deciding to care and act, although there are no guarantees of success. It is not easy, she says, as such action requires immense deep daring. At the same time, however, it also enables deep joy.[54] As Welch contends,

The aims of an ethic of risk may appear modest, yet it offers the potential of sustained resistance against overwhelming odds. The aim is simple—given that we cannot guarantee an end to racism nor the prevention of all war, we can prevent our own capitulation to structural evil. We can participate in a long heritage of resistance, standing with those who have worked for change in the past. We can also take risks, trying to create the conditions that will evoke and sustain further resistance. We can help create the conditions necessary for justice and peace, realizing that the choices of others can only be influenced and responded to, never controlled.... We cannot make their choices; we can only provide a heritage of persistence, imagination, and solidarity.[55]

THE WEAKNESS OF CATHOLIC SOCIAL TEACHING

As could be seen in the last two sections of this chapter, the CST provides a rich source for mapping out an ethical perspective to the problematic dimensions of migration. Critics of the CST, however, say that it still needs some improvements when it comes to gender perspective. First, CST documents are written by men and, to a certain extent, may privilege men's experience and perspective. Secondly, a patriarchal perspective underpins the CST, particularly the earlier documents. Pre–John XXIII documents, for example, seldom mention women except implicitly under generic statements regarding the dignity of "man" and under the category of "family." Workers, as understood in *Rerum Novarum*, are men.[56] Moreover, women are not seen as autonomous adults, for example, *Quadragesimo Anno's* section on "Support of the Worker and His Family."[57]

What could be perceived as a gendered problem for migrant women is reinforced in the CST in the way motherhood is presented as the locus of the dignity and vocation of women. Within the CST one gets the impression that women's duties are, first and foremost, to be a good mother and wife.[58] In her study of papal teachings (up to John Paul II) on women, for example, Christine Gudorf posits that despite the shift toward equality for women in Church social teaching, papal teaching on the nature and role of women still demonstrates a romantic pedestalization of women. The predominant theme, Gudorf submits, is motherhood.[59] It stresses that women's particular or special nature and, consequently, their full proper role is as wives and, in particular, as mothers. *Laborem Exercens* stipulates:

It will redound to the credit of society to make it possible for a mother ... to devote herself to taking care of her children and educating them in accordance with their needs, which vary with age. Having to abandon these tasks in order to take up paid work outside of the home is wrong from the point of view of the good of society and of the family when it contradicts or hinders these primary goals of the mission of the mother (LE, no. 17).

Indeed, one could get the impression that as far as the CST is concerned, women's duties are, first and foremost, to be a good mother and wife. Maria Riley singles out and critiques what she considers to be at the heart of this oppressive duty and responsibility for women:

The image of family in the doctrines is the patriarchal family with very clear delineations and authority structures. The ideal is the so-called "traditional family" with a father who is employed and a mother who takes care of the home and children ... This image does not reflect the reality of today's post-industrialized world [and even the Third World where the mother has to work] Because the doctrines place so much stress on the meaning and role of womanhood, the meaning and role of fatherhood is insufficiently recognized ... It disenfranchises men from the full potential of their fatherhood, while it disenfranchises women from the full potential of their personhood.[60]

An approach and perspective, which puts motherhood at the locus of the dignity and vocation of women, may be problematic for migrant women especially for migrant women workers. First of all, the idea of the family is not only that of a patriarchal family but also and, as could be seen in John Paul II's *Letter to Families*, that of a nuclear family.[61] The nuclear-family-centered perspective is problematic (especially in view of the situation of the transnational family) since it is eurocentric or, at the very least, very much Western.[62] Moreover, it overlooks how migrants transform the meanings of motherhood and fatherhood to accommodate spatial and temporal separations. Last but not the least it overlooks how migration and labor market policies contribute to the spread of transnational families between home and host societies as well as to the creation of new transnational family forms by marriage to and/or family formation with a wide selection of nationalities. This bifurcation of the notion of the family plays out in the very decision and act of women to migrate.

The contention is that the ideal of the so-called traditional family in the CST is a reflection of the middle-class family that emerged during the Industrial Revolution. As such it does not represent a universal experience of families.[63] Moreover, the use of complementarity as a foundational sexual ethical concept in magisterial pronouncements on human sexuality poses difficulties.[64] As Cahill submits in her analysis of John Paul II's *Letter to Families*,

Given the pope's view of women's unique role in recognizing the individuality of persons and in making a loving response to all, the special vocation of the family would then seem to rest especially with women. Women, it would seem, are more closely associated by nature than men with the upholding of a "civilization of love"...the fatherhood of men is interpreted in relation to and by virtue of the maternal role of women. Both the civilization of love and the successful raising of children will depend on the father's "willingness...to become willingly involved as a husband and father in the motherhood of his wife."[65]

Indeed, while John Paul II was deeply cognizant of and influenced by the changing roles and various injustices done to women in modern societies, he also espoused this "equal but different" model of the sexes.[66] In *Familiaris Consortio*, for example, while he says that the equality of the sexes "fully justifies women's access to public functions" and rightly points out that a number of indignities suffered by women, for example, prostitution and discrimination against unmarried mothers, are rooted in the attitude that a woman is a "thing" or mere "object of trade," he also insists that "the true advancement of women requires that clear recognition be given to the value of their maternal and family role, by comparison with all other public roles and all other professions."[67] "This biologically determined view of women also becomes evident in the documents," Riley writes, "when they purport to be speaking of human nature and human rights. Women's ability to participate fully in all arenas of the human community is consistently being circumscribed by their so-called nature."[68] Cahill echoes this critique by pointing at how *Familiaris Consortio* and other papal writings have repeatedly affirmed that men and women have distinct personalities that are equal but complementary. Cahill submits that while CST traditionally regards all members of society as having reciprocal rights and responsibilities, the ways in which this is true for women and men differ.[69]

Like Riley and Cahill, some theologians find problems with a complementarity model of gender because, aside from giving the impression that women's social contribution is limited to motherhood and domesticity within the home, it also holds up an ideal of self-sacrificial love for women that could result in inequity and injustice in family and social relationships.[70] In her excursus on *Familiaris Consortio*, Cahill herself argues that John Paul does not address the possibility that women's "nurturing" characteristics might reflect adaptation to social expectations, and raises the feminist concern that elevation of certain "feminine" qualities could reinforce hierarchical arrangements of adults in the family.[71] Katherine E. Zappone articulates this criticism more sharply[72] by saying, "women's 'specialness' really meant woman's confinement to secondary status and specified social roles."[73]

Christine Gudorf, in the meantime, points the source of the problem to the "schizophrenic quality" between papal social teaching, on the one hand, and papal teaching on the private realm of church and family, on the other. Gudorf contends:

Papal social teaching on politics, economics, and social policy in the public realm is characterized by a social welfare liberalism assuming equality, pluralism, democracy, social dynamism, and optimism about creating a just egalitarian order through gradual altruistic efforts within existing social structures. Papal teaching on the private realm, on the other hand, continues to be characterized by assumptions of static institutions rooted in divine and natural law, hierarchy, and paternalism.[74]

Gudorf notes further that papal concern for the stability of family and reluctance to support any equality that might free women of double workloads is influenced by a traditional theology of marriage.[75]

Obviously, the desire to go on being a family in the context of female migration means that theological understanding on the nature of women and, consequently, the idea of the family must be re-imagined. In cases where mobility is a way out of poverty and death-dealing situations, for example, it offers women and their families opportunities for survival or greater well-being. Migration and transnationalism also give women opportunities toward greater freedom and autonomy economically, politically, socially, and culturally. Hence, as Charles Curran argues, the three epistemological presuppositions of CST, namely universality, impartial and universal perspectives, and certitude, must be nuanced in view of developments within the Catholic tradition itself and challenges arising from postmodernism as well as recent liberationist and feminist ethics. A few points raised by Curran on the matter of an impartial and universal epistemological perspective are relevant here. Curran notes:

The early documents were almost entirely Eurocentric. The authors and their experience were heavily European, especially in their intellectual and cultural formation.... The Eurocentric approach still comes through ... Furthermore, the male perspective comes through in almost every document of Catholic social teaching. Women tend to be invisible in the earlier documents, except in discussions of the family. Within the family, however, the earlier documents clearly portray and extol the subordinate position of women. Even today the role of women is primarily as mothers and educators of their children in the home.[76]

Hence, Curran thinks that with regard to the voices of women, the CST faces a structural problem. As Curran points out, women have played no role in the formation of the papal documents of CST.[77]

Still, one must not discount or overlook the fact that there is a growing sensitivity to women's experience and perspective in the CST. The Synod of Bishops gives credence to this by pointing out that women should have their own share of responsibility and participation in the community life of society and likewise of the Church (*Justice in the World*, no. 42). It is also noteworthy to mention here how more recent documents explicitly tackle the sad plight of women migrants. *Erga Migrantes Caritas Christi* notes: "The emigration of family nuclei and women is particularly marked by suffering. Women migrants are becoming more and more numerous. They are often contracted as unskilled laborers (or domestics) and employed illegally. Often migrants are deprived of their most elementary human rights....when they do not become outright victims of human trafficking...This is a new chapter in the history of slavery."[78]

Even pope emeritus Benedict XVI shows the same awareness and sensitivity as could be glimpsed in the following excerpts from his 2006 World Migration Day message:

With regard to those who emigrate for economic reasons, a recent fact deserving mention is the **growing number of women involved** ("feminization"). In the past it was mainly men who emigrated, although there were always women too, but these emigrated in particular to accompany their husbands or fathers or to join them wherever they were. Today, although numerous situations of this nature still exist, **female emigration tends to become more and more autonomous**. Women cross the border of their homeland alone in search of work in another country. Indeed it often happens that the **migrant woman becomes the principal source of income for her family**. It is a fact that the presence of women is especially prevalent in sectors that offer low salaries. **If, then, migrant workers are particularly vulnerable, this is even more so in the case of women.**[79]

What is clear is that the idea of integral humanism might be a way forward for the CST in order to address a perceived gender gap that underpins its contents. As Kenneth Himes posits: "An incorrect view of the human person will inevitably lead to an inadequate theory of political economy....Attainment of the proper understanding of the human person is essential if we are to develop political, economic and cultural institutions that will promote the authentic development of humankind."[80] Mexican-American feminist theologian Maria Pilar Aquino speaks along these lines by pointing out that

[w]hen we speak of humanity we must integrate individual differences into our structure of knowledge. Humanity expresses itself in intrinsically different ways; men and women, though different, are two actual ways of being human. This difference does not in any way imply that one is greater or lesser. It simply indicates a single equal equality in two different modes. Although the modes are different, they possess one same original quality. A notion that makes the differences between women and men antagonistic creates competition and not mutual solidarity.[81]

Hopefully, the increasing awareness and understanding of the plight of women on the move will intensify and help address the weakness when it comes to gender perspective in the CST.

Conclusion

What is notable about CST is that it exhorts people to be citizen-disciples. As the long list of courageous, active, and hopeful Christians has shown, many things are possible when discipleship animates citizenship. But, of course, CST still needs sharpening and further development, not only in light of the political and economic impact or changes brought by globalization, for example, changing notion of nation-states, but also with regard to women. CST, in other words, is not just a fixed truth that needs to be discovered and applied but also one that must evolve and deepen in view of the changed and changing contexts. As Heinrich Bedford-Strohm argues, a sound theological-ethical treatment of migration and flight should not define its objective as primarily addressing "society" in order to simply "hand down" the thoughts of Christians on these issues.[82] Faith insights are not a precise roadmap for normative reforms but they do set a framework within which to move.[83] Consequently, what I propose in this chapter is to look at CST as an alternative approach to the liberal egalitarian and political realist perspective, particularly in view of the promise CST offers in seeking a critical rapprochement between the politics of the common good and the politics of rights.[84] Appropriating Thomas Massaro's words, the CST is not so much an ideology, a blueprint, or a "third way" but a distinctly *religious* contribution to human society.[85] Indeed, despite its inadequacies and weaknesses, one could still arguably say that CST provides an important source and impetus in daring to take the risk in imagining an alternative future toward the flourishing of human beings no matter what color, race, ethnicity, or language they represent. The next three chapters, which constitute the second part of this book, explore how migrants and migration contribute to human flourishing as far as religious experience is concerned.

PART II

MIGRATION AND RELIGIOUS EXPERIENCE

CHAPTER 4

JOURNEYING (TOGETHER)
IN FAITH: MIGRATION, RELIGION,
AND MISSION

Having been to a number of very diverse cities in various parts of the world and having lived in the Netherlands, the United States, and currently in Australia, I consider myself no stranger to the population density and religio-cultural diversity that contemporary migration has brought globally. When people move, they bring not only a literally visible backpack or suitcase but an invisible one as well. This invisible "baggage" is their culture, which consists of, among others, their language, cuisine, music, and intertwined with these, their faith. As Will Herberg points out

in the case of the early US immigrant, it was expected that sooner or later, either in his own person or through his children, he will give up virtually everything he had brought with him and the "old country"—his language, his nationality, his manner of life—and will adopt the ways of his new home. Within broad limits, however, his becoming an American did not involve his abandoning the old religion in favor of some native American substitute. Quite the contrary, not only was he expected to retain his old religion, as he was not expected to retain his old language or nationality, but such was the shape of America that it was largely in and through his religion that he, or rather his children and grandchildren, found an identifiable place in American life.[1]

In earlier times, particularly in the West, religions have clearer or more discernible geographical locations such that one could more or less say Europe or the United States is Christian. Contemporary migration, however, has muddled this claim. In the case of the United States, the very title of Diana Eck's book *A New Religious America: How a "Christian Country" Has Become the World's Most Religiously-Diverse Nation* points to this blurring of geographical religious boundaries.[2] Not surprisingly, migration brings religious diversity both across and within religious traditions. Gregg Easterbrook, for instance, directly attributes the rise of spiritual diversity in the United States to the influx of immigrants. Most Asian migrants, for example, do not give up the religions of the East and the subcontinent like Hinduism, Buddhism, and Islam just as many Afro-Caribbean and Afro-Brazilian migrants do not give up Santeria and Candomblé, which are hybrids of African religion and European Christianity. They celebrate their own festivals, build their own places of worship, conduct the service in their own language, and even import a priest or religious leader from their home countries.

And while most (inter)religious relations are usually smooth in cities worldwide with significant migrant populations, there are serious tensions related to religion that calls for theological (re)consideration. The increasingly complex and critical role of religion in the very process of migration and, in particular, in the life of migrants themselves deserves theological attention, as well.[3] The next section explores this multi-faceted and complex role of religion in the lives of migrants as well as churches or religious communities in destination countries, which is presenting some serious theological challenges.

Religion in the Context Of Migration

Despite its share of charlatans and hypocrites, religion undeniably continues to have a near-universal appeal. William Portier, for example, maintains that human life has a religious dimension such that one can note that wherever we find human beings we usually find a god or gods, religious behavior, and religious faith.[4] Muslims and Christians alone account for more than half of the world's population[5] and these two religions are still growing. This continuing role and power of religion in the lives of human beings lives on—in ever more creative forms—in migration and in the lives of migrants. Even historians and sociologists point out the salience of religion in the lives of migrants[6] and contend that any study of migrants that ignores the role of religion will most likely be incomplete and skewed. This critical role of religion in the lives of migrants could be discerned in two forms, that is, as comfort and challenge.

Religion as Comfort

Religion's enduring role and power in the lives of human beings has often been attributed to the way it serves as "the fire around which people gather." To most adherents it provides not just a sense of identity but also a semblance of security, especially in moments of crisis. Religion, in other words, serves as a source of comfort. This is true in many cases among migrants not just after migration but even before or during the journey itself.

First of all, support from religious leaders and institutions has become an important resource before, during, and after migration. Oftentimes, prayers are sought from the priest or congregation or Masses are offered for the migrant(s). In *Migration Miracle: Faith, Hope and Meaning on the Undocumented Journey,* Jacqueline Maria Hagan notes the increasing practice of migration counseling among ministries in the western highlands of Guatemala for prospective migrants. Services sought by migrants from their pastors as part of the migration counseling range from group prayer (by the migrants and their families and sometimes with the congregation) before setting off by foot toward the Mexican border or asking their pastor to meet with their *coyote* to determine whether the guide is honest or a scoundrel.[7] For these migrants and many other migrants from Latin America who cross into the United States via the southern border of the country, the riskier the endeavor, the greater divine help is sought.

Religious groups themselves sometimes become a direct part of the actual journey itself[8] either by facilitating it or supporting it. There is a relationship, for instance, between the emergence of neo-Pentecostal movements and the upsurge in migration as new charismatic churches are often connected to international or global networks that facilitate migrant movement.[9] In the United States, religious groups' involvement during migration, especially for those who cross the southern border without proper documents, is well known. Pierrette Hondagneu-Sotelo identifies some of these groups in *God's Heart Has No Borders: How Religious Activists Are Working for Immigrant Rights.* These include the Scalabrinians—a Catholic order of priests— who operate a network of migrant shelters along the US-Mexico and Mexico-Guatemala borders that provide spiritual, religious, and practical support for unauthorized migrants in transit; Humane Borders, an interdenominational group that offers emergency assistance to migrants in transit along the Arizona–Mexico border, particularly by maintaining a network of water stations along treacherous crossing points; Border Angels, a similar but smaller version of Humane Borders in the desert hills of east San Diego; No More Deaths, an interfaith group that established emergency camp aids for undocumented migrants in the desert; and Samaritan Patrol, a coalition of Quakers, Jews, Methodists, Catholics, and Presbyterians. Samaritan Patrol is an improved version of Humane Borders because, instead of building water stations, trained volunteers roam the desert in jeeps and vans from daybreak to nightfall looking for migrants in distress.[10] These and other groups, which will be mentioned in the succeeding section, arose in the 1990s and combine advocacy, service, and civil disobedience. Hondagneu-Sotelo reckons that they constitute a new civil society of biblically inspired social action groups.

Today, religious groups worldwide continue to play a major role in working for better living conditions for migrants in the way local churches provide various services that welcome and help migrants. To help migrant women domestic workers, for example, the churches in Hong Kong have a variety of strategic activities designed to mitigate the abuse and exploitation of the domestic workers.[11] The churches help organize the domestic workers as well as provide hotlines and shelters for those in distress. The churches also help in pursuing cases, give counseling and religious formation programs, and offer livelihood courses designed for reintegration.

Churches built or established by migrants themselves often become veritable centers of social and religious life. Take the case of the Chinese Gospel Church in Houston, Texas. It created various social services, which include language classes, welcome party for new Chinese students, charity as well as special crisis funds to help members during emergencies, scholarship funds, and a bulletin board that displays important ads and information, for example, used cars for sale, real estate and insurance agents, jobs like babysitting, food donations, etc. Classes on critical issues such as applying for a job or how to get various kinds of insurance are also conducted. They also formed fellowships, made up of 50 people, which hold religious meetings with activities that include regular training workshops and Sunday school classes for doing one-on-one evangelism, singing, praying, Bible studies, and religious lectures on topics such as married life, children's education, and workplace relationships. The fellowships met, as well, for potluck dinners, picnics, and camping trips, thereby becoming a formidable source of intimacy and mutual support.[12] All in all religious institutions provide comfort for migrants in the way religious organizations play an important role in immigrant integration.[13] This role is notable as it extends well beyond the churches into the religious schools and other faith-based community programs.

Migrants themselves seek solace, hope, and courage in religion before, during, and after migration. They may pray, attend religious services, do their novenas and devotions on their own or with their families for the safety and success of the endeavor. They may also use religious icons or practices for protection in their often perilous journeys. One gets a glimpse of this in items left in abandoned migrant camps in the desert along the southern border of the United States, which include, among others, crosses, rosaries, and prayer books.

Religion serves, as well, to reinforce ethnic identity. One can most strongly see this in the so-called ethnic churches. Janet Mancini Billson sheds light on this close link between religion and ethnic identity in the case of Ukrainian immigrants in Saskatchewan in Canada. In the 1920s every Ukrainian community in Saskatchewan had the so-called Ukrainian National House, which is actually a church and a hall where people could get together. Today, churches, whether Orthodox or Catholic, have relatively remained as a source of well-being, security, and meaning. They also serve as a conduit into Ukrainian heritage and a bridge across generations. Youth choirs, women's associations, and summer camps generate endless opportunities for learning the culture.[14] Migrant religion as a kind of "ethnoreligion" could also be seen in how religious icons, rituals, customs, and traditions that are particular to the migrants' home country or region are re-created in their host countries, churches, and communities. For example, in a parish in Texas where 95 percent are of Mexican descent, one can still see varieties of Mexican Catholicism that are defined by regions and hometowns. They bring practices that are common to Mexican Catholics like home altars, rosaries, novenas, pilgrimages, processions, Day of the Dead celebrations, and lighting candles in front of an image of the Virgin, but they also bring their own saints from either their home towns or family of origin.[15]

Lastly, religion also serves, for better or for worse, as a last line of defense in moments of desperation. In the words of an immigrant mother frantically searching for a cure for her ailing daughter,

[D]esperate times require strong measures, no matter their source. Take, for example, when my youngest child, my daughter got polio.... Already the doctors told me she was a goner. A neighbor brought me some oils and herbs, which I mixed just as she told me, but nothing seemed strong enough.... I prayed to every saint that I could remember. I couldn't find a priest so I carried her down the street to Fulana's house and banged on the

front door.... Once I entered it, I knelt down in front of the Virgin and
begged that she help heal my daughter. After crying and praying for awhile
I returned home. About an hour later my father came in the door from work
and he told me, "Elena, take a cup of drinking water and add a pinch of salt
to it, then from it take a mouthful of water, bless yourself with the sign of the
cross and spray it over your little Maria. If you have faith she will be cured.
I did just as he said and within a short period of time, her fever broke. After a
few more days she recovered completely without any paralysis. I was so happy
with my daughter cured that we went on a pilgrimage to San Benito to stay
with relatives so that we could visit with the Virgin of San Juan.[16]

Religion as Challenge

Part 1 of this book drove home the point that global migration is
embedded in inequities. At the same time it cannot be denied that
the migration of people is an area of human activity in which change
is foregrounded. It comes as no surprise, therefore, that religion in
the context of migration goes beyond being a source of comfort and
charity or playing harmless and less risky roles. Religion, in other
words, takes on the form of challenge. Whether internally or exter-
nally, in word or in deed, migrant or religious groups' perspective,
this challenge is reflected in a number of ways.

First and foremost, religious groups and organizations often play
important roles in contesting not only the social inequities that compel people to move but also the restrictive policies and practices in
destination countries. In the United States, religion could be seen as
a challenge in the way it serves as a means to contest the status quo
or forms of injustice at the border. The religious groups at the southern border mentioned in the previous section, for example, Samaritan
Patrol, illustrate this role of religion since some of the groups' humanitarian acts could be seen as civil disobedience. Other groups at the
border also reflect this role of religion as a challenge through critical
advocacy work. Borderlinks—an ecumenical organization founded by
Presbyterian minister Rick Ufford-Chase—offers experiential education and border tours for US citizens as it seeks to provide a theological understanding of conflicts and inequalities at the US-Mexico
border. Meanwhile, the American Friends Service Committee—an
ecumenical organization by the Quakers—offers migrant advocacy
information, outreach, and referrals through the Immigration Law
Enforcement Monitoring Project to challenge violence at the border, particularly along Texas.[17] Hondagneu-Sotelo maintains that the
actions and some of the principal actors of these groups are direct heirs
to an equally well-known and powerful religious-led movement for

migrants in the United States in the 1980s, known as the Sanctuary[18] Movement. The movement, led by a lay Quaker named Jim Corbett, aided and advocated for just treatment for Central American refugees, particularly Guatemalans and Salvadorans who have been detained and denied legal status as officially sanctioned refugees.[19] The group, which included Jewish clergy, posted bond, offered legal assistance with deportation hearings, and prepared asylum applications. Some who were frustrated with their best legal service efforts resorted to sheltering Central Americans in their homes and churches. Their actions on behalf of migrants took a radical turn when Presbyterian minister and Samaritan Patrol founder John Fife, followed by five San Francisco Bay churches, publicly declared his church as a sanctuary church. The letter sent by Fife to the US attorney general goes straight to the point:

We are writing to inform you that Southside United Presbyterian Church will publicly violate the Immigration and Nationality Act, Section 274 (A). We have declared our church as a "sanctuary" for undocumented refugees from Central America.... We believe that justice and mercy require that people of conscience actively assert our God-given right to aid anyone fleeing from persecution and murder. The current administration of US law prohibits us from sheltering these refugees from Central America. Therefore we believe the administration of the law to be immoral, as well as illegal.... Obedience to God requires this of all of us.[20]

This tradition of active involvement by religious groups in the United States in view of having more humane immigration policies and practices lives on today. At the height of Obama's initiatives to tackle the issue, for example, some of the information campaign or sessions conducted by his party's members were organized with the help of religious groups. The meetings organized by Representative Luis Gutierrez in Chicago have all been held in churches with clergy members from various denominations including, in several places, Muslim imams in attendance.[21]

One could say, indeed, that religious institutions serve as a challenge in the context of migration through the various and sustained ways in which they try to counter the xenophobia that has been present throughout US history. Despite these institutions' efforts, however, religion in the context of migration continues to face some formidable challenges. First, there is the question of the status of the migrants' religious affiliation in their home and host countries. One can see this in the study of two groups (one Buddhist and one Christian) of Chinese immigrants in Texas. Up until a temple was built in their area, the Buddhist immigrants who didn't have much problem finding a temple from their predominantly Buddhist home-land of Taiwan had to resort to going to Chinese Christian churches in order to satisfy their religious and social needs.[22] The Christian Chinese immigrants who were in the minority in mainland China, however, have no shortage of churches to choose from as Christians are the dominant religious group in the United States. In some cases immigrant congregations who do not share the host community's dominant religion encounter hostility. The experience of a Hindu dur-ing the early years of their temple in a southern suburb of Houston reflects this:

When we first built the temple there were feelings of animosity toward us by members of the surrounding community. They were a farmland community that had never seen such a structure before in their life. It was a conservative community, and a few miles before the temple there is a church located on the left side. We were not worried about any harm that would come to us, but we were a little apprehensive about how the community would treat the temple. One day, a crazy man came running into the temple. I believe he was a Christian fanatic, but anyway, this person came in telling us that we would all go to hell, and that we should leave before any bad thing came to us.[23]

The situation is worse, of course, when the migrants' religion itself is not just in the minority but also subjected to suspicion and associated with grave social problems such as terrorism. This is particularly true for Muslim migrants in the West where the religion and its adherents continue to experience backlash from terrorist attacks perpetrated by fundamentalist Muslims. In the United States, which has suffered the most from terroristic acts and campaigns, a Pew poll conducted dur-ing the controversy over the proposed mosque near the World Trade Center found that the American public continues to express conflicted views over Islam.[24] Moreover, mosques have been vandalized and pub-lic opposition or protests have been lodged or held against proposed mosques in some towns and cities.[25] This politicization of the alleged problems posed by Muslim migrants creates social tension and division and, and on few occasions, have turned violent.[26]

For other migrants, being in the minority is worsened by state-sanctioned intolerance of religions other than the dominant religion. This is very much the case in Saudi Arabia, where foreigners are prohibited from performing any kind of religious worship except Islam. In 2010, for example, about 100 foreigners were arrested for practicing Christianity.[27] When I attended a pre-departure orientation seminar—as part of an exposure program for my students—the nuns running the seminar for Middle East–bound Filipina migrant domestic workers even warned those going to Saudi Arabia against bringing any non-Islamic religious materials, for example, Bible and rosary.

In any case, sharing the same religious affiliation with the receiving society or community does not automatically put migrants in good terms with receiving communities and churches, especially when there is a prevailing general anti-immigrant sentiment. In the United States, religious practice becomes challenging for certain groups like Latinos who have unfairly become the symbol of the unwanted immigrant. Take the case of the following Mexican immigrant church, which had to ask the Bishop for their own church because they were rejected by the members of the local Catholic Church:

[I]t was really hard work and long days, still we were happy to have our Sundays free. Yet, even then we could not feel at home in the Catholic Church since we were denied pews at Our Lady of perpetual Help (pseudonym). The Italians would tell us, "all seats are taken." No matter how early we arrived the pews were always reserved for Italians. That is why we asked the Bishop for our own church.[28]

Indeed, while it is true and good that immigrants can use most local churches for their own services, Martin Luther King's statement that the most segregated hour of the week is 11:00 a.m. on Sunday morning still rings true in places of worship worldwide as cultural differences inhibit the formation of integrated churches.

At the same time migration is likely to be among the most conspicuous agents of change of religious systems, primarily because it exposes migrants to new ideas, challenges the power of control and religion in places of origin, and raises profound questions of community and personal identity and affiliation. Consequently, religion itself is challenged and transformed in the context of migration. Fenggang Yang and Helen Rose Ebaugh identify a couple of ways in which religion is transformed among immigrant religious groups, particularly in the United States.[29] Yang and Ebaugh posit that immigrant religious congregations in the United States tend to adopt the dominant American religious (Christian Protestant) model, that is, the congregational form, in two ways, namely organizational structure and ritual formality, which then leads to various changes. The shift from denominational hierarchies—which many immigrant religious groups are more used to in their home countries—to a congregational structure lends itself to voluntary membership. Consequently, joining or leaving a religious group is more likely a conscious, personal act rather than due to family or ethnic heritage or pressure. Moreover, the congregational structure facilitates (greater) lay leadership. The Greek Orthodox Church, which was part of the study, reflects this. Whereas the priest would usually have supreme legislative authority in Greece, the said church in Texas is governed by a priest and parish council cooperatively, along with a board committee consisting of elected members. The congregational structure also makes the expansion of types of services provided to members much easier. Furthermore, some immigrant congregations are developing regional, national, and international networks and organizations. The Taiwanese-speaking Evangelical Formosan Church that was studied has built 30 churches throughout North America and has expanded to Central America, Australia, and New Zealand.[30]

The adoption of congregational ritual, meanwhile, also brings a few changes to immigrant congregations.[31] One change involves the times for worship and the use of Sunday for religious activities. For example, Yang and Ebaugh point out that the Buddhist, Hindu, and Zoroastrian congregations that were studied are increasingly gathering on Sundays rather than on their traditional day of worship. While immigrant Muslims in Houston continue to gather for the traditional Friday prayer, some mosques also regularly hold Sunday gatherings and Sunday school classes. Another change relates to ways of worship. One of the Buddhist temples, for example, adopted the pews-style of Christian churches instead of the traditional empty space with cushions where people often sit cross-legged. Meanwhile, Hindu and Zoroastrian temples, which used to be places primarily for individual prayers and devotion, have also begun collective chanting and praying.

The roles of the clergy for these non-Christian religions are also changing. In traditional societies where immigrants mostly come from the clergy are usually experts in religious rituals and scriptures. In the context of migration, however, they are sought for various kinds of help, particularly those that are normally defined as pastoral work. Last but not the least, there are also changes in the language of worship, which often happens (and is often described) in three stages. Immigrant congregations purportedly usually start as monolingual, that is, in the ethnic group's language. They then progress into the second stage characterized by a bilingual minister who conducts services in English as well as in the ethnic language as an accommodation to the needs of both immigrant and later generations. The third and final stage is a monolingual, that is, English, often multi-ethnic church.

Last but not the least, Yang and Ebaugh note how the adoption of congregational forms is accompanied by increasing inclusiveness in membership. However, with the exception of intermarriages, which are broader in scope, this growing inclusivity in membership is usually still heavily influenced by ethnic or religious affinity. Certain Hindu congregations, for example, are expanding to include diverse Hindu subtraditions just as the Chinese and Hispanic churches expanded by integrating other Chinese or Hispanic immigrants. In any case there are also multiethnic churches among those studied whose racial membership and/or expansion go beyond regions and continent. The Southwest Assembly of God, for example, has membership that includes people of 48 nationalities speaking 49 different languages.

In a few cases even gender hierarchies undergo certain transformations as immigrants get exposed to more liberal worldviews as well as different social, cultural, and economic experiences. Traditionally, women are stereotyped as the "keepers" of religion. Generally, this is still in place among immigrants. But while there are a number of situations that legitimate or allow women's traditional subordinated status to persist, migration also provides some conditions under which congregations promote an improvement in the status of women. Gertrud Hüwelmeier sheds some light on this, examining the dynamics of gender and power relations among Vietnamese Pentecostals in Berlin composed mainly of male pastors and female believers.[32] There are a couple of interesting points to consider in this case. First, a church made up primarily of women, with their own female pastor, was established (albeit as a branch and under the general leadership of a male pastor) due to the women's initiative and on account of their shared experience as migrant Vietnamese women in Berlin.[33] Then, due to problems with their paternalistic male pastor and dissatisfaction with the female leader, a small group of women within the church split and formed their own "prayer circle" under the leadership of a woman whose house became the group's spiritual place.[34] Their routine during their meetings offers a window into some of the unique activities that are woven into the practice or celebration of the faith in the context of migration, particularly by migrant women: reading the Bible, chatting, cooking, and sharing news about problems in their workplace, finances, health issues, relatives in Vietnam, and visas and marriage documents.

Thomas Douglas also gives an example of some semblance of women empowerment in migrant religious practices in his study of changes in religious practices among Cambodian immigrants in Long Beach and Seattle. In the said essay Douglas writes how Cambodian Christian women who were originally Buddhists acknowledge that they had more public faces and greater opportunities for religious participation in Christian churches than in the *wats* (Buddhist houses of worship).[35]

Transformations in religion in the context of migration are also expressed in the phenomenon of multiple religious belonging, which could be seen in the abovementioned case of the Chinese Buddhists in Houston who initially went to churches due to the lack of a temple. Multiple religious belonging arguably becomes a way of life for migrants due to a number of factors that include, among others, the lack of availability of a house of worship for them, exposure to more liberal religious views, and close encounters with other Christians or practitioners of other religions in their host societies. Such encounters, on top of concrete psycho-social, political, and economic needs, filled by other religious groups could broaden migrants' perspectives and openness toward other religious groups and influence the way they understand and practice their faith. The following remark of a Mexican immigrant who shuttles back and forth within different Christian denominations illustrates the complexities such situation poses:

God is not so narrow that he divides us up into groups because of the particular church's roles. I think that God only separates the bad from the good. . . . To me God is giving and Catholics are just as much followers of Christ as are the Pentecostals and the members of the Fellowship of Excitement. But I can't tell the Catholic priest that any more than I can try to explain this to my Pentecostal minister. They don't want to hear it. So I don't tell them. I learn something from each of them and find that I am a much better person for studying the Bible with the Pentecostals and raising my children Catholic as well. It was also good to volunteer with the members of the Fellowship by delivering food baskets to the many people who are less fortunate than me and my family. I think there are many people who do just as I do and we are perhaps the more committed members of our churches.[36]

For others, particularly Asian migrants who were converts to Christianity, multiple religious belonging is a more prominent or "normal" way of life. A scenario and question posed by a Cambodian-American Catholic reflect the tricky situation this poses. She said, "On Sunday morning I go to church where I'm an active member. When I come home from church I then do my ancestor veneration. Does this make me a bad Catholic?" She later opined that this does not make her less Catholic and that this is actually the reality for many Asian-Americans who converted to Christianity when they came to America. Kathleen Sullivan echoes this (inter)religious way of life among Asian-Americans when she noted how home altars of Asian parishioners in a church in Texas[37] are designed for both Catholic and ancient rituals associated with ancestor veneration, with images of the Virgin, Jesus, Buddha, and/or saints, flowers and/or fruit, candles, photos of a person (alive or deceased), and instruments of devotion (rosary, Bible, prayer book, hymnal, and Buddhist beads) all occupying a space in the home altar.

Religious change also occurs literally in the context of migration through religious conversion by migrants within and across religious traditions. To be sure, various reasons related to the realities and conditions of migration play a critical role in these conversions. It could be on account of ethnic affinity. In the Argentine Protestant evangelical church that Yang and Ebaugh studied, for example, there were many members who converted from Catholicism upon their arrival in Houston because of the large community of Argentine members of that Protestant church. They also left Catholicism because of the absence of a specifically Argentine Catholic church in the city.[38] Others, like the Filipina migrant domestic workers in Hong Kong who converted to Islam, have far more complex reasons. Their reasons include exposure to the multiple religious traditions in Hong Kong; a desire for "greater autonomy and liberation," especially from what they perceive as stifling marriage–related policies of Filipino Catholicism (like the ban on divorce and abortion and the severe restrictions on birth control methods); friendship with Sr. Madiha (a Filipina convert to Islam who is also a domestic helper); romantic involvement and inter-marriage with the Pakistani men; previous work experience in the Middle East; influence from converted family members, employers, or co-workers; mere curiosity; or a desire for enlightenment. The Filipina domestic workers struggle, however, with a number of Islamic rules and practices, for example, praying five times a day and wearing a *hijab*, not just because of adjustment to the new religion but also because of the restrictions imposed by their job and by their predominantly Buddhist employers. Not surprisingly, a lot of the converts also revert to their religion when Islam becomes repressive or less able to contribute to the mitigation of their oppression. Sitthi Hawwa attributes the reversion to the inability of Mosque to fund sisters in terms of financial crises, the absence of a physical space for converts with terminated contracts, the unwillingness of fellow Muslims to employ them, and the dissatisfactory behavior of Muslim men.[39]

MISSION IN THE CONTEXT OF MIGRATION

Mission is another area that merits theological exploration in the context of migration as migrants arguably become (more) missionary in a number of ways.[40] In their receiving countries, religious assembly and affiliation constitute the most powerful means available to migrants in their search for self-identity, communal acceptance, and social integration. Consequently, Jehu Hanciles posits in his book *Beyond Christendom: Globalization, African Migration and the Transformation of the West* that immigrant congregations potentially have a missionary function not only because they represent the most effective instruments through which immigrants can impact the wider society but also because immigrant churches model religious commitment, apply the message of the gospel directly to daily exigencies, and comprise communities that interact on a daily basis with other marginalized segments of society.[41] In the United States, for instance, immigrants have played a significant role in shaping American religious life[42] not only by contributing to the de-Europeanization of American Christianity but also in witnessing to a kind of public Christianity or by becoming a "social congregation." Hanciles points at how Catholic congregations that were predominantly made up of immigrants were the first to keep their churches open throughout the whole week. Then, as now, immigrant churches were bastions of fervent religiosity and communities of commitment as they "bore faithful witness to the claims of the gospel, experienced significant growth through innovative ministries, catered to the most urgent needs of the most vulnerable communities, provided religious instruction and training for the next generation of Americans, and supplied vital social services that contributed to public well-being."[43] This transformation of the role of the church within American society as a result of the realities of the immigrant religious community and by the very presence, active participation, and witness of immigrants themselves renders the immigrants missionary.

Today, migrants are also strongly described as missionary on account of the dynamism they bring to the faith communities of their destination countries. In the words of the Hong Kong Church,

Our churches are very alive on Sundays because of their presence. The Filipinos have brought their religiosity and faith to the Church of Hong Kong—they enhance the faith of our local people with their presence, witnessing hospitality, joy, and love for music. The diocese is truly blessed in many ways because of the Filipinos, and their dynamism will keep alive the faith in the territory... In short, **the Filipinos are to be called missionaries first before they are labeled as domestic helpers** (emphasis mine).[44]

Owing to the organizational structure, nature, and vision of their congregations, immigrants also literally become missionaries. This is illustrated in the boost that the early immigrant Christian influx in the United States gave to the overseas or foreign missionary movement in America. The Black Church Movement, for example, stimulated African American missionary consciousness, particularly in relation to Africa, while the wave of Eastern European immigrants between 1900 and 1920 saw the explosion in the number of American mission agencies and forces for overseas missionaries.[45] This missionary impulse, which is more intense and has a broader scope today, is reflected in the Chinese Gospel Church in Texas mentioned earlier in the chapter. This church has developed an evangelistic ministry that not only created a daughter church and actively supported missionary work in China (with a USD 50,000 annual donation) but also sends missionaries to South and Central America, to various Asian nations, and to Britain and other European countries. It works, as well, at the Houston Port with Chinese seamen. Furthermore, fellowship meetings include regular training workshops and Sunday school classes for doing one-on-one evangelism, singing, praying, Bible studies, and religious lectures on topics such as married life, children's education, and workplace relationships.[46]

Such missionary endeavors or active evangelization, however, do not always elicit positive responses and could become a source of tension. Some homes in a largely Catholic neighborhood in Texas, for instance, are marked with the following sign warning those who approach with an intent to proselytize: "This is a Catholic home and your Protestant literature is not welcomed here."[47] Nevertheless, migrants today also arguably witness to new ways of understanding and doing mission. Gerrie ter Haar sheds light on the former by pointing at the link between the evangelistic zeal of African immigrants and colonial Christianity. She says that African Christians in Europe themselves see their evangelism as a form of a reversal of colonization. ter Haar notes that

just as European missionaries once believed in their divine task of evangelizing what they called the dark continent, African church leaders in Europe today are convinced of Africa's mission to bring the gospel back to those who originally provided it. Thus, many African Christians who have recently migrated to Europe, generally to find work, consider that God has given them a unique opportunity to spread the good news among those have gone astray.[48]

Hanciles, meanwhile, points at the role of transnationalism or transnational networks in doing mission. He points, in particular, at how migrant Pentecostal churches make use of their transnational networks to facilitate migrant movement and recruit so much so that churches initiated by them often become veritable centers of transmigration and transnationalism.[49] Hanciles contends that contemporary processes associated with globalization has made possible some actions by migrants, which are missionary in nature. Many transmigrants and/or migrants with dual citizenship, for example, maintain close connections and are very invested in the socioeconomic and political issues in their countries of origin. As described in the section on social capital in the first chapter, migrants contribute, to a certain extent, in lifting the poverty of their home countries. African immigrants in the United States that Hanciles talks about in his abovementioned book even actively participate in the political process in their countries of origin by lobbying political leaders through letter writing and sponsorship of political activities in the United States, which are meant to call attention to particular issues at home and to coordinate action.[50] Because they are relatively well-off and quite organized, their voice does carry some weight in the political establishment in their countries of origin.

THEOLOGICAL REFLECTIONS

So what are the theological implications of the characteristics of religion and mission in the context of migration? What are the facets of a Christian theology that takes into account the new or more pronounced issues and questions put forward by migrants' and receiving communities' experience and practice of religion and Christian mission? Lastly, what are the areas in Christian theology that needs re-appropriation if it is to dialogue with the religious and missionary experience of migrants?

A Church of the Stranger

The comfort and challenge with which religion is experienced in the context of migration lends itself to an image of the church as a church of the stranger. A church of the stranger is, first and foremost, a catholic church. Catholicity is the ability to hold things together in tension with one another.[51] From such a perspective, catholicity is not about the superficial coming together of cultures where migrants and their culture-based expressions of the faith are confined to the basement or to marginalized church times and spaces but one where they can freely breathe, equally make a difference, and flourish. When plurality is approached from the perspective of catholicity, it becomes accepted as richness. Authentic Christian catholicity then calls us not only toward openness but also toward embracing diversity. As Miroslav Volf writes, a catholic personality is "enriched by otherness, a personality which avoids exclusivism and, at the same time, transcends indifferent relativism. It does not simply affirm the otherness, as otherness, but seeks to be enriched by it."[52]

In the church of the stranger, churches are challenged by the brokenness of communities and the social fabric of life as experienced by uprooted people like migrants to become what they (churches) really are: sanctuaries for everyone in need and a table around which people of diverse and even opposing positions can converse and break bread together, for a church of the stranger is supposed to be a church without borders. It loses its *raison d'être*, particularly its catholicity, when it closes itself to the strange-r or when it becomes indifferent to the different and does not strive for an inclusive community, that is a sign and foretaste of God's *kin*dom.[53]

A church of the stranger thrives on difference, diversity, and plurality. It envisions not so much a "melting pot" but a mosaic society. It builds harmonious relationships with people regardless of their gender, class, race, ethnicity, and religion. Consequently, the church of the stranger is an intercultural church. It respects and is open to all cultures. It welcomes fellow believers, including converts, from/with other cultures regardless of class. Moreover, its members struggle to be church by "becoming strangers together." It is a church that does not simply focus on the multiplication or amalgamation of cultures but, most especially, on the dynamic interaction between and among cultures. It is a church that views other cultures and other religions as gifts that enrich the catholicity of the church of the stranger, individually and collectively. It is my belief that an intercultural church is the fullest potential of the church.

Come to think of it, it is not that the church is experiencing multiculturality for the first time or that it is facing the challenge of learning how to be a church of the stranger for the first time. The early Christian churches across the Roman Empire, especially those with a significant number of Gentiles who converted to Christianity, are familiar with this experience. The apostle Paul, who advocated for and struggled to build churches that include and embrace non-Jews (as reflected especially in his letter to the Galatians) could enlighten us on this predicament. Going back much earlier, Jesus himself, as the stranger *par excellence*, paves the way for forging a church of the stranger. As the stranger *par excellence* Jesus profoundly identifies, shares, and struggles with strangers' primary condition of alienation and discrimination. There was no room for his parents at the inn, so Mary had to give birth to him in a manger. His family fled to a foreign land (Egypt) to escape from Herod. Like many migrant parents, who constitute a significant number of the "strangers" in American churches, necessity forced Jesus' parents to go to Egypt for their child's sake. Moreover, while he went around preaching and teaching, Jesus sought the hospitality of friends and strangers. He also experienced not being welcomed (Luke 9: 52–54). Last but not the least, as the master/teacher who practiced the "hospitality which causes scandal," by associating with and eating with the least, the last, and the lost of Jewish society, Jesus is the "perfect (fellow) stranger." He not only knew what it means to be an outcast and excluded; he also connected with the "estranged" people in his time. Thus, it could be said that Jesus not only forged the path for struggle for the "estranged" of this world; he also laid the foundations for a church of the stranger.

As could be seen in Jesus' practice of it, hospitality is an important foundation. While it is often regarded in its tame and pleasant dimension, that is, welcoming only friends and acquaintances, hospitality in its "subversive countercultural dimension"[54] could provide a framework for critiquing xenophobia. This radical hospitality is the opposite of cruelty. It entails welcoming socially undervalued persons, like migrants. It means challenging "other-ing" and paving the way toward the respect for and visibility of strangers. As Mike Purcell posits, hospitality is an ethic that ought to be constitutive of the culture of immigrant societies. For Purcell the law of an unconditional hospitality is *a priori* and realizable even though it must be enacted within a particular, and possibly perverse, historical space.[55] This ethically inscribed notion of hospitality, Purcell says, becomes even more important and urgent in places where the state attempts to juridically circumscribe it.

Hospitality, in this way, becomes resistance for or toward humanization rooted in the power of recognition.[56] Matthew 25:31–46, where Jesus says, "Come...inherit the kingdom prepared for you...for I was hungry and you gave me food...thirsty and you gave me drink...a stranger and you welcomed me," offers a very good basis for this. It goes to show that the hospitality that recognizes the stranger is a *kin*dom value that is actualized in the recognition of a neighbor in the stranger and, most especially, in the recognition of Jesus in every stranger. The author of the letter to the Hebrews, in fact, reminds us that it is a moral obligation to offer hospitality for, like Abraham and Sarah, we might be entertaining angels (Heb.13:2).[57]

Luke goes so far as asserting that refusal to extend hospitality can have greater consequences than those endured by the people of Sodom (Luke 10:12; cf. 9:54).

Hospitality, as a practice that integrates respect and care, recognizes and enriches human dignity. It not only creates a safe and welcoming space for the guest but also provides an enriching experience for the host. Parker Palmer points at this common grace in hospitality: "Through the stranger our view of self, of world, of God is deepened and expanded…we are given the chance to find ourselves…and God finds us and offers us the gift of wholeness in the midst of our estranged lives."[58] Hospitality in this way is seen in terms of what John Koenig describes as "partnership with strangers." But then I find this limited in articulating the depth of hospitable encounters. For one, the idea still carries elements of, at best, charity and, at worst, paternalism. The best to way to avoid this paternalism, I believe, is to see hospitality directly in relation to God. Hospitality has been characteristic of the way God has been described in the Bible as well as presented in tradition.[59] I posit that imaging God as the host provides a way of not falling into the trap of paternalistic hospitality. Seeing God as the provider of hospitality destabilizes the usual roles (with the migrant as the usual guest and the citizen as the usual host) and the unbalanced order of relations these roles spawn. God as the host presents, instead, both the migrant and the citizen as guests and, consequently, as both strangers.

I argue that this is a more egalitarian way of looking at the experience of hospitality. In fact, it is very much Christian as exemplified in our experience of creation, grace, healing, and forgiveness as God's gifts. This means that whenever we receive or practice hospitality, we are actually sharing in God's hospitality. In this way God becomes not just the host but also the guest we receive in others.[60] This challenges theology to go beyond the notion of partnership *with* strangers to partnership *of* strangers and from hospitality *to* strangers to hospitality *of* strangers. Moreover, this means Christian theology must go beyond *koinonia*, or communion among Christians, to the more egalitarian and inclusive community that Elisabeth Schüssler-Fiorenza describes as *ekklesia* or discipleship of equals.[61]

Letty Russell weaves together the question of power dynamics, the primacy of the outsider, and the sacred dimension of hospitality in *Just Hospitality: God's Welcome in a World of Difference*. Russell does this, first, by critiquing how the doctrine of election has been used in Christian theological tradition in such a way that "difference" becomes a means of oppressing people. Russell points out that the

Christian doctrine of election, which carries with it an understanding of chosenness for some, has been used historically to exclude and divide, rather than as God's mandate for radical hospitality. Russell goes on to say that the divisions of chosenness have often served religiously, politically, racially, gendered, and economically dominant groups.[62] One could see this play-out in the drama of contemporary migration in the way the chosen ones—skilled workers, skilled transients, or wealthy migrants—are encouraged, even invited, by destination countries to migrate by providing these potential migrants much easier and quicker process to enter or immigrate.[63] Meanwhile, the undesirable or excluded ones—the poor and unskilled, sometimes even refugees—are often given an unwelcome message either by putting them in detention centers; granting them temporary visas; making the immigration process long, difficult, and expensive; or outrightly denying them entry.

The Christian tradition of election is rooted in the covenant stories in the Hebrew scriptures (Gen. 15: 18–21; Exod. 3:17; Deut. 7:2). Russell writes that Christians, claiming the superior revelation of God's redemption, carried the biblical story of chosenness as Christ's universal messianic mandate to them. The problem, Russell posits, is that they carried an understanding that they were a chosen people because they thought they have special qualities. The reality, Russell goes on to say, is that they were chosen simply because God loved them. Consequently, Russell offers the Christian tradition of hospitality as a way of resisting the deformation of the doctrine of election. More specifically, Russell suggests a feminist hermeneutic of hospitality that (1) pays attention to the power quotient, (2) gives priority to the perspective of the outsider, and (3) rejoices in God's unfolding promise.[64] The doctrine of election, thus, becomes a matter of mission and not of privilege, and chosenness becomes more about responsibility rather than superiority.

Christian Theology of Religions

Migrants' experience of religion and religious identity also presents a theological challenge from an interreligious perspective. First, it intensifies religious diversity that presents challenges to destination countries, in general, and creates tension between and among migrants and communities who find it difficult to deal with difference, in particular. Second, migration opens up—through multiple religious belonging—new commitments not just to the migrant's dominant faith but to two or more religious traditions. Third, migration also lends itself to religious conversion as migrants get exposed to other religions or to experiences that encourage or compel them to convert. Last but not the least, global migration patterns' facilitation of the mobility of terrorists, who admit to committing violence in the name of their religion, create tensions and conflicts between the adherents of the religion that is perceived as "violent" and the adherents of the aggrieved religion, for example, the case of Muslims in the United States. It could be argued that such challenges could be addressed by a broader Christian theology of religions, which recognizes and respects the integrity of other religious traditions.

Such a broader theology of religions could entail a number of approaches. One could be the Asian approach. Just as multiple religious belonging seems more prevalent among Asian (im)migrants, most theological discussions on interreligious relations in Christian circles have been arguably provoked by the particular context of Asia, where there have been substantial theological reflections on interreligious relations. For some Asian Christian theologians, the whole thesis of the theology of religions poses problems. They ask: Why do we need to measure other religions against our own religious ideals and theological systems? Why do we need to categorize them in terms of their salvific efficacy? Why do we need to evaluate if peoples of other religions are saved or headed to eternal damnation? Felix Wilfred, for example, points to the predominantly Western epistemology grounded on the principle of non-contradiction as shaping the exclusivist-inclusivist-pluralist paradigm.[65] This epistemology hinges upon history where particular events or persons and their uniqueness matters. However, for many Asians, what matters is that the various religions are thriving, giving life, and at peace with one another. After all, they have been partaking in the inexhaustible search for the divine for centuries.

Moreover, the Asian psyche is open to diversity and ambiguity. As renowned Vietnamese-American theologian Peter Phan notes:

Scratch the surface of every Asian Catholic and you will find a Confucian, a Daoist, a Buddhist, a Hindu, a Muslim or more often than not, an indistinguishable mixture of all of these religions. Asian and Pacific Christians live within a society in which they rub shoulders daily with non-Christians and have direct experiences of the moral values and spiritualities of non-Christian religions. They are socialized into these values and spiritual traditions not only through formal teachings but also, and primarily, through thousands of proverbs, folk sayings, songs and, of course, family rituals and cultural festivals. Many Asian and Pacific Catholics do not find it strange or difficult to inhabit different religious universes.[66]

Phan goes on to say that this rich and varied as well as latent but pervasive religious heritage constitutes a significant contribution by Asian and Pacific Catholics to the American church. Ordinarily, Asian Christians have no problems embracing a sort of epistemological humility by refraining from judging the religious other. If anything, the religious other's presence encourages Asian Christians to give witness totheir own faith with greater zeal. In the words of Indian theologian Michael Amaladoss: "People then learn to relativise their own belief systems without in any way relativizing the Absolute to which they are committed and which they witness to and proclaim."[67] Problems begin when they are told that their Christian tradition make claims to Christianity's uniqueness or the absoluteness of their savior or religion. But as Phan argues:

If non-Christian religions contain "elements of truth and of grace" and if they may be considered ways of salvation from whose doctrinal teachings, sacred texts, moral practices, monastic traditions, and rituals and worship Christianity can and should benefit through dialogue, then there should be no theological objection and canonical censure against someone wishing to be a Christian and at the same time to follow some doctrinal teachings and religious practices, let's say of Buddhism or Confucianism or Hinduism, as long as these are not patently contradictory to Christian faith.[68]

Another approach toward a broader Christian theology of religions could be the engagement of specific thorny issues. Evidently, Christian theologies of religions have come a long way. At the same time one could not deny that Christianity's relations with other religions remains a bone of contention. It is in need of what John Hick calls a Copernican revolution.[69] Christianity has to realize that it is not the center of the universe and has to come to terms with the fact that two-thirds of humanity have never and probably will never ever share in its faith and conviction. Besides, contemporary efforts toward interreligious dialogue in the context of migration could still be problematic in three ways. First, any mention or talk about God will inevitably be from a religious lens and, most likely, a particular religious lens. Second, what about religions like Buddhism, which does not use the term "God" as the Christian tradition has understood it? Last but not the least, even if God as incomprehensible mystery is supposed to be a transcendent category,[70] we still have to contend with the reality that the word "God" is overwhelmingly tied with Christianity. In fact the word "God" has often been understood by ordinary Christians to refer to the *Christian* God and has been used by Christians themselves to engage in exclusionary practices. Eck illustrates the point I am trying to make with a story:

> When Muslims in Edmond, the suburb of Oklahoma City where the University Central of Oklahoma is located, planned to build a mosque in 1992, a move was made to deny a building permit because, as a Pluralism Project researcher reported, One of the minister's wives [*sic*] attended the first public hearing and vehemently opposed it. She said, "The constitution says One nation under God, and that's a Christian God. These people have no right to be here."[71]

Then there is the issue of gender. The religions (Christianity included) have to recognize the seriousness of women and gender issues that continue to plague them as well as acknowledge the critical role women (can) play in interreligious engagements. Last but not the least, is the thorny question on whether religious pluralism exists *de facto*, meaning just a fact of the world today that is meant to be overcome or *de jure* meaning it is a good intended by God in principle.

Another helpful approach in articulating a broader Christian theology of religions could be seen in what Jeanine Hill Fletcher suggests in *Monopoly of Salvation?: A Feminist Approach to Religious Pluralism*, that is, engaging in a dialogue that takes into account people's hybrid identities. Hill Fletcher argues that human beings, in all the dimensions of who they are and in their particularity, are the self-communication of God. In a sense she submits that it is our and the other's hybrid identities whether it's religion, class, gender, etc. that allow, challenge, and give us several ways or possibilities to engage the religious other without erasing his/her (religious) particularity in the process.[72]

James Kroeger articulates what could be seen as the practical demands of the abovementioned approaches in the context of migration in what he calls "dialogue decalogue for migrants."[73]

1. Be aware of the new, unfamiliar experience you are entering; no longer are you living in a monocultural-religious milieu. This is one important factor in the constellation of pressures you and your family will experience.
2. As a Christian migrant, know that the Catholic Church encourages interfaith relationships and that "interreligious dialogue is part of the Church's evangelizing mission" (*Redemptoris Missio*, no. 55).

3. Embrace a positive view of other religious traditions and faiths; this will facilitate the building of constructive personal relationships with your neighbors and fellow-workers, Recognize the goodness and genuine faith of others.

4. Honestly and straightforwardly examine your own fears, biases, and prejudices regarding other religions and their adherents.

5. Realize that everyone can always begin in simple ways to promote the "dialogue of life." Ask how you can collaborate with persons of other faiths to serve the needy and poor in your midst.

6. Explore "common ground" with the followers of other religions, seeking to know and appreciate the similar elements and values that are found in both faith traditions (e.g., holiness, morality, spirituality, or prayer).

7. Recognize that there can be various levels, areas, or approaches to interreligious dialogue. One commonly accepted view acknowledges four basic forms (dialogue of life, dialogue of deeds, dialogue of specialists, and dialogue of religious experience). Remember that for the Church, dialogue is not an abstract idea, but a personal encounter.

8. Be aware that migrants can serve as "dialogue catalysts" in their concrete living, working, and worshipping situations.

9. Be committed to your own faith; practice it, develop it, share it in genuine, respectful ways (cf. 1Pt. 3:15–16). Develop a "spirituality of dialogue."

10. Remember dialogue and interfaith living are difficult endeavors and a challenging commitment; ask in prayer for God's grace to practice them well.

Mission as Incarnational Evangelization

The missiological dimension of migration is arguably a new area of theological exploration.[74] This does not mean, however, that mission's close link with migration is a new phenomenon. In the first place Christianity has always been a migratory religion. The most extensive missionary movement in Christianity's history even corresponded with one of the great migrations in human history, that is, the European expansion (especially between 1800 and 1925). In the United States each wave of immigration has been known to bring dynamism to the missionary movement, local and overseas. Of course one should not discount the fact that each wave of immigrants also literally increased the number of adherents of the different religious groups. For example, the new wave of Christian immigrants, that is, Hispanics, has undoubtedly increased the number of American Catholics, which declined in the 1980s when some of the nation's larger dioceses were losing number and closing schools.

Mission in the context of contemporary migration could be characterized as evangelical. First of all, every Christian migrant is a potential missionary. As such huge movements of people from Asia, Africa, and Latin America—today's bastions of Christianity—means a huge number of potential missionaries. So, as Hanciles muses, just as European migrations from Christianity's old heartlands provided the impetus for the largest missionary movement in Christian history, massive migration from Christianity's new heartlands could galvanize a phenomenal non-Western missionary movement. This argument holds ground in view of the reality that many new immigrants have a Pentecostal spirituality. This is true among United States immigrants, particularly those from Korea and China, who tend to be evangelistic and place a lot of importance on conversion. One could see this in the case of the Chinese Gospel Church in Texas mentioned earlier in the chapter.

This evangelistic preoccupation takes a new missionary dimension as immigrants, particularly those in Western secularized countries, even see themselves as missionaries to the people of their destination countries, creating a phenomenon called "reverse-mission." One could see this reversal in missionary activity in the case of African Christians in Europe cited earlier in the chapter and in how African migrants in the United States see America as a mission field.[75] But, of course, with their transnational networks, and as transnationals themselves, migrants' missionary capacity and sustained missionary engagement goes beyond American society and spills over into the wider global context. Indeed, the much stronger forces of transnationalism, which allow migrants to simultaneously engage multiple networks to finance and conduct missionary activity in multiple places, make the transnational aspect another unique feature of Christian mission as understood and practiced in the context of contemporary migration. The congregations, communities, and missionary endeavors by new immigrants in the United States, for example, are more strongly intertwined with transnational networks than those of earlier immigrants. As veritable centers of transmigration and transnationalism, immigrant congregations consequently have a great potential to play a critical role in global Christian missions. Many African immigrant pastors, for instance, find that living in America produces avenues and resources for global outreach unavailable to them before they moved. As Afe Adogame points out,

The significance of local and global networks among African churches in both home and host contexts cannot be overemphasized. Such networks are assuming increasing importance for African migrants. The range and nature of ties include new ecumenical affiliations, pastoral exchanges between Africa, Europe, and the US, special events and conferences, prayer networks, internet sites, international ministries, publications, audio/video, and tele-evangelism. The "flow" between the links is two-directional, sending and receiving—globally and locally.[76]

Missionary dynamics in the context of contemporary migration, however, is seen not always through conversion but also in the exchange and communication that happens across Christian traditions and across cultures, including among those belonging to the same Christian denomination.[77] The majority of new Christian immigrants in the United States, for example, are generally evangelical in faith and practice. This means that they are more likely to be Bible-believing, emphasize evangelism, uphold strict moral lifestyles, and affirm divine intervention in daily life. But, as Hanciles insists, new immigrants' type of evangelicalism is different in that its religious practices and institutions, having been decisively shaped by the experiences, priorities, worldviews, and primal spirituality of African, Asian, and Latin American contexts, cannot be seamlessly absorbed or assimilated into Anglo-American evangelical Protestantism.[78] Latinos, for example, bring with them new devotional expressions and spirituality that do not always and necessarily sit well with Euro-American Christians. This is reflected in the following statements of a Mexican Catholic immigrant who converted to Protestantism and then went back to Catholicism:

At home in Jalisco, Mexico, my mother always had holy water at the entrance to the house and it was a fountain with the image of the Guardian Angel protecting two small children outside their home. My mother always had us bless ourselves before we left and I somehow liked the image of knowing that there was this invisible guardian watching over me. So even as a Baptist I continued this custom. I know they did not like it.[79]

Thus, mission in the context of contemporary migration is inevitably intercultural. It is about Christians learning from one another (and non-Christian religions) the manifold ways and faces of forging a relationship with the sacred. It goes without saying that mission is also about embracing and practicing inculturation or interculturation (more on this in the next chapter), which naturally entails a dialogical attitude.[80] The de-Europeanization of American Christianity and the increasing Pentecostalization of American Catholicism[81] reflect some of the results of this contextual approach and perspective. Such an approach and perspective is vital in developed countries like the United States, where the majority of immigrants come with particular ways of being Christian. Equally important, most of these immigrants come from countries in the global South, which are now the heartlands of the Christian faith[82] and the chief sources of missionary movement.

It is this southern character of global Christianity and global migration patterns, on top of the problematic conditions inherent in migration, that compel mission in the context of migration to take on a prophetic dimension. Mission, as it is in the biblical tradition, has inescapable social justice implications. So, if mission is to be rooted in Jesus' mission, it must be liberating. At the heart of the biblical tradition and Jesus' missionary vision is the gift of a "home"—a place and space where justice is done and respect and compassion unite everyone. Today death-dealing and life-giving conditions inherent to contemporary migration are redefining all our notions of "home" and challenging our very understanding and approach to mission. The call, therefore, is to engage in a mission that brings about contextual, borderless liberation, especially to all marginal(ized) persons like migrants. In doing so, missionary engagement becomes incarnational.

Such missionary engagement, also described as "witness as *with*ness," is critical in the United States, where congregations, particularly immigrant congregations, are increasingly filling the void for outreach to the areas and sections of the American population that need serious and urgent attention. This is particularly true in the cities where most of those in need are highly concentrated,[83] for example, homeless and unemployed. Immigrant congregations play a strategic role whether they like it or not since they are predominantly located in urban neighborhoods and often forced to occupy the most unlikely places—cramped living rooms, hotel ballrooms, thousands of storefronts, rented halls or office buildings, even ornate churches whose membership has declined—they serve constituencies (both immigrant and native) long abandoned by more established and affluent American congregations.[84] An incarnational type of missionary engagement that focuses on interpersonal exchange and emphasizes effective presence and participation as the basis for proclamation is, without doubt, an important dimension of mission in the context of contemporary migration.

Conclusion

The changes and challenges faced by religion and mission in the context of migration obviously confront Christian theology to explore more deeply the catholic character of Christianity. Catholicity, as mentioned earlier in the chapter, is the ability to hold things together in tension with one another. As a heuristic means, it can help in situating ethnicity in the context of the radical universality that is humanity's call and deepest identity. As it is about wholeness and fullness through exchange and communication, catholicity can address the questions raised and/or experienced by migrant religion in view of internal and external pluralism. By focusing on wholeness as the physical extension of the Church, catholicity strikes at the exclusivity that could arise as a response, either wittingly or unwittingly, among migrants and between migrants and the local people, whether they share each other's religion or not. By speaking about fullness as orthodoxy in faith, it (catholicity) allows more room for doctrinal re-appropriation or re-interpretation as particular traditions of a religion interact with one another, hence addressing the problems or difficulties posed by internal pluralism. Lastly, and most importantly, catholicity as exchange and communication provides a theological framework for dealing with the interaction or relations among the members of a multi-ethnic church or congregation.

While all these may sound great, they are, unfortunately, easier said than done. Moreover, they leave certain dimensions that beg for further discussion that the succeeding chapter will attend to. For example, how do we go about creating intercultural churches? Is it enough that migrants can use the church or church grounds? Is it enough that they are given time slots (often the less popular time) for their own services, hence have separate worship in different languages? Moreover, is it best to just always let them have their own service in their own time and their own language while the local members stick with their old group and their old ways? Will it suffice to have occasional exhibits or have icons or religious symbols from the migrants' home countries displayed in churches or observe their religio-cultural festivals during or after the services? Is knowing and singing one or two songs or having one or two scripture readings in the migrants' mother tongue sufficient? These are questions the next chapter will more fully explore.

CHAPTER 5

TOWARD AN INTERCULTURAL
CHURCH: MIGRATION AND
INCULTURATION

It was my first Sunday in the United States, so my husband and I decided to go to the main church for my first experience of the "American" Eucharistic celebration in our new home, a medium-sized city in the Midwest. As we walked around the church grounds I came face to face with a statue of Mary I had never seen or heard of before: Our Lady of La Vhang. At first I wondered who this Mary was and wondered what it—a seemingly atypical American name and face—was doing in what I thought was a largely Euro-American city. Things became clear to me when I went inside and found a church filled with mostly Vietnamese-American parishioners, complete with a Vietnamese-American priest and a bilingual Mass. Welcome to the American church or, for that matter, the church of the twenty-first century!

Without a doubt the cultural landscape of city churches has never been as diverse as they are today. Moreover, this diversity is true not just in the West but also in cities worldwide, particularly in migrant-receiving countries.[1] I have seen this myself in Malaysia—a migrant-receiving country in Asia—at a Mass on Epiphany Sunday at St. John's Cathedral in downtown Kuala Lumpur. There was an overflow crowd (the church has a seating capacity of more or less 1,500) of about 200. What was striking aside from the sheer number of people that packed the church is the diversity of the church goers. Aside from the local Catholics, that is, Indians and Chinese, there were Westerners as well as Asians and Africans from various countries.

I have previously seen the strikingly large number of Filipino migrants who flock to this cathedral every Sunday, but what amazed me that Sunday was the significant presence of Africans. Most of those who were part of the procession with the priest at the beginning of the Mass were even Africans! I have been to Eucharistic celebrations in this cathedral in the past few years that I have been to Malaysia to visit relatives and I could literally chart the dramatic increase in and participation of African migrants in the cathedral. In that moment, in that huge cathedral overflowing with people of various colors from various parts of the world, one gets a sense of the world church and a glimpse of what is probably the future of the church, that is, an intercultural church brought about or, at the very least, reinforced by migration.

Forms of Inculturation in the Context of Migration

As could be seen in the previous chapter, religion has, arguably, never gone through so much significance, dynamism, expansion, and transformation as in the context of contemporary migration. To be sure this revitalization of religion is rooted in as well as intensified by the increase in density and multiculturality of people on the move today. Within Christianity the significant presence of migrants, who inevitably have particular ways of understanding and living the faith, bring not just wonderful gifts but also immense challenges, especially in the area of inculturation. The succeeding section will describe these wonderful gifts migrants bring to churches through a discussion of the ways in which they express and incorporate their particular ways of living the faith.

First, however, a general description of inculturation might be useful here. In Asia, where the word "inculturation" was arguably used for the first time in Church parlance, early documents of the Federation of Asian Bishops' Conferences (FABC) interchangeably used it with terms like "adaptation," "incarnation," "acculturation," and "indigenization."[2] The word often used by the World Council of Churches, that is, "contextualization,"[3] also carries more or less the same meaning as the abovementioned terms. For purposes of a general framework this book will more or less subscribe to Aylward Shorter's definition, which describes inculturation as "the on-going dialogue between faith and culture or cultures" or "the creative and dynamic relationship between the Christian message and a culture or cultures."[4]

In the Liturgy

Most forms of inculturation in churches where there are migrants are done through the liturgy. Often regarded as the more "official" form, by virtue of the fact that the liturgy is considered by the Church as the official public worship of God, liturgical inculturation is "the process whereby pertinent elements of a local culture are integrated into the texts, rites, symbols, and institutions employed by local churches for its worship."[5] In Western churches liturgical inculturation in the context of migration often means a reinvigorated church in terms of worship and spirituality. Gerrie ter Haar notes, for example, how new immigrant Christian groups in both North America and Europe bring new life and vitality in the worship and spirituality of their host churches because they reproduce or exhibit the same dynamic, creative, and celebratory character of religious rituals in their homeland.[6] I argue, however, that this type of worship and spirituality is intensified or made more exuberant and dramatic by the often difficult situations inherent to migration, for example, alienation, discrimination, and harsh working conditions. Noted Filipino sociologist Randy David offers us a glimpse of this in the case of the Filipino domestic workers in Hong Kong:

I recently sat through a Sunday service in one such gym in Hong Kong, and wondered what it was that drew in the participants. It could not have been the long high-pitched and thoroughly uninspiring lecture-sermon of the *pastora*, who certainly did not deserve her audience's reverential attentiveness. I am more certain now that it was the community, and the bonding and the comfort they derived from each other's sheer presence that made them come ... For when it was time to sing ... the gym came alive. A band started to play a rousing tune and costumed dancers with ribbons and tambourines took center court. I thought for a while it was a prelude to a basketball tournament. Three thousand Pinoys, almost all of them women, stood up. **With eyes closed and arms raised, they swayed their bodies to the rhythm of a prayer. They cheered, they clapped and they shouted God's name; and in that anonymous collective drone, they cried out their individual pain.**[7]

The liturgy includes, above all, the Eucharist and the other sacraments.[8] Consequently, most expressions of liturgical inculturation among migrants could be seen in and through the sacraments. In a rite for the ordination to the diaconate that I attended in Chicago, for example, Filipino and Korean songs were sung.[9] Moreover, the choir and the parents of the deacons, who brought the gifts for the offertory, were in their native (Filipino and Korean) costumes.

The USCCB's *Planning Your Wedding Ceremony*, in the mean-time, mentions various additions and alterations by Americans to the prescribed wedding liturgy, which are gaining wider usage among US faith communities. The document mentions, for instance, the cross-cultural occasional practice in American wedding ceremonies of having a symbolic offering for the poor given during the presentation of the gifts[10] and the more common practice of the bride being escorted down the aisle by both her parents (not just by her father as is traditionally practiced). The document mentions, as well, a practice more common at African-American and Vietnamese-American wedding ceremonies, that is, a brief commentary that parents or invited guests give to the couple after the post-communion prayer.[11] The US Bishops' Committee for Pastoral Research and Practice, which came up with the said document, also mentioned four faith expressions frequently used at Mexican-American weddings, namely the *arras* (13 gold or silver coins), *lazo* (a band that looks like the number eight, often comprised of two rosaries), bouquet to the Blessed Virgin Mary, and parental blessing of the couple.[12]

In parishes where there is a considerable presence of particular ethnic groups or, in some cases, when a particular group has its own parish liturgical, inculturation chiefly happens in the Eucharistic celebration. Oftentimes the priest himself comes from the same ethnic group sponsoring the Mass and, on certain occasions (depending on the priest), the priest's chasuble has an ethnic symbol or design. Almost always, however, inculturation is practiced through language. In fact the presence of priests and religious who can minister in the immigrants' mother tongues is often high in the list of priorities among immigrants.[13] In the Eucharist forms of linguistic inculturation could either take the form of celebrating the Eucharist solely in the dominant group's native language, for example, Polish, or having a bilingual religious service, for example, English and Spanish. The latter is often done in the Liturgy of the Word; for example, the first reading is in Spanish while the second reading is in English and the gospel is read in both Spanish and English. The songs (oftentimes the entrance, offertory, communion, or closing hymns) are either bilingual or multilingual as well.

In more diverse churches, inculturation is also practiced by having the Prayers of the Faithful read in the language of the different groups, particularly during special Masses that celebrate cultural diversity. Among extremely diverse groups such as the Asian and Pacific Catholic Network the challenge is more daunting. However, there are various efforts by these groups toward integrating the language, rites, and symbols of the different ethnic groups, including those that go beyond the Mass or language. As I was writing this chapter, for instance, my husband and I received an invitation to speak at a gathering of the pastoral leaders of the network. The schedule of activities for the gathering is a testament to some of the many laudable efforts toward inculturation within the American Church. There is a multicultural Mass (Korean, Indonesian, Sri Lankan, Laotian, Pakistani, Vietnamese, Cambodian, Japanese, Bengali) and a multilingual call to prayer (Montagnard, Vietnamese, Pakistani). There is also a procession of the different images of Mary (with an emphasis on different Asian and Pacific Marian images) and a multilingual rosary (Vietnamese, Filipino, Chinese, Burmese, Indian). The procession itself, which concludes at the Basilica of the National Shrine of the Immaculate Conception in Washington, DC, constitutes a pilgrimage for the group and a culmination of a one-day event organized by the network to celebrate the tenth anniversary of the USCCB document *Asian and Pacific Presence: Harmony in Faith*.[14] This brings me to the second most common, albeit usually "unofficial," form of inculturation in the context of migration, that is, popular piety.

Popular Piety

For various reasons inculturation also happens in the context of migration through popular piety.[15] Leonardo Mercado maintains that popular piety itself is a form of inculturation.[16] Popular piety is the quest for more simple, more direct, and more profitable relationships with the divine.[17] It usually comes in three forms. The first involves devotions to Christ, Mary, and the saints. These devotions are commonly expressed through pilgrimages and processions—as illustrated in the activities of the Asian-Pacific American Catholics mentioned above—novenas, patronal feasts, and other acts of popular devotions such as having an *altarcito* or home altars. Among Chicanos in the United States, for example, there is the well-known devotion to Our Lady of Guadalupe.[18]

The second form involves rites related to the liturgical year, particularly to the Christmas and Lenten season. For Mexican-Americans these rituals include the *posada* ("hospitality" or "shelter" reenactment), the *Via Crucis* (Way of the Cross), *siete palabras* (the seven last words of Jesus from the cross), and the *pésame a la Virgen* (condolences to the Virgin).[19] Among Filipino-Americans there is the *Simbang Gabi*, *Visita Iglesia*, and *salubong*.[20]

The third form of popular piety involves institutions and religious objects that are often connected with the first two forms. Religious objects, for example, include symbols linked to devotions to Mary, Jesus, or a saint, for example, rosary, miraculous medal, or the statue of the saint. Other more general symbols include holy water, oil, or candle.[21] Institutions, in the meantime, include national, diocesan, or parish organizations, for example, confraternities or religious brotherhoods that promote popular devotions. We see examples of these groups in "Companion of the Immigrants: Devotion to Our Lady of Guadalupe Among Mexicans in the Los Angeles Area, 1900–1940" where Michael Engh, S.J., describes how the leaders of parish organizations, particularly the *Santo Nombre* for men and the largely female *Asociación Guadalupana*, led weekly prayers and presented social activities for important occasions when Mexican priests were unavailable.[22] The home-based prayer circles among Filipino-American Catholics in modern-day northeast Florida also serve as an example here.[23]

While the clergy often recognize most of the forms of popular piety among migrant Christians, there are also instances when these are not encouraged, especially when they compromise the centrality of Sunday or the integrity of the liturgical season. Keith Pecklers, S.J., sheds light on this based on his experience:

Several years ago I presided at the Sunday Eucharist on the Third Sunday of Lent at a very Irish-American parish...As Saint Patrick's Day was only two days away, Patrick and Ireland won out. The church was aglow with green shamrocks, complemented by the parishioners themselves all done up in green. Most of the liturgical music that day was chosen from Irish hymns tunes and texts. After Communion the soloist did a rather sentimental rendition of "Danny Boy." Little was mentioned about Lent.[24]

Forms of popular piety also do not get warm reception from the clergy when problematic indigenous religious practices enter into the mix. Thomas Tweed's essay "Identity and Authority at a Cuban Shrine in Miami: *Santería*, Catholicism, and Struggles for Religious Identity" sheds light on this.[25] The shrine is a social space in which the clergy struggle with some lay followers over competing meanings of "Catholic" and "authentic" religion. The clergy and lay elite actively try to correct what they perceive as the "deficiencies in evangelization," which has led to the association of Yoruba *orishas* with Catholic *santos* (saints) and, in particular, the mixing up of Our Lady of Charity with pagan imagery, particularly *Santería* and *Ochún*.[26] Using every form of communication for catechism, for example, homilies and publications, the clergy struggle to cleanse the supposedly "syncretis-tic" popular piety of pilgrims[27] while *Santería* initiates who come to the shrine are either asked to leave or encouraged to change. The suc-ceeding section will further explore these problems and prospects that forms of inculturation in the context of migration pose to Christianity.

Problems and Prospects for Doing Inculturation in the Context of Migration

As the struggle to integrate faith and culture(s), inculturation clearly involves a process of ecclesial self-discovery. In the first place, con-temporary migration enriches and, at the same time, complicates inculturation in the way it intensifies the desire to affirm one's iden-tity in the midst of a need or demand to assimilate, integrate, or create a new identity in a culturally different society and faith com-munity. Contemporary migration also brings gifts and challenges for inculturation in the way it is likely to be among the most conspicu-ous agents of change of religious systems and relationships. Hence, inculturation in the context of migration, particularly as reflected in the preceding section, also comes with a host of problems and prospects.

From "Multi" to "Inter" Perspective of Cultures

As could be gleaned in the previous section, one limitation of the cur-rent ways or strategies with which inculturation is done in churches where there is considerable number of migrants is that they tend to be superficial or do not go beyond the externals.[28] In many cases I believe this is because the understanding and practice of inculturation do not fully take into account the fact that faith or the Gospel is not dealing with only one culture or only one homogenous group (as it has mostly done in the past) but rather multiple cultures and extremely heteroge-neous group(s).[29] This tricky situation is complicated by the fact that the inculturation process also has to take into account not only the dif-ferent groups' complex (sometimes bitter) histories (past and present) but also the regional, political, and economic differences—within a culture or across cultures—which could lead different groups to disso-ciate from or be indifferent toward one another. Within ethnic groups, for instance, one problem for inculturation is intra-ethnic differences between recent immigrants and their American-born counterparts or earlier immigrants.[30] Others, as Peter Phan laments in the case of Asian immigrants in the United States, are afflicted with petty conflicts and quarrels that often have to do with rivalries among various associations, vying for positions of honor within the parish council, and fights with allegedly despotic pastors.[31] The differences, however, are usually more pronounced and more problematic between the minority ethnic "guest" group(s) and the majority or dominant "host" ethnic group. This situation that often leads to segregation is affirmed by the following excerpt from the national report on Hong Kong at the Symposium on Filipino Migrant Workers in Asia:

We also recognize the difficulties in establishing a Church that is both Filipino and Chinese. We are aware that we still need to inculcate among our Chinese people that the Church is universal and that two cultures can proclaim the same faith in the same Church, in different ways and languages. The Diocese of Hong Kong would like to see the Chinese and the Filipinos join one another at Mass and gatherings, as equals and as friends. We may still be a long way from the reality of our dream.[32]

The desire of Hispanic parishioners of a church in Texas to have more Masses in Spanish in church and not at the community center also reflects this segregation, which covers not only parish time (best Mass times are given to the dominant group) but also space (migrant congregations are relegated to the basement, community centers, or parish hall for their Masses or religious services).[33]

What may be the missing link here is the desire and effort on the part of both new(er) ethnic minority group(s) and old(er) dominant ethnic group to learn from one another in view of having a richer and more meaningful faith. Phan eloquently illustrates this in the case of Asian and Pacific Catholic immigrants and the American church. Phan suggests that the American church could learn from four values that characterize Asian and Pacific Catholics. First, American individualism could be countered by the Asian and Pacific Islanders' understanding of the human person as "embedded selves," that is, as constituted by relationships, with the family, with the neighbors, and with God. Second, Asian and Pacific Islanders' traditional simplicity of lifestyle, frugality, deep sense of transcendence, and introspection may help overcome the American culture of consumption and materialism. Third, the American propensity to use arms and violence to resolve political conflicts might be critiqued by the Asian and Pacific Islanders' tradition of nonviolent resistance and harmony. Finally, Asian and Pacific Islanders bring plurality and diversity in ethnicity, culture, and religions to the American tendency toward the melting-pot conformity.[34] At the same time Phan submits that Asian and Pacific Catholics have learned from the American church's new ways of being church. The idea and practice of "public Catholicism," for example, have enriched the former who have been traditionally brought up in a Catholicism that emphasizes the afterlife and individual salvation at the expense of the church's ministry for justice and peace. Phan contends that the American church's commitment to be a transformative agent in society, especially in issues concerning peace and justice, the economy, gender equality, human rights, and ecology enhances Asian and Pacific Catholics' faith.

Moreover, Phan notes that Asian and Pacific Catholics could learn more from the American church's strong tradition of voluntarism and philanthropy as opposed to Asian and Pacific Catholics' tendency to be concerned mainly, if not exclusively, with the welfare of their own families, thereby tending, as well, to neglect the wider common good of society and church. Last but not the least, Phan writes that the consultative, almost democratic style of collaborative ministry that is exercised in many American parishes offers Asian and Pacific Catholics a unique opportunity to exercise their baptismal priesthood and to break away from the more authoritarian and clericalist model of church they have inherited.[35] There is, indeed, a dynamic and conflictive process that goes on in the encounter between and among cultures in churches that even theology, as a "multicultural" discourse, does not sufficiently capture. Consequently, I believe that inculturation could benefit well from an expanded and more fluid way of understanding cultural encounters by looking at cultural plurality from the perspective of "multi" to the perspective of "inter."

"Multi" is a prefix, which means "having many," "more than two," or "many times more than." It could also be the shortened version of the word "multiple." Hence, "multicultural" may mostly refer to a situation where two or more cultures exist in a detached manner from each other. In other words, "multicultural" could primarily refer to the existence of two or more cultures in a society or to a state of plurality of cultures, thereby capturing only what is happening on the surface and not necessarily the currents underneath. It could, in other words, just signify, indicate, or denote the presence of two or more cultures in a certain place without necessarily speaking of the dynamics involved. To say, for instance, "multicultural parish" may just mean a parish that has members from different ethnicities and not necessarily refer to the actual relations, interactions, or power dynamics between and among the groups.

Meanwhile, "inter," which is also a prefix, means "between," "among," or "with" each other. Most importantly, it means "mutual." To speak of "inter," I believe, is to grasp what is in between, to discover whatever it is that is born out of the inter-action between cultures. To view cultures based on the "inter" perspective is to capture the encounter, whether positive or negative, superficial or deep, between and among cultures. To look at it the "inter" way is to probe the depth and bring out the subtleties in the encounter. An intercultural perspective attends to the interaction and juxtaposition, as well as tension and resistance when two or more cultures are brought together sometimes organically and sometimes through violent means.[36] Mark Francis sheds light on the perspective I am arguing for here by pointing out that "this cross-cultural dynamic is most important since [Hispanic] liturgical inculturation in the United States takes place within an increasingly multicultural context and will both influence and be influenced by trends in other cultural groups."[37]

An "inter" perspective is desirable then in the sense that it could capture the experiential and dialogical character of inculturation, particularly the multiple layers of dialogical encounter within and among culture(s) that the Gospel has to engage individually and collectively in a multiethnic parish.[38] While looking at the encounter from the "multi" perspective can be just quantitative, regarding it from an "inter" perspective can be both quantitative and qualitative. While the former can be just descriptive, the latter can be evaluative. As such, the latter, I believe, is a more fruitful and faithful way to doing inculturation in the context of migration as it indicates an inculturation with a view to (and done in the spirit of) mutuality, justice, hospitality, and catholicity.

Political, Economic, and Pscyho-Social Dimension

In many cases inculturation in the context of migration is rooted in how religion becomes a means to deal with or struggle against the alienating forces embedded in contemporary migration. Away from their home country and in search of company, intimacy, identity, and better living conditions, religion becomes a formidable anchor in migrants' lives. Consequently religious acts, rituals, symbols, and institutions permeate and inform almost every aspect of their lives. Hence, one challenge for inculturation is to take the understanding and practice of faith's engagement of/with culture(s) beyond the purely religious realm and take into account both faith's and culture's fluid connections with the other key dimensions of migrants' lives.

Popular piety, for example, denotes "much more than a series of religious practices, symbols, narratives, devotions" but also "a particular worldview, an epistemological framework that infuses and defines every aspect of the community's life"[39] such that it becomes not only a particular way of being "religious" but also a particular way of living life. Migrants "need that sense of family in order to survive in an alien world; they need to celebrate God's future in the midst of an oppressive and alienating present."[40] Popular piety, despite its problematic tendencies,[41] answers this need not only because it serves as support of identity[42] but also because it has liberating potential.[43]

Orlando Espin explicates on this less elitist and more pastoral approach to popular piety in *The Faith of the People: Theological Reflections on Popular Catholicism*. Using primarily the experience of Latino Catholics in the United States, Espin contends that popular piety mainly operates on a worldview that the divine, who is encountered in and through the symbols of popular religion, intervenes daily and constantly in a world marred by the conflict between good and evil. Espin argues that popular piety could be regarded as an epistemology of suffering[44] insofar as it is the religion of those treated as subaltern by both society and the Church.[45] For instance, "Latino popular Catholicism," Espin posits, is "an effort by the subaltern [Latinos] to explain, justify, and somehow control a social reality that appears too dangerous to confront in terms of and through means other than the mainly symbolic."[46] Mexican-American theologians themselves maintain that the rites and practices that comprise their people's symbolic world not only reinforce their ethnic identity but also function "as a defense and protest against the demands of the dominant culture."[47] This living faith, according to Virgilio Elizondo, is an expression and/or means of resistance and survival.

Karen Mary Davalos illustrates Espin's and Elizondo's point in "The Real Way of Praying: The *Via Crucis*, Mexicano Sacred Space, and the Architecture of Domination," where she writes on how the practice of the *Via Crucis* by Mexican-Americans in the Pilsen and Little Village neighborhoods in Chicago is a witness to "a theology that is also a politically grounded concept of culture"[48] in the way it is engaged within a space and architecture of domination experienced by these neighborhoods. That is why *Via Crucis* as understood and practiced by these neighborhoods is, in the words of a young Mexican-American, "a reenactment of a historical event, but **it is not a play**" rather a **"relieving (of) that moment which is actually happening now."**[49] Consequently, it becomes not simply the Way of the Cross but the *Living* Way of the Cross.

Wayne Ashley describes a similar approach to a Good Friday practice in a primarily Puerto Rican parish.[50] In what is both a public prayer and critique, participants enact each of the stations in strategically chosen problem areas within the parish: a controversial health clinic, a deteriorating public school, a street corner where drugs are sold, a luxury condominium, and a park associated with danger and vice. By traversing through the neighborhood's volatile areas, the participants create two overlapping narratives: one about Christ's suffering, the other about the topography of the East Village and its residents' suffering. What we see here is a cultural practice (outdoor processions are common in Puerto Rico) and traditional text and performance (Stations of the Cross) repositioned and inserted into a new and political discourse such that ongoing social debates and conflicts surrounding housing, welfare, and morality are assimilated into the Christian narrative.[51] A similar form of politicization has also been used in the case of the *posada* in Chicago whereby Mexican-Americans and about 250 Catholics from all walks of life used the *posada* to demonstrate the need to change the immigration system. Instead of traveling from house to house, like Mary and Joseph did in their search for an inn, the group traversed the city, stopping at the federal Metropolitan Correction Center, DePaul University, the Federal Plaza, and ending up at St. Peter's Catholic Church. Prayers and dialogues at each stop were tailored to the nature of the public places where they stopped.[52] Interestingly, as Gioacchino Campese points out, this engagement of popular piety in migrant protest and advocacy is restricted not only to the *Via Crucis*, *posada*, or the Stations of the Cross; neither are they done only by immigrants nor confined to the mainland but also at the border.[53] This is what inculturation needs to do more, that is, make the Gospel enter into a dialogue with the faith and culture(s) of migrants as these are embedded in their social-psychological, economic, and political struggles as marginal(ized) strangers. In so doing, inculturation becomes more powerful as it also becomes a tool for liberation. In fact this is a face of inculturation that is increasingly critical in this postmodern globalized world. As Robert Schreiter points out, the second decade of globalization calls perhaps for two strands of inculturation, namely those focused upon identity and those committed to liberation.[54]

The Ecclesiastical Role

The fact that the abovementioned forms of inculturation exist and, to a certain extent, flourish tells us that the Church hierarchy has the ability to deal with cultural diversity without imposing a rigid uniformity of practice. Historically, the Catholic Church has proof of this ability as exemplified in the very formation of the different liturgical families in the East and West, for example, Byzantine, Roman, Gallican, Syro-Malabar, Syro-Malankara, and Visigothic/Mozarabic. However, the multiethnic context of inculturation in the context of migration makes the task more difficult for the hierarchy today. Hence, in some cases their efforts fail not just due to the usual suspects, that is, hierarchy's control mechanisms or "tribalism" and ethnic tension, but also due to a number of other factors. Michael Pasquier sheds light on these other factors with regard to popular piety in "Our Lady of Prompt Succor: The Search for an American Marian Cult in New Orleans," where he not only traces the transatlantic origins of the devotion to Our Lady of Prompt Succor but also chronicles the Catholic hierarchy's valiant but failed efforts in recasting the cult as indigenous to America and creating a multiethnic devotion. Pasquier writes:

Rome and the Archdiocese of New Orleans tried to do something different with Our Lady of Prompt Succor. They wanted a relatively mundane, unpopular cult to **transcend ethnic boundaries and thus incorporate a broader range of Catholics in America**. However, without the initial ferment of a popular movement, and without a supernatural tradition to activate the imaginations of potential devotees, Our Lady of Prompt Succor never became what the Catholic hierarchy had intended—**an American Mary with multiethnic appeal**.[55]

What the Archdiocese of New Orleans did is arguably a more desirable practice of inculturation in the context of multicultural churches that, as concretely shown in the case of New Orleans, are usually fashioned by migration. It also shows that the hierarchy is usually an ally in efforts toward inculturation. In the case cited earlier in the chapter on a predominantly Puerto Rican parish with a politically charged outdoor Stations of the Cross, it was the parish priests who conceptualized and pursued the practice despite protests by more traditional parishioners. Initially created as an experimental church in 1967 by the archdiocese in the spirit of Vatican II (the church had a team of three priests instead of having the traditional organization of a senior pastor aided by associates), which was also the period of intense liturgical experimentation, these priests not only sponsored block parties and neighborhood clean-up programs by opening the rectory to help drug addicts and troubled teenagers; they also brought the Spanish Mass out of the basement into the main church, added folk instruments and Puerto Rican songs, and made many innovations in the liturgy and festival life of the parish.[56] However, there are potential ecclesiastical problems, particularly in current efforts toward liturgical inculturation, due to "a centralizing tendency among the Roman liturgical authorities that seems to downplay or even disregard the legitimate demands for more local and regional control over the liturgy on the part of bishops and national bishops' conferences."[57] In certain cases it is not so much the Roman authorities but priests and other local religious leaders themselves who pose problems to inculturation. Joseph Sciorra points outs that, in the case of the Italians in Brooklyn, one reason why the Mount Carmel Society and the groups affiliated with our Lady of the Snow, St. Sabino, and St. Cono moved the celebrations of their respective Masses from Our Lady of Mount Carmel Church (to St. Francis Padua Church) is that the priests from the former church attempted to wrest control of religious feasts from the different lay societies allegedly because they (clergy) wanted to be the sole recipient of money collected during the celebrations.[58]

In this sense the hierarchy offers both prospects and problems for inculturation. In relation to this one phenomenon that is noteworthy to mention here for the possible problems and prospects it offers for inculturation is the increasing practice, especially in the West, of having foreign parish priests. Initially most occasionally sought the assistance of foreign priests because the parish priest was sick, on a day-off or on leave. Similarly, most churches used to ask only those foreign priests who happen to be in the country for various reasons, for example, sabbatical or study leave. For instance, when I was doing my doctoral studies in the Netherlands I lived in a student house made up mostly of priests from Africa and Asia. Most of these priests will be gone on Sunday (some as early as Friday or Saturday evening) as they fan out across the country (a couple of Africans go as far as Germany) to celebrate the Eucharist either to migrant congregations or in remote parishes. After their studies at least three of these student priests applied for and was accepted to serve for a number of years in a parish either in the Netherlands or Germany.

Today an increasing number of dioceses, particularly in the United States and Canada, are resorting to actively recruiting foreign men from their homelands and giving them their formation in the receiving country. A priest friend of mine, for example, was recruited by an American diocese while he was in his home country in Asia. He is now serving at an overwhelmingly white parish in a city in the southern part of the United States together with another "imported" but "trained in the US" African priest. In Canada I also have a couple of priest friends who have the same story. One who is serving in a parish in a remote area and acts as a circuit-riding priest to a couple of other parishes says there is a priest from India who takes care of his parishes—also made up of mostly white parishioners—when he is on vacation.

The increasing presence of foreign priests as (assistant) parish priests not only in minority congregations but also in predominantly white parishes deserves attention as it holds both problems and prospects for inculturation. While it is, on the one hand, a boon for the migrant parish(ioners) on the basis of similarity in terms of language and ethnic ways of living or celebrating the faith it could also pose problems, particularly for members who are now used to the American or Canadian way of life and prefer a more democratic system of relationship and leadership in the church. Since many foreign priests come from Third World countries and largely patriarchal societies, where priests are treated with considerable deference, these priests struggle with the less deferential treatment they get from their parishioners. This problem is understandably more pronounced in the case of foreign priests from the global South serving in predominantly white and affluent parishes. On top of class differences and the expectation for a more transparent, more democratic or more western style of leadership there is the problem of language and other ethnic ways of celebrating the faith which these foreign priests might find hard to shake off, especially at the beginning.[59]

Allen echoes these problems by noting how South-North movement of priests promises to be a growing source friction especially since, in some cases, more liberal congregations in the North are uncomfortable with what they perceive as the conservatism of foreign priests. Allen goes on to say how sometimes the difficulties are more practical. He cites the case of a Nigerian priest working in a diocese in Pennsylvania. The priest shared to Allen how when he first began delivering homilies in America, his congregation always looked askance at him whenever he described something as "important." The priest found out later that it was actually because the church-goers thought he was saying "impotent."[60]

On the other hand, these priests also hold promise for inculturation, especially if they are not ashamed, inhibited, or prohibited from sharing or integrating their particular ways of living and celebrating the faith in their parishes. In parishes that are more multicultural these foreign priests could facilitate the integration of other ethnic groups' particular ways of living the faith, hence pave the way toward a more intercultural sense of the church.

Whether coming from the same ethnic group or not the role and attitude of parish priests toward inculturation is critical since they are at the frontline and remain key decision makers in parishes. They can either make possible or stifle deeper and wider inculturation. The situation of a multi-ethnic parish in Texas depicts this ecclesiastical dimension to the problems and prospects for inculturation. Things look ideal on many fronts. The various ethnic communities (at least 12) have their own patron saints enthroned upon the back wall of the church and ethnically-specific feast days are celebrated, complete with novenas, Eucharist, and a meal in the community center or parish hall. There are ten Eucharistic celebrations each Sunday and various Marian devotions, many of which are specific to one nationality. The words of the pastor, however, on inter-ethnic celebrations and relations sound patronizing. Asked on the separate celebration of immigrants' national saints he says "I am tolerant. As long as they don't get in my way and we can fit them into the schedule, they are always welcome." The priest goes on to say that "they need to keep out of each other's way" while acknowledging the fact that "tension exists between the Anglos and the rest and the Anglos don't realize that they are dominant. **Parish Council members are almost all Anglo and they are insensitive.**"[61] In this case it is obvious that there is a need to foster not only deeper cultural sensitivity but also parity through more inclusive membership in key organizational structures in the parish, e.g. parish council. The priest's or pastor's leadership and initiative is naturally vital here.

Robert Schreiter offers some concrete ways with which inculturation could take place in the Church in the postmodern globalized world.[62] First, Schreiter draws attention to the importance of celebrating difference and honoring culture, including the need for aligning inculturation's focus on identity with that of commitment to liberation. Secondly, Schreiter contends that the Church needs to have a deeper understanding and appreciation of the non-western faces of Christianity as well as for the varieties of popular piety.[63] Lastly, Schreiter contends that, in seeking to embody the whole today, the church needs to find non-dominative, inclusive and liberating ways to embrace the entirety of Christian faith including attending to silences that may be sites of suppressed speech or detecting hidden patterns of hegemony that need to be exposed. This is important in view of the church's monarchical, absolutist and imperialist history.

There are other factors that affect current and future efforts toward inculturation in the context of migration which will be briefly explored together in the succeeding section not only due to space limitations but also because not much has been said about them yet in relation to inculturation.

Other Factors to Consider

Other emerging and/or equally important factors that pose problems or prospects for inculturation in the context of migration also deserve attention in this chapter. First, there is the concern about the participation and involvement of the children of immigrants. Like many young people today, children of immigrants tend to feel alienated, hostile, and even indifferent to the Church because they find their religious needs, experiences, and expectations to be vastly different from those of their parents. Moreover, the Church does not often engage these needs or, at least, engage them enough for young people to feel they are an important part of the Church. Likewise, parents find their children's relative lack of care for the family's faith and church bewildering and frustrating.[64] In many cases the problem lies in the fact that the children do not speak or understand the ethnic language (or the language of their parents), which is often the language used in religious rituals and services. I have read this over and over again in the papers of my undergraduate students who lament how the service is rendered less meaningful as far as they are concerned because they do not understand what is being said or what is happening. Others end up being hostile to ethnic religious rituals and celebrations (and sometimes to the ethnic religion itself) especially when they are unwillingly brought to church by their parents. Understandably, the preservation of ethnic languages, customs, and rituals usually rank high on the list of immigrant parents' and immigrant parishes' priorities. But then this, especially the insistence of immigrant parents and parishes for the youth to learn the ethnic language, may not always be the most adequate or practical solution. I submit that it would be best to, at the same time, have English ministries to immigrant youth[65] not only because that is the language they are most comfortable with but also because it could serve as a unifying factor with the American youth population in general and young people from the other ethnic groups in particular. The latter is vital since, as Phan predicts, panethnic parishes may be necessary in the near future when it is no longer possible to have separate parishes for each ethnic group, either because there will not be sufficient priests or because third generation immigrant children no longer speak the ethnic languages.[66]

Beyond the ethnic aspects there is also the matter of intergenerational differences when it comes to religious beliefs and practices. What a young Mexican-American hopes the religious leaders in her

Catholic Church would do gives voice to this gap which is obviously not just generational but also cultural and religious in nature:

> Maybe someday they will allow us to have an electric band, to use slides for the words of the songs for we can barely buy but a few books for the choir anymore. And some of the parishioners attend the Charismatic Center frequently and see how nice it can be to have a really good choir that encourages everyone to sing along with them.[67]

Indeed, problems lie also in the fact that children and their parents do not share a common vision of being Church together and this could be addressed by critical and creative approaches to cultivating a sense of community and faith life between the immigrant (parent) contingent and the following generations (children).[68]

This, of course, is easier said than done. In the case of St. Brigid's Parish, for instance, the outdoor Stations of the Cross was initially staged by the priest in the traditional devotional style, with mildly contemporized prayers forging connections between Christ's suffering and the parishioners' own grievances. The parishioners were ambivalent and charged the priest with "bringing politics into the church." The priest attributed the negative response to the inability of older and more "traditional" Puerto Rican parishioners to accept innovation. Thinking that the younger parishioners would be more open to his changes he resorted to dividing parishioners along generational lines. Adults would stage half the Stations in the traditional devotional style while the parish youth would stage the other half as a series of short social dramas which they create (and perform on a flatbed truck) based on their own social biographies, for example, on abortion, drugs, and relationships among racial groups. However, what started out as a plan to increase young people's involvement in the church and the neighborhood resulted in a generational conflict within the parish.[69] Tensions rose several times between the younger generation and their parents over changes in liturgical practice. Many older parishioners objected to the new music introduced into the Mass,[70] the liturgical dancing and what is perceived as a shift away from the awesome, mysterious element of the divine toward the humanistic. Clearly there has to be a common ground for the three groups, that is, church leaders as well as older and younger parishioners to meet. The young people are not just the future of the church but also the future of the faith in immigrant families. Hence, what is stake here is far too important for church leaders and the older generation to be immovable and absolutely adamant about.

Secondly, there is the women and gender question. Migrant women are critical in inculturation since they are the keepers of the faith. In almost every ethnic group they are often the ones left with the responsibility to raise the children in faith.[71] Moreover, they are usually the ones who more faithfully go to church and play an active role in it.[72] Not surprisingly they are also often the ones who keep popular devotions alive whether through the maintenance of pious associations in the parish or organizing processions, pilgrimages, or prayer circles in the neighborhoods or communities. In particular, older women like the *abuelas* (grandmothers) in the Hispanic community play a critical role in popular piety as they are regarded as carriers *par excellence* of tradition. An Orthodox priest sheds light on this in the case of Ukrainian women in Canada:

If you go across Canada, you'll see a similar pattern coast to coast. We don't rely on bingos and casinos for raising funds. Our women make cabbage rolls and meals. This is how our churches exist! If you go to any parish, whatever size, where there's a thousand families or ten, the parish is held on the backs of women. They do everything. They decorate the church. They provide the ecclesiastical embroideries. They provide care for the children; they make sure the altar boys have their vestments and everything else. Their ministry is very, very supportive.[73]

Women's marginalization in society (and by most religions) is a well-known fact. Migration then provides an opportunity for women to circumvent or undercut some of the marginalization, especially when they migrate to a more liberal and egalitarian society. In fact, religious involvement offers some kind of visibility and empowerment for migrant women such that they volunteer or take on roles in the churches, including those that somehow reinforce traditional gender roles.[74] Helen Ebaugh and Janet Chafetz, for instance, point out that along with participating in social services and in the ethno-religious education of children, women's most ubiquitous role within their congregations is that of ethnic food provider.[75] While the role of food provider reinforces domestic stereotypes Ebaugh and Chaftez says that migrant women often use the opportunity to relate information, discuss problems, and provide mutual support, turning meal preparation into an experience of shared sisterhood.[76] In any case the preparation and consumption of ethnic foods reinforce traditional religious and ethnic identities[77] so to the extent that women monopolize this role they constitute a critical lynchpin in the reproduction of ethnic religion and, to a certain extent, inculturation.

Ebaugh and Chafetz also point at women's groups in religious communities, which provide both practical and socioemotional support for their members and other female co-ethnics, as possible vehicles for women's mitigation of their marginalization. They maintain, however, that while such groups could, in the future, also constitute the bases from which women work collectively to improve their status, as yet, this has only rarely occurred. These rare cases, which mostly occur in Western societies, hold promise and possibilities for inculturation in the context of migration since the migrants' patriarchal culture is challenged and evangelized by the socio-religious culture of their host society.[78] What is also interesting is that the challenge and the critique of the patriarchal aspects of the migrants' culture come not only from the outside but also from the inside.[79] Francis, for example, points at how problematic characteristics of Hispanic culture such as *machismo* and its devastating impact on marriage and family are increasingly being explored by Hispanics themselves.[80]

Conclusion

Migrants' struggle to express and integrate their particular ways of living the faith in the context of migration could be regarded as a new if not reinvigorated model of ecclesiological praxis in the way it is both dialogical and prophetic. This is because despite the challenges inculturation efforts face, including the fact that these have yet to go well beyond their ethnic enclaves, the influence or changes these are bringing to the Christian faith in their host churches or communities cannot be ignored.[81]

First, the expressions or symbols of worship and spirituality get expanded and the universal character of Christianity becomes more real and alive. It is not uncommon, for instance, to see images of saints of various cultures, for example, Our Lady of Guadalupe in churches across the United States. Secondly, the means of evangelization is challenged and, in certain cases, changed. As documented by Engh in his abovementioned essay Protestant evangelizers actually resorted to distributing the pictures of the Virgin to attract Mexican immigrants to their churches. One minister even permitted Mexican women to continue to pray the rosary in recognition of the deep attachment of many Mexicans to the Virgin,[82] illustrating what religion scholars today call the "Guadalupe Protestants" and, consequently, a more ecumenical form of Christianity. This is because inculturation in the context of migration, particularly popular piety, also tends to foster some kind of social and religious unity with its ability to transcend economic and religious divisions. This could be seen at the height of the so-called "Massachusetts Miracles," which not only drew Catholics all over the US (and the world) but also other Christians (as well as a Jew) even if the devotion was largely associated with Irish Catholics.[83] Even the prayer circles in Florida occasionally have non-Filipino faces turning up to observe or participate.[84] The *salubong* I attended in a church in Illinois certainly had a significant number of participants from various ethnic groups including the priest who lauded the social and religious significance of the ritual.

The need for inculturation in the context of migration also makes possible clergy-initiated changes in the liturgical and pastoral life of churches to connect with and integrate migrants. This is strongly illustrated in the changes made by the three priests for their marginalized Puerto Rican parishioners in the abovementioned case of St. Brigid Parish. This is also reflected in various developments in St. John's Cathedral in Kuala Lumpur designed with its migrant parishioners in mind, e.g. the addition of two huge containers of holy water in the church (which attracts mostly Filipino migrants), a small Marian shrine in front of the church, and the allocation of parish space for the prayer meetings of African migrants.

It could thus, be argued, that inculturation in the context of migration is bringing some kind of *ecclesiogenesis* in the way migrant congregations are redefining the idea of who, where and what a church is. Aside from drawing us back to the time of the early Christian community when members gather for religious services in household churches migrant congregations have revolutionized what "sacred space" or what a church is by creating their own "church" out of parks, gyms, auditoriums, and community centers especially when they are ignored, isolated, and discriminated to the point that no church building, church space, or church time is available for them. Consequently, they also bring more profound meaning on what it means to be church since the "church" is not just the principal site of celebration for migrants' identity and community; it is also their refuge in times of crisis and their home when they want to shout for joy. This transformative power of religion in the context of migration extends, I believe, to religions in general and Christianity in particular. Insofar as migrants are breathing new life and infusing new energy and vitality to churches worldwide migration could very well be a source and impetus of an *ecclesiogenesis*, either in terms of rebirth, new beginnings, or a new way of being church. Virgilio Elizondo's description

of the impact of Mexican-American Christians in the religious landscape in the United States, particularly in Catholic churches eloquently
illustrates such a perspective:

> Today our Good Friday processions through the middle of the cities of the
> US, or our Guadalupe celebrations on December the 12th and the many
> other public expressions of our faith are bringing new life not only to us
> Mexican-Americans who are reclaiming them, but to all the people of the
> US who are finding new life and a source of unity and communion in these
> religious rituals...[85]

Indeed, insofar as the various forms, problems and prospects of
inculturation in the context of migration articulate and reflect contemporary forms of forging relationship with the sacred in the modern globalized world, migration could very well be the birthplace
of a new church. The next and last chapter further pursues this
idea of migrant contributions toward understanding and renewing
contemporary Christianity, this time in relation to spirituality.

CHAPTER 6

A PILGRIM PEOPLE: MIGRATION AND SPIRITUALITY

The epic nature of many migration stories today often inspires a quickening of faith and an attentiveness to the matters of the Spirit. Theologians agree that spirituality is concerned with the depth dimension of human existence insofar as it is about the authentic human quest for ultimate value or the human person's striving to attain the highest ideal or goal.[1] The spiritual core, therefore, is the deepest center of the person to the extent that spirituality is the experience of conscious involvement in the project of life-integration through self-transcendence toward the ultimate value one perceives.[2] Lawrence Cunningham and Keith Egan say that when we discuss Christian spirituality, we must pay attention to Christian *experience*, how that experience gets *articulated*, and how we are to understand it both for its own sake and for whatever it might teach us about our own spiritual journey.[3]

THE MIGRANT WAY OF LIFE

A recent study by the Pew Research Center's Forum on Religion & Public Life on the religious affiliation of migrants shows that Christians comprise nearly half (49 percent) of the world's migrants.[4] This dominance of Christians among people on the move opens up the possibility and significance of the migrant way of life as a window into contemporary Christian spirituality. When one explores the migrant way of life in view of what it could teach us about the Christian spirituality, there are four values that, I believe, embody that which is at the heart of the migrant experience, and could teach us a thing or two about Christian life in the world today. These values, which are what drive, sustain, empower, and strengthen migrants, are courageous hope, creative resistance, steadfast faith, and festive community spirit. It is to these values that I now turn to discuss.

Courageous Hope

If there is one thing that all people on the move will agree on, it is the fact that migrating is never easy. It takes courage to migrate. It is a long, complicated, and difficult process that never truly and fully ends even long after people have successfully moved from one place to another. First of all, migrants have to make the agonizing decision to leave. Because it is often forced (even irregular), especially for those who migrate in search for work, it carries with it tremendous misery. Even those who go through proper channels have their fair share of negative experiences. They part with their hard-earned cash (sometimes life's savings), mortgage or sell their properties (even their own house and land), or borrow large amounts of money to pay for the journey and the recruiter and have some money to get through the first few weeks or months. On top of these they do not have much choice but face the reality that they will be leaving familiarity and some kind of stability in exchange for an uncertain future and life in a strange (and maybe even hostile) country. As Juan says, "the most painful thing is leaving the family behind, especially the children, but we do it in the hopes that some day we will have something in Mexico."[5] For migrant parents the discernment process could sometimes be a long, drawn-out, and excruciating one such that they consult not only their spouse, friends, and family members but also priests and other religious leaders. The pain and guilt of leaving their children is such that some migrant parents, especially mothers, do not tell the truth about their travel or do not even say goodbye to their children.

Despite these difficulties tens of thousands of men and women, especially from the global South, migrate to escape death-dealing situations in their home countries. In the name of their families (or together with their families), they risk their life and their limb just to get into the land of their dreams. For instance, among the Filipino women who led the migration across the dangerous borders of Italy many hid in cargo ships without ventilation, storage areas of tour buses, or the dust-filled ceiling of trains, or walked across the mountainous terrain of Europe to reach Italy. Some even died along the way due to hunger and cold.[6] It is often worse, indeed, for those who brave the elements. What makes it worst for these migrants is when unscrupulous people facilitate their migration. Irregular migrants crossing the southern border of the US, for example, must entrust themselves to the coyote and sometimes this is a fatal mistake for a number of reasons:

the coyote will lead people over the border only to rob them on the other side. Other times, coyotes will leave immigrants stranded in the middle of the desert, to become disoriented and die of dehydration. Still other times, they will have unsuspecting migrants carry the coyote's backpack, which may have drugs in it. If officials apprehend a group, sometimes these same immigrants can be the ones sent to jail.[7]

What is striking is that migrants still decide to take the journey despite being aware of the possible perils that await them. In the words of Julio: "We are aware of the dangers, but our need is greater. There's always the risk of dying in the desert but the desire to survive and keep going is even more important. It's a gamble."[8] Some of these dangers could be seen in Pepe and Maria's harrowing experience: "Our coyote told us that we had to hit the ground because an (immigration) helicopter was coming overhead and we threw ourselves on the desert floor. When we got up my wife was covered in cactus spines and for eight days I removed them from her body."[9]

The enormity of the threats and dangers for migrants during their journey is such that Dante's inscription over the gates of hell *Lasciate ogne speranza, voi ch'intrate*, "Abandon hope all who enter here" might seem appropriate. And yet migrants never lose hope. In fact it is their last enduring weapon. They fiercely and desperately believe in the promise of a better future and continue to do so . . . despite the odds . . . against all odds. It is there in how countless continue to move across borders despite the difficulties and dangers. It is there in how they put up or fight against isolation and discrimination, in how they refuse to leave and give up, and, most of all, in how they continue to weave and nurture dreams for a better life, especially for their loved ones. It is a courageous hope in the sense that it is a "hoping against hope," a sense of hope that continues to believe and open itself to possibilities of transformation that can never be fully spoken of.

Creative Resistance

As Chapter 1, 2, and 3 illustrate migration is fraught with problematic conditions that, in many cases, amount to oppression. Migrants, however, do not simply submit to or resign themselves to death-dealing situations associated with their migration. Under certain circumstances, and using strategic means, they actively fight against oppression in their quest for full humanity and liberation. These active attempts to resist oppression and transform their lives are not just on the level of the local but also that of the global; social not just individual; personal as well as structural; formal and informal; public and private.

What is most instructive to the Christian spiritual life when it comes to migrants' resistance strategies is the way in which some of these strategies are creative and imaginative. An example of these creative strategies are the more subtle or covert ones, that is, those which are not necessarily aggressive and are a combination of active and passive yet creative and potentially liberating strategies. They are akin to what Yale professor and anthropologist James Scott describes as unconventional ways in which subjugated peoples refuse to give in to their oppression.

Scott argues that the oppressed have strategies that, at first glance, may look negative, passive, or weak but are actually quite potent. Scott calls these strategies "hidden transcripts" or "weapons of the weak."[10] Scott refers here to a politics of disguise and anonymity among subordinate groups that is partly sanitized, ambiguous, and coded. He says this is often expressed in rumors, gossip, folktales, jokes, songs, rituals, codes, and euphemisms that usually come from folk culture. Hidden transcripts, according to Scott, do not contain only speech acts but a whole range of practices that contravene the public transcript of the dominant group.[11]

A few of these weapons of the weak could be seen among the migrant domestic workers in Hong Kong. Take the case of the use of songs. During Sundays their fellow domestic workers serve as accomplices to their cash-strapped compatriots who sell the illegal *halo-halo* (a concoction of fruits, milk, sugar, and shaved ice), by providing the vendor a human camouflage every time the Urban Services Guard passes by.[12] When one of them is caught selling food by the patrol for illegal hawking, the cluster of customers suddenly sing "Happy Birthday," and instantly transform the activity into one of many birthday parties celebrated at the square. In 1994 when much fuss was made by the management of the Dynasty Court, an affluent apartment building, about Filipina maids washing their feet after washing their employer's car, the domestic workers did not only call the management's notice as an act of "upper class inanity." They also have a song to express their disapproval at the seemingly snotty or elitist notice. The song, which has the tune of "*Magtanim ay di Biro*"—a popular folk song in the Philippines—has the following lyrics: "Washing car is little fun. Rub and scrub in morning sun. Water flooding down the street. Maid wash car but not her feet."[13] The choice of "*Magtanim ay di Biro*" alone is already significant. It is a song every Filipino knows. Moreover, it is some sort of a "resistance song" against planting rice and, in effect, against agricultural work, a physically strenuous work that the American colonizers tried to inscribe among Filipinos by peddling the idea that the Philippines is better off as an agricultural country.

Jokes and laughter, which is upheld by folk wisdom as a means of resistance, are also utilized by the Filipina domestic workers in Hong Kong to deal with the difficult conditions of their migration. Like most Filipinos who love a good joke the domestic workers have many jokes that poke fun not only at their condition but also (and mostly) at their employers. Their jokes about themselves even have a caricature in the person of "Maria the stupid DH". To many domestic workers, jokes are their way of getting back at their employers in a covert manner. Most jokes, especially chicken and cooking jokes, make fun of the employer's English. An example is that of Maria's employers going out for dinner and the conversation goes like this:

Sir (in broken English): Maria, come—eat outside.
Maria: Sir, you mean you're going out for dinner?
Sir: Yes, come . . . you like?
Maria: Thank you, sir. But I prefer to eat here.
Sir: All right. Just cook yourself![14]

The use of folktales, in the meantime, could be glimpsed in the urban legend on Father Toribio Romo, which many Mexican migrants who cross the desert into the US recount over and over again. What is striking with the folktale is how the countless stories about Fr. Romo are almost always the same: he appears to distraught migrants, helps them, gives them his name, then asks them to visit him in Jalisco. Ben Daniel recounts the story:

I was crossing the border and became separated from my group. I was tired and thirsty. My feet were blistered and I could barely walk. It was dusk and I was cold. In my despair I collapsed, giving up my spirit. Suddenly I was approached by a young priest. He had blue eyes and he spoke perfect Spanish. He gave me water and food and bandages for my feet. He handed me some money and showed me the quickest way to the nearest town, where, he assured me there would be a job waiting for me. As we parted I asked him how I ever could repay him. "Don't worry about repaying me," he said, but when you return to Mexico, come visit me in Santa Ana de Guadalupe in Jalisco. My name is Toribio Romo.

I followed the young priest's directions. I found a job and made a good life for myself in El Norte. When I returned to visit my family in Mexico, I kept my promise. I drove from my home in Sinaloa to Jalisco, to Santa Ana de Guadalupe. It's a small village, and I assumed that everyone would know the young priest who saved my life. When I asked after Toribio Romo, the villagers directed me to a local church. Upon entering I found myself looking at a photo of the same priest who had come to my aid; only here in the church at Santa Ana de Guadalupe did I learn that he had been dead for many years.[15]

Hundreds of testimonies are written out and displayed in Santa Ana de Guadalupe's hilltop chapel, which Toribio Romo helped design and build. Fr. Toribio Romo, a saint himself, was not well known outside of the Jalisco highlands. All that has changed since stories of Fr. Toribio's benevolent ghost began to appear sometime in the 1970s. Today, many Mexican Catholics both in the US and Mexico consider him as the patron saint of undocumented migrants.

The emphasis and re-appropriation done by the Hispanic community in the US on the story of Our Lady of Guadalupe by focusing on the Virgin's "empowerment" of Juan Diego is also an example of how stories serve as tools for resistance and empowerment. Ana Maria Bidegain points this out in "Living a Trans-national Spirituality: Latin American Catholic Families in Miami," in the way Virgilio Elizondo and other theologians re-frame the story around defense of the rights and dignity of immigrants. Bidegain also notes how the figure of the Virgin of Guadalupe has been strongly bound up with the Latin social movement in the US[16] since the era of mobilizations by Cesar Chavez in 1960s in defense of the dignity of immigrant workers.

For many migrants crossing via perilous routes like the sea or the desert their situation gets worse before it gets better. The documentary *Wetback: The Undocumented Documentary* shows some of the extremely imaginative ways, which migrants come up with, to deal with the dangers and difficulties of the migrant journey along the southern border of the US. For example, to avoid losing the little money they have to thieves, migrants roll dollar bills to fit into a specially-made thin cloth belt hidden inside the waist area of their pants.[17] Indeed, migrants resort to creative survivalist strategies. Some drop names that elicit suspicion and discrimination or change into names that will more easily blend with the general population.[18] Chinese immigrant Te-Sheng Cheng became "Tommy" Cheng to more easily blend in the small town of Rothschild, Wisconsin[19] just as many immigrants from Cape Verde who settled in New Bedford, Massachusetts in the early twentieth century anglicized their names.[20] Others like Japanese-American immigrants from Okinawa in the first few decades of the twentieth century,[21] and more recently some Christian migrants in the Middle East,[22] change their religion not just for better living and working conditions but also to more easily blend and be accepted in destination countries.

For refugees who brave the perils of the sea only to be kept in detention centers for an indeterminate amount of time hunger strike is one common strategy. In Australian detention centers lip-stitching is one way in which asylum seekers express their anger and frustration in the strongest possible way at the prolonged detention. It was also a radical way of drawing attention to their desire to have their application for refugee status dealt with immediately, be moved to open camps in the city while they waited, or be given bridging visa which allows them to live with the general populace and work while waiting for the result of their application.[23]

Last but not the least, creative resistance is also evidenced in the way migrants re-constitute or transform marginal public places into spaces which help them in their struggle for greater well-being. Women migrant domestic workers in Hong Kong and Singapore who work in the same building and are under strict surveillance by employers, for example, create "safe meeting places" out of the garbage area and the car park since these are places where employers do not "tail" them. The domestic workers then utilize garbage-throwing and car-washing time for S.O.S. and socialization.

La Missión Católica de Nuestra Señora de las Américas in Georgia also reflects this reconstitution of marginal public places into spaces. The congregation's sanctuary is a former warehouse. The only clue that it is a place of worship is a statue of Our Lady of Guadalupe in one of two plate-glass windows on the building's exterior.[24] Nothing is probably more striking, however, than the following case of women migrants in Japan as narrated by sociologist Randy David:

I once visited a bar in a suburb of Tokyo where the hostesses were very young *Pinays*. I was very impressed with the way they dealt with the more aggressive among their Japanese customers. These girls were in total command of themselves and of the situation, even if their Japanese was barely understandable. One of them told me that all five of them prayed together at the beginning and at the end of every night—before an image of the *Santo Niño* (Infant Jesus) which was magnificently enshrined right among the cognac and whisky bottles.[25]

Spirituality involves the totality of life. It includes the social, political, economic, and cultural dimensions that shape it. For migrants the challenge lies in integrating these dimensions in view of their quest for authentic human liberation.

Steadfast Faith

"When we started the journey the first thing we did was make the sign of the cross."[26] This statement by a migrant captures, in a nutshell, the most powerful window into the spirituality of migrants, that is, their steadfast faith. As could be seen in chapter 4 and 5 migration is not just about economics and politics. It is also a religious phenomenon. For many migrants, particularly those moving to the US from Mexico, migration is a deep physical journey through a spiritual landscape marked with deep faith and peopled, as often as not, with angels, demons, and a crowd of folk saints, and motivated by a sense of divine purpose.[27] For migrants, the world is a religious universe; God's grace permeates the earth and meets us constantly in our daily lives be it in our relationships, in the created world or in the events of our daily lives. This deep religious faith is like a treasure trove that migrants draw from, right from the beginning of their journey. The following observation by a sociologist on a migrant, whom he happened to sit beside with on a plane, reflects this prominent role of faith as migrants undertake the journey:

She must have carried with her more than a dozen novenas to various saints. She did nothing but mumble her magical prayers through the entire trip, her contemplative pose only occasionally disturbed by the chatter of her Japanese recruiter. I asked her if she was nervous and if this was her first time to leave the country. No, she was not, and this was her third time.[28]

Prayer and doing their devotions are, indeed, the most common expressions of faith by and among migrants. As Chapter 5 illustrates these prayers and devotions can either be on an individual or communal level. Moreover, these acts of faith are not just expressed or passed on to their children in strictly religious settings. A Mexican-American immigrant recounts of his mother: "My mother, as her mother did before her, uses the meal to teach our kids about the use of food and its relationship to St. Mary's, to our family tree and how sharing a meal means thanking the Creator for all of our blessings. So sitting at the table means blessing yourself and listening to a prayer just as much as it means enjoying a good Mexican food."[29]

Going to church or attending church service (especially the Sunday Eucharist) ranks next among migrants' expressions of deep faith.[30]

In the case of a small Haitian Pentecostal community in South Florida the church is the center of life outside their jobs. They spend long hours in church, including most evenings after work, part of Saturday, and most of Sunday. Those with young children take them along into the pews.[31] In the case of the thousands of Asian migrant women domestic workers in Hong Kong Sunday is the preferred "day-off" as it enables them to attend religious service and meet their compatriots or friends who also go to church. For these migrant Christians the day will not be complete without going to the Sunday service. Even the lack of actual church buildings does not deter them. If there is no church building available for them, they find places, create, and build their own "church" out of parks, gyms, and auditoriums. This is confirmed in the Asian Migrant Workers Center' study of foreign domestic workers in Hong Kong, which revealed that they seek out Christian fellowships and churches for refuge and solace. The study also affirmed that many spend a longer a time in church and related activities for strength and support.[32] Eliseo Tellez Jr. says that Filipino NGOs in Hong Kong even establish and forge links with them by "visiting churches and hanging around church grounds" since the church is where the Filipina domestic workers meet. Even "the physical structure of a church is sometimes enough to assure them that things will improve."[33] In a sense, the establishment of ethnic churches provides for migrants what could be the single most important source of continuity in their world that has changed in so many ways.

Shu-Ju Ada Cheng, in her comparative study of migrant women domestic workers in Hong Kong, Singapore, and Taiwan singles out the practice of stronger attendance in church or church activities by domestic workers as a factor that explains their ability to break the isolation and engender visibility. Cheng specifically extols Church attendance as one that "provides an important opportunity and space for Filipino women to establish their support system and networking, which is essential for breaking the isolation of the household."[34] Indeed, many admit to a feeling of "homecoming" whenever they join other domestic workers for a Eucharistic celebration. Wherever it is held, "it's another home" where they can "forget [the] misgivings induced by being a stranger in another country."[35] They do not care whether they have to stand instead of sit, kneel on a rough floor, or put up with the noise and the stares of curious passers-by. For them, it is the spirit with which one attends the Mass that counts. In a sense this is a reflection of a deep Christian conviction that date back to the first followers of Jesus that the Eucharist is the very heartbeat of Christian life. The Eucharist, in the first place, is the source and summit of the Christian life.

Deep and unwavering religious faith could also be glimpsed in migrants' accounts of their own experience of migration. This is especially true for those who experience great difficulties before, during, or after migration. This, of course, is even more acute for those who cross into Europe or Australia via the merciless sea or those who cross into the US via the unforgiving desert. Like the desert fathers and mothers in ancient Christianity, migrants discover that the desert is a place that often strips them of illusions about life, a place for purification that helps them realize central truths about who they are before God. As Cesar reminisces

When I was in the desert I thought about Jesus' temptation. It was like God was testing me in some way.... For me the temptation was not to trust God, to give up, to admit defeat, to allow myself to die in the desert. But I couldn't do it.... I felt God was calling me to fight, to keep going, to suffer for my family. I did not want to let myself be conquered by death least of all.[36]

Undeniably, religion is one of the institutions whose influence is not usually radically changed by migration. As a matter of fact it is, in many cases, strengthened and even transformed. It serves as a social glue for the migrant community such that many big or prominent social gatherings are based on religious feasts or religious occasions. And because their religious rituals and faith are bound up with their ethnic customs and other elements of folk culture, e.g. music, dance, and holidays, or to life's rituals and passages, e.g. weddings, funerals, and coming-of-age celebrations, e.g. *quinceanera* among Mexican-Americans religious faith then plays a prominent role in the lives of migrants. In the US the strong ties of religious faith with the maintenance and reproduction of ethnic identity has been the subject of numerous studies at the turn of the twentieth century from the Italians to the Irish, the Jewish, and the Greek. In more recent times the study of the intersection of religious identity with ethnic identity has gained ground in the case of Hispanic or Latino/a communities as could be seen in the works of Espin and Elizondo cited in this book.

For Asian-American communities, meanwhile, Pyong Gap Min's article titled "Religion and Maintenance of Ethnicity among Immigrants: A Comparison of Indian Hindus and Korean Protestants," echoes what is happening among Hispanic or Latino/a communities.[37] Min's survey of 131 Korean immigrant churches in New York City showed that Korean churches contributed to the preservation of ethnicity among Korean immigrants by helping them increase their co-ethnic fellowship as well as maintain Korean cultural traditions. The significant role of the church among the Korean-Americans surveyed by Min is such that most of them even celebrate traditional Korean holidays in church eating traditional Korean food and playing traditional games with their ethnic co-members, rather than at home.[38] Thus, religious faith takes on a central role in relation to ethnic identity insofar as it is strongly linked with the three critical goals for ethnic identity or ethnic attachment in the context of migration: retention of ethnic subculture (cultural), involvement in ethnic networks and interaction (social), and group self-identification (psychological).

Migrants' enduring religious faith is also manifest in the way they keep or hang on to it in the midst of hardship or in the way they use or engage it to view or deal with the problematic conditions inherent to migration. First of all, migrants are uprooted people and they often rely on or draw from their faith to deal with the ruptures and discontinuities born out of their state of "uprootedness." Secondly, most migrants—regardless of religious affiliation—know that most religious leaders and places of worship, especially churches, will provide charitable or social services no matter who they are or what their immigration status is. For many migrants, indeed, turning to religion is another strategy to deal with or resist their oppression. The church, for example, is not just the principal site of celebration for ethnic identity and community. It also serves as the central source for dealing with and combating their various difficulties or experience of injustice. It is both a religious and a social center: the place where they hold meaningful rituals and forge ties with their compatriots. It is their refuge in times of crisis and their home when they want to shout for joy.

Migrants' steadfast faith could also be seen in the various religious icons or decorations that grace their homes. Many have either a cross, pictures of Jesus, Mary, and the saints or framed biblical passages inside their homes. Some would have statues of Mary or Jesus in front of their homes or an altar right inside their homes. Other indications of migrants' steadfast faith include reading the Bible, singing hymns, or listening to religious programs at home, while driving, or at work.[39] Whether it's simple or grand, overt or covert, religious faith occupies a central place in the lives of migrants.

Festive Community Spirit

The festive community spirit, which characterizes migrant communities, could also teach us a thing or two on matters of the Spirit. To be sure, there are usually vibrant social circles within the migrant communities, which serve as surrogate extended families. Most migrants would belong to one or more of these social circles. These "spontaneous extended families" or subgroups are strong networks of social interaction as well as mutual support. Among the Finnish-Vietnamese community in Turku, Finland, for example, this strong mutual assistance include various types of practical help such as interpreting assistance, help with paperwork such as tax declarations, extending financial loans for larger purchases like a car or for larger emergency remittances to relatives in Vietnam, temporary lodgings, etcetera. As Kathleen Valtonen observes this extended family role structure, which the Vietnamese-Finnish also applies in their relationship with the natives,[40] could be seen as one form of sociocultural capital that invigorates the integration process.

The ways in which this sense of family and community is reinforced or nurtured through festive gatherings, especially around food and/or the Eucharist, is instructive. On Sundays, for example, a paved lot in Georgia that is used as parking lot on weekdays is transformed into a *plaza del pueblo*, in conjunction with the religious services of the La Missión Católica de Nuestra Señora de las Américas which uses the warehouse—which the parking lot was built for—as its sanctuary or worship space.[41] The lot is filled with people as vendors sold *paletas* or ice cream popsicles, religious items, and other foodstuff from stands as music played from loudspeakers. The vibrant scene is not surprising. In many of the church members' *pueblos* and *ranchos* of origin, local parishes are usually adjacent to the town square and on Sunday afternoons after Mass, vendors gather to sell food and worshippers linger to chat with their neighbors and family members.

In particular, the fellowships or shared meals that usually follow migrant communities' Eucharistic celebrations, prayer meetings, Bible study or any religious gathering give us a glimpse of the rich possibilities that migrant religious faith can offer for Christian spirituality. First of all, migrants usually go to great lengths to procure the necessary ingredients for the ethnic viands, which are usually the staple food whenever they gather. They exert so much energy and creativity just so they can come up with the real or, at least, close to the real recipe.[42] Hence, one could imagine the joy of a migrant not only at seeing compatriots but also at seeing, smelling, and eating "home" food.

I for one remember how delighted and, at the same time, amazed I was at seeing and eating Philippine viands and native delicacies on a table in a house in The Netherlands on the third Sunday of my first month in my former host country. And the women-dominated Filipino migrant community in the Dutch city where I lived for a number of years do this once a month, as does all the other Filipino communities in the Netherlands, most of whom are led and sustained by women. I have been to a number of similar gatherings of migrants in the United States, Malaysia, and Australia and I am very much inclined to say that the *salo-salo* (shared meal) is iconic of the Eucharist. Seeing one is, indeed, like witnessing the Gospel at table. The spirit of joy, the atmosphere of warmth and affection, and the sense of community are such that the experience itself becomes a God-experience. It is like seeing "the substance of religion and more . . . the strength that comes from valuing the intangibles, the meanings that are continually created and understood, when human beings come together to share their lives and their fears, their meals and their memories."[43] It is the Eucharist in the flesh rooted in the resiliency, tenacity, and beauty of the human spirit. In many ways such gatherings fit Eddie Gibbs and Ryan Bolger's description of emerging churches which "include the outsider, even those who are different. . . . place a great emphasis on the Eucharist as a central act of worship" and where "the ethos of the service is one of hospitality"[44] such that at times, the eucharistic celebration takes place in a home or café setting to enable the group to demonstrate hospitality in a culturally appropriate manner.

The Eucharist, in the first place, anticipates the messianic banquet. It is also a potent tool in the search for ecclesial unity as it makes the church present. As a celebration of Christian spirituality, the Eucharist keeps our spirituality from deteriorating into an individualistic piety.[45] To be sure, these shared meals are potent reminders that Christian life is not just about individual salvation but also about collective liberation. These meals teach us that Christian spirituality must not just be about fasting but also about celebrating; it must not just be about families but also about communities. Most of all, these meals remind us that spirituality must not be confined to prayer or any other religious activity but to everything that celebrates our humanity.

What makes this festive community spirit even more striking is its inclusive character. This inclusive character could be glimpsed in terms of how religion-based activities not only facilitate closer relations for migrants but also opportunities to involve and engage other ethnic groups and/or the wider community. Religious activities organized by Vietnamese migrant congregations in Turku, Finland, for example, are generally inclusive and open to nonmembers.[46] The St. Patrick's Day celebrations I have experienced in Chicago, where I used to live, are not only a huge family and communal social event for the Irish. These celebrations also attract the participation of the general population, e.g. the parade. The devotion to Our Lady of Guadalupe and the annual celebration of the Virgin's feast in Miami captures very well the inclusive character of the festive community spirit among migrant communities. Bidegain points to how the Marian devotion involves not only every national Hispanic community but also the whole Anglo community in all its ethnic diversity, as well as the Haitian community. There is even an annual pilgrimage to the Virgin of Guadalupe involving all the parishes of the archdiocese.[47] Indeed, migrant spirituality is first and foremost about relationships and providing for others, sometimes through their presence but often in their absence.

THEOLOGICAL REFLECTIONS

Faith-based language for the migration experience, particularly the journey is not new. The Bible, which is dotted with stories of people like Abraham, Joseph, and Ruth who found hope and liberation by crossing borders, frequently uses migration as a metaphor for human spiritual journeys. From their human condition, from tragedy and hope, from their situation of grace and disgrace, migrants make known the passing of God through history. The following section explores the connections and implications of migrants' struggle to "become a person in the fullest sense,"[48] as they relate to Christian spirituality.

The "Crucified People"

A spirituality of suffering clearly marks migrants' lives. In fact, migrants and theologians alike regard the migrant experience as a way of the cross. From this perspective Christian spirituality in the context of migration could be articulated not so much as an ascent to the mountain of God but as a descent into the valley of injustice. Such a perspective makes sense in view of how migrants' experience is almost like Jesus' self-emptying or kenosis, whereby Jesus empties himself of everything but love, a love that reaches its greatest self-giving expression on the cross.

Korean-American theologian Jung Young Lee gives voice to such perspective based on his own experience as an immigrant: "Immigration is the most vivid and profound symbol of marginality. Through immigration we are completely detached from a country that had protected and nurtured us. Immigration also estranges us from a centrality that previously protected us. We become displaced and must re-adjust our lives."[49] Fellow Korean-American theologian Anselm Min echoes Lee's observations, saying

The migrant is the marginalized person *par excellence*, suffering economic deprivation, political disenfranchisement and cultural displacement as an excluded minority, almost always exposed to the worst possible human passions, racism and xenophobia. In many ways, the suffering of the migrant worker is the representative, paradigmatic suffering of our time, embodying all the contradictions of a global capitalism in the process of often inhuman and degrading globalization...[50]

For many migrants crossing a border means leaving behind much of what gives meaning, value, and cohesion in their lives. Indeed, even when migrants do not suffer or die physically in their courageous and hopeful journeys they undergo a suffering or death culturally, psychologically, socially and emotionally. They suffer an agonizing movement from belonging to non-belonging, from relational connectedness to family separation, from being to non-being. Groody argues

Within the particular stories of their lives, we see echoes of the universal experience of suffering. The poor often bring forth truths that are the most basic to human life. They penetrate the superficialities of a cosmetic culture and reveal the naked truth of human existence. Through them we can glimpse hints of the hidden presence of God who lives with them on the margins of society. Within their particular stories of hunger, thirst, estrangement, nakedness, sickness and imprisonment we can begin to see the face of a crucified Christ.[51]

Thus, the suffering migrants experience is an important starting point for a discussion about their spirituality which, like the suffering of the poor and oppressed, is revelatory. Irregular migrants, for example, could be regarded as the "crucified people" today.[52] Coined by Ignacio Ellacuria and further developed by Jon Sobrino "crucified people" refers to "that collective body which, as the majority of humanity, owes its situation of crucifixion to the way society is organized and maintained by a minority that exercises its dominion through a series of factors which, taken together and given their concrete impact within history, must be regarded as sin."[53] They are, in other words, "those who fill up in their flesh what is lacking in Christ's passion, as Paul says about himself. They are the actual presence of the crucified Christ in history."[54] In this crucified people Christ acquires a body in history; the crucified people embody Christ in history as crucified.

Groody considers the idea of the "crucified people" as analogical language for speaking about the social reality of undocumented immigrants in terms of Christian theology, a way to conceptualize what immigrants are experiencing in the contemporary world. The immigrant poor, Groody surmises, see their own story in Jesus' story, and from their story we can also reread the Jesus story. He explains the comparison in the way irregular Mexican immigrants experience an agonizing movement from life to death:

Economically, undocumented Mexican immigrants experience a movement from poverty in Mexico to poverty and exploitation in the United States. Politically, they experience oppression. Legally, they are accused of trespassing. Socially, they feel marginalized. Psychologically, they undergo intense loneliness. And spiritually, they experience the agony of separation and displacement.[55]

Well-known Latino activist Cesar Chavez himself compares the jobs irregular immigrants do to a crucifixion saying

Every time I see lettuce, that's the first thing I think of, some human being had to thin it. And it's just like being nailed to a cross.... [Like working with sugar beets] that was work for an animal, not a man. Stooping and digging all day, and the beets are heavy—oh, that's brutal work. And then go home to some little place, with all those kids, and hot and dirty—that is how a man is crucified.[56]

Thus, the cross of Jesus is not only a comfort to migrants but a challenge to the structures and systems that continue to regularize and legitimize the crucifixion of migrants. Phan explains this double-edged meaning and symbol of the cross:

Jesus' violent death on the cross was a direct result of his border crossing and ministry at the margins... Even the form of his death, that is, by crucifixion, indicates that Jesus was an outcast, and he died, as the Letter to Hebrews says, 'outside the city gate and outside the camp' (Heb. 13:12–13). Symbolically, however, hung between heaven and earth, at the margins of both worlds, Jesus acted as the mediator and intercessor between God and humanity.[57]

Consequently, when followers of Jesus witness the crucifixion of the innocent, the encounter functions as a real sign drawing them into the reality of the paschal mystery such that they are challenged, according to Jon Sobrino, to "take the crucified people from the cross." When followers of Jesus take the "crucified people" down from their cross, they then become a living sign for the universal church of both the coming of the Kingdom of God and the resurrection of the crucified Jesus from the dead.[58] The eschatological horizon of migrants' realities, consequently, leads us to consider ways in which the "crucified people" of today are integrally related to the salvation of the world. As Robert Lasalle-Klein points out "crucified people" embody a luminescent faith, hope, and communal solidarity that have helped desperate communities to survive in the face of overwhelming odds.[59] In the case of immigrants Lydio Tomasi goes to the extent of claiming "it's not the . . . the Church [that] saves the immigrant, but the immigrant who saves the Church."[60]

In a world of suffering what is at stake is the humanity and faith of believers.[61] Insofar as in Christian terms all sanctification, all inner transformation, is ultimately for the sake of transformative action and redemptive practice in society[62] the suffering of migrants all over the world strongly calls for Christian witness to make humanity's quest for salvation even more strongly linked with one another. Indeed, in this day and age when the situation of the stranger in our churches is once again calling us to accountability for our responsibility toward our neighbors, particularly the voice-less and power-less in our communities, God's exhortation to the Israelites to take care of the stranger because they too, like us or our ancestors, were once strangers challenge us to foster social equality based on anamnestic solidarity.

A Spirituality of Pilgrimage

A Christian spirituality that arises from the experience of migrants today could also be understood and articulated as a spirituality of pilgrimage. To be sure, the journey that migrants undertake is more than a trip. It is more than an adventure, more than a vacation, more than a sojourn. As a people who brave deserts and seas, and struggle against death-dealing conditions in destination countries in their unwavering search for "greener pastures" and their own "promised land," migrants experience mobility as a spiritual journey or a pilgrimage.

The multiple, multi-directional, and difficult but transforming journeys that migrants undertake remind us, indeed, of the character of Christian life as a journey, as a constant coming and going, as a continuous departure and arrival, and of Christian life as a process. A pilgrimage unites the seeker and the traveler and insofar as migrants' journeys force them to struggle to survive and, to a certain extent, thrive in strange places their journeys are a pilgrimage in the wilderness. They are like Israel in the wilderness that embarked on a journey believing that the promised land lies ahead. Using the experience of struggle and hope by the Israelites in the wilderness as heuristic lens, for instance, Chad Rimmer contends: "In the wilderness,

nations are recreated, people are renamed, sacrifices are made, call-
ings are discerned, spiritual acumen is honed, God's grace is revealed,
and God's people are renewed."[63] This perspective challenges us to
rediscover the God of revelation in the context of leaving, of going
out to other places as Abraham, Jesus, Paul, and countless Christian
missionaries over the ages did.

In the context of Christian spirituality the experience of migration as a spiritual journey is as yet incomplete, tentative, and forward
looking but may not necessarily relate to everything that a pilgrimage connotes. For example, Christian spiritual commentators speak of
a model of Christian life as ascent or climbing up toward God in a
manner analogous to the angels ascending and descending the lad-
der in Jacob's dream or Moses climbing up the mountain of Sinai
where he meets God. Indeed, in Christian spirituality there is an entire
ascent literature in which spiritual commentators have even mapped
out steps which had to be taken to move up from this world to the
world of God. While such an understanding relates to the idea of pilgrimage it probably could not fully speak of/to migrants' experience
of spiritual journey. First of all, the spiritual journey for migrants is
probably not a direct and immediate ascent. In fact, it is more of a
descent. For refugees and those taking perilous routes, for example,
the quest for well-being and justice ironically entails a further descent
into the valley of injustice where they are forced to surrender everything. They literally put their lives in the hands of God, whom they
believe will uphold, guide, and protect them even as evil threatens to
crush them.

Secondly, implicit in the ascent understanding of spirituality is the
idea that as one ascends one leaves mundane realities to be closer to
God. For migrants, however, the search for God and the encounter
with God is rooted precisely in what may amount to mundane things
and activities such as food and water or eating, sleeping, drinking,
and, oftentimes, just the simple joy of rest from the daily grind of
work. Thus, their spirituality as pilgrimage is more of a spirituality of
lo cotidiano (daily life). Such an understanding makes sense in view
of the fact that the basis of living spirituality today, especially from a
Third World perspective, is preceded by a radical encounter with that
which gives life.[64] For migrants, memories of their loved ones and the
dreams they have for themselves (and their loved ones) enable them
to situate themselves fully in the reality of daily life with its uncertainties and precariousness. Ivone Gebara maintains that our ability to
deal with and appreciate daily realities helps us to touch the very heart
strings of the meaning of existence. It allows us to open ourselves to

receive that which is temporary, that which is passing in all its multiple expressions with all its vulnerability. Gebara goes on to say that spirituality in that which is provisional, that which is fleeting, is an expression of faith in life. It is a search for confidence and hope, so necessary to live today so as to achieve a better tomorrow for all. And this hope, continues Gebara, lived within passing reality is the spirituality of large masses of people (like migrants) who hardly have any certitude of survival. Theirs is a day-to-day spirituality with no long terms, for it is experienced in the constant struggle for life.[65]

For the in-between, like migrants, reality is always someplace else and the pilgrimage is a journey of hope and faith. They hope against hope, believe even when they do not see, and give even when it hurts. They are a pilgrimage in that they are difficult journeys nourished by courage rooted in hope, love, generosity, and faith. Indeed, life in the context of migration is also a test case for faith. Lee further illustrates this perspective in the case of Abram and Sarah by pointing out how it is with faith that they took the risk to leave everything that is familiar and secure to them, even if they do not know where they were going (Hebrews 11:8). Lee drives home the point by describing how the faith of Israel deepened in the throes of migration, particularly during their sojourn in the wilderness.[66] For Lee the life of wandering in the wilderness for 40 years was an experience of being in-between for the Israelites. They were uprooted without belonging anywhere. The experience, however, clarified for them their need to shift their focus on God.

Like the Israelites' experience in the wilderness, the pilgrim represents a type of mobility long venerated in the Christian tradition.[67] Migrants' experience somehow continues this tradition since they have a profound experience of God as a pilgrim community. As they move from one reality to another, so does their God, who is not established in a solid temple but shares in their provisional life. God walks alongside them and becomes a pilgrim on the roads of this uneven world nurturing and blessing them by the power of renewed relationships and community within the household of life. In fact, solidarity is more real in such situations than in stable communities. Because it is an improvised community, the pilgrim community is less attached to the institution. It enjoys more flexibility and freedom, and is more open to other cultures and to less clerical ways of being church.[68] Thus, migrants reveal

the underlying reality of the church as a pilgrim people . . . almost a sacrament, for it is like a mirror in which the People of God views its own reality not only as a problem but also as grace that . . . transforms the church when its members embrace their [migrants] poverty as wayfarers in a passing world.[69]

As a people of faith, we are also like people on the move. The phenomenon of contemporary migration drives home this point as it brings to mind the eschatological destiny of all humanity. To migrate is to wander away from home and whether we are migrants or not we are, all of us, as human beings, migrants, pilgrims or travelers on a journey to our eternal homeland, the new heaven and the new earth. As the *Letter to the Hebrews* points out, "here we have no lasting city, but we are looking for the city that is to come" (Heb. 13:14).[70] The words of Augustine illumines this biblical passage: "Our hearts are restless until they rest in God."

A Spirituality of Hope and Life

Last but not the least, a Christian spirituality of hope and life is discernible among migrants. To be sure, Christian spirituality deals with the highest aspirations of the human life. It deals with, and reveals, what one values (Mk. 10:17–25), how one spends one's time (Lk. 10:38–42), where one stores one's treasure (Mt. 6: 19–21), how one lives out one's relationships (Rom. 12:18) and, ultimately, how one loves (1 Cor. 13:4–8a).[71] Nowhere is such understanding of Christian spirituality reflected in the context of migration than in the consistent ethic of hope and life that is woven into the fabric of migrants' lives. Michael Downey writes in *Understanding Christian Spirituality* that there are two spirituality constants or two essential components in any approach to spirituality. First, there is an awareness that there are levels of reality not immediately apparent. Second, there is a quest for personal integration in the face of forces of fragmentation and depersonalization.[72] Human authenticity, then, is the outcome of a continuous dynamism of self-transcendence toward that which is true and truly good. Migrants reflect this orientation and struggle toward what is true and truly good consistently in their very decision to migrate and their persistence to struggle for justice.

While often pushed to live on the borders of society migrants refuse to do so completely and create spaces for themselves to survive. Their creative use of "imposed shrunken places" e.g. garbage area and car park and their occupation of public places have a revelatory quality.[73] Migrants' transformation of "shrunken places" gives us a glimpse on how marginal(ized) places can be transformed into spaces of presence. With their creative resistance and festive community spirit they, like

Jesus, create with other maginal(ized) people new all-inclusive centers of reconciliation and harmony, because and despite of their status as strangers and guests.[74]

This dogged orientation towards what is life-giving is also rooted in the survival nature of migrants' lives. This survival way of life has theological implications. For example, African-American womanist theologian Delores Williams asserts that survival struggle and/or struggle for quality of life are inseparable and are associated with God's presence with the community. She maintains that this "survival quality of life" runs through both the Hebrew and Christian testaments so much so that one can detect a survival tradition and not just prophetic and liberation tradition in the Scriptures. An example, which she has eloquently elaborated on, is the story of Hagar, a biblical survival story which has nourished the African-American community for generations.[75]

Cuban-American theologian Ada Maria Isasi-Diaz is more direct, however, as she points at the struggle for survival of Hispanic women, especially those in the U.S.[76] She posits that survival is not just about sustaining physical life but also about being agents of our own story or destiny. She especially argues for a hermeneutic of survival in evaluating culture from within and shares Williams' position that the struggle for survival is ultimately relational or that it is integrally linked with the survival of the community. Naming survival as Hispanic women's daily bread, Isasi-Diaz maintains that to survive is "to be" or "being fully." She weaves all of these with her phrase *la vida es la lucha* (to struggle is to live). Since to struggle is to resist to creatively resist, therefore, is to fully live.

This survival quality of life is, without a doubt, nourished by a deep spirituality of hope. Hope, as it is understood and used in this text, differs from emotion or mere optimism. Rather, it is employed here as both an ethical activity and theological virtue. Anthony Kelly's writings on hope are instructive in this regard.[77] First, Kelly contends that, as an ethical activity, hope has a conscience and intelligence which mere optimism lacks. Moreover, hope looks beyond self-regarding satisfactions to the transcendent values that alone can nourish life and give it direction. Thus, hope refuses to see the ultimate meaning of life as simply "more of the same". It is patiently open to what is, and must be, "otherwise". It cannot rest except in the truly meaningful and the genuinely good, thereby increasing the scope and energies of the human spirit in the quest for the fullness of life. Hope, then, breathes the conviction that what is deepest in our aspirations is not ultimately worthless or self-defeating.

Kelly notes further that hope is not mere *wishing* for something more. It is a conduct of life, a mode of living and acting which inspires action. It engenders a deep moral sense and points in the direction of a more passionate self-involvement in the making of the world, and risking even life itself for the greater good of oneself or others. Kelly goes on to say that, as theological virtue, hope is not only about giving thanks for what is already given but also being open to what is beyond all imagination and control. Hope for oneself then expands to hope for others, interceding for all who are our companions in the light and shadow of the history we share.

This hope is, in turn, nourished by faith. Faith and hope, in themselves, are part of the triad of theological virtues, that is, faith, hope, and love. Hope without faith would be blind. It would not know who it was trusting or what it was hoping for. At the same time, faith without hope would be closed in on itself. It would tend to imagine the future as a mere extension. Benedict XVI provides a clear link between faith and hope in *Spe Salvi*. In the said encyclical Benedict draws upon key biblical texts on hope such as the *Letter to the Hebrews* which closely links the "fullness of faith" to "the confession of our hope without wavering" and the *Letter to the Ephesians* where Paul reminds the Ephesians that before their encounter with Christ they were "without hope" because they were "without God in the world" (Eph. 2:12).[78] From this perspective the cross or the crucified Christ is a critical element of a Christian spirituality of migration insofar as it is juxtaposed with hope rooted in faith. Like Jesus, migrants do not actively seek the cross. They seek the Kingdom values of justice and accepted the cross as part of it. For many migrants their destination country is the place where they experience a contemporary Golgotha. It is, however, also the place where many equally experience the rising to a new way of life. Indeed, many a migrant's journey to their destination countries is like Jesus' journey to Jerusalem. It is both a journey toward a great promise and great suffering.

It is within this spirituality that prayer also finds a place. In Benedict XVI's words prayer is a "school or setting for learning and practicing hope."[79] Migrants' devotions, in themselves, already indicate an element of holiness, of the mystery which is larger than life, and of that "something more" which has to do with the ultimate. Groody's reflections on prayer is helpful here. Groody reckons that prayer opens up the door to the one unchanging relationship that promises stability amid the vicissitudes of life and the uncertainties of the contemporary world. Because it taps into some of the deepest places of loneliness and longing lodged in the human heart, prayer allows us to develop that intimate conversation with Christ that enables us to abide with him and know each other as intimate friends (Jn. 15:4). It is the doorway to spiritual depth, human meaning, and genuine intimacy and allows us to perceive more clearly the truths of life. Exercised in private and in community, prayer builds and nourishes our relationships on all levels and is expressed in many forms.[80] The use of prayer or religious rituals by migrants as well as Christian churches and advocacy groups in their struggle for life-giving conditions, e.g. *Posada sin Fronteras* also makes a lot of sense from a Christian spiritual perspective.[81] This is because prayer is not just a psychological tool for self-actualization but a spiritual grace that facilitates human transformation. It is a fundamental human need and is especially important for those involved in the work of justice. Prayer and justice are two sides of the same spiritual coin: justice without prayer quickly degenerates into frenetic social activism, but prayer without justice is hollow and empty.[82]

Within this spirituality of hope and life we also understand the festive community spirit which characterizes migrants' view and way of life. As hopeful and hope-filled people migrants embody the central tenet of Christianity, that is, Easter. Even in death Jesus did not remain within the boundaries of what death means: failure, defeat, destruction. By his resurrection he crossed the borders of death into a new life, thus bringing hope where there was despair, victory where there was vanquishment, freedom where there was slavery, and life where there was death. In this way, the borders of death become frontiers to life in abundance.[83] In the same manner, the resurrection of Jesus from the dead offers migrants hope that they will also overcome all that threatens their lives even as they surrender in trust without knowing the final or even intermediate outcome of their journey. Indeed, migrants are Easter people. They cling to an active enduring hope. Most importantly, they know how to celebrate individually and communally even in the midst of hardship. It is precisely this Easter spirituality that enables migrants to celebrate in the midst of their struggle, even crack a joke or laugh about it.

Such a hearty spirituality is biblical and Christian. In the Old Testament laughter is attributed directly to God. The name of Isaac—the son of Abraham and Sarah—means "God laughs." Karl-Josef Kuschel even provides a link between laughter and the resurrection. According to Kuschel, the Jesus story did not end in His suffering and death that elicited derisive laughter among his oppressors. The Jesus event culminated in the resurrection, the expression of God's power, specifically through laughter at death. In the story of Jesus, then, the final act is laughter and the final experience is joy.[84] Kuschel echoes Harvey Cox's position on laughter as "hope's last weapon"[85] by saying "Christians who laugh are insisting that the stories of the world's sufferings do not have the last word."[86] This celebratory attitude cannot be ignored or downplayed in the face of what Lawrence Cunningham and Keith Egan say:

> But to celebrate the eucharist well we must learn, first of all, how to celebrate, to make festival, to make "Sabbath." What does not happen outside of eucharist will not happen at the eucharist: we cannot become instant celebrators, festive people merely by walking through a church door. We cannot celebrate the eucharist well if we do not celebrate elsewhere.[87]

There are a few other spiritual notes that could be drawn from migrants' festive gatherings. First of all, like Jesus during his ministry and in his post-resurrection appearances, a shared meal plays a key role in these events. The use of the Eucharist as the focal point for these gatherings is also important to highlight here because from the perspective of Christian spirituality the way of discipleship in community finds it highest expression in the sharing of the eucharist. Authentic Christian spirituality has an ecclesial character to it and among the many meanings of the eucharist is its significance in shaping as well as nourishing the community which affirms Jesus as Lord.[88] Thomas Aquinas even calls the Eucharist the "sacrament of church's unity."[89]

Second, these gatherings are occasions when migrants celebrate milestones and achievements or moments when they come and share their triumphs not just their tragedies. Oftentimes, the celebratory character comes from the simple joy of coming together and seeing each other as they nourish themselves not just with food from their home countries but also the Eucharistic bread. This scene, in some ways, is reminiscent of the early Christian community making Jesus present once again by coming together to pray and celebrate through the breaking of the bread. To the extent that migrant religious gatherings like those in Turku, Finland are inclusive, they reflect what Cunningham and Egan say as one hallmark of authentic Christian spirituality, that is, its ability to reach out to everyone regardless of class, gender, social condition, etcetera.[90] Ultimately, our task as disciples of Jesus is to invite others to share at the table.[91] As such these gatherings are proofs of what contemporary Christian spiritual writers say that spirituality is not simply concerned with interiority or the interior life but seeks an integration of all aspects of human life and experience[92] or that what we do as followers of Jesus must include a concern not only with our immediate community but with humanity as a whole.

CONCLUSION

For centuries and generations people have sought to express quite particular forms of Christian spirituality based on the actual historical and existential conditions in which they find themselves. Thus, for example, we find in the history of Christianity monastic or ascetic spirituality, spiritualities informed by liberation theology, or feminist spiritualities.[93] What this chapter shows are the sources and contours of a Christian spirituality of migration.

While spirituality in general deals with what people most value, Christian spirituality involves living out what Jesus most valued. In other words, it is about how one lives out what Jesus most valued, particularly the values of the Kingdom of God. Lived out in its personal and public dimensions, Christian spirituality is the way in which the invisible heart of God is made visible to the world. The tremendous faith and resilience of the human spirit in the face of unimaginable difficulties, that migrants steadfastly exhibit, is an eloquent testament to Christian spirituality as a way of discipleship. To know Christ is to follow Christ. And like the story of Jesus, migrants' stories and lives are not just about suffering and death. They are not just victims but also subjects and agents of their own destiny. Indeed, their experience shows us that in the midst of pain and sin it is possible to discover God's abundant grace in unexpected and amazing ways in the context of migration.

CONCLUSION
ONE BREAD, ONE BODY, ONE PEOPLE

This book explored the human and religious dimensions of contemporary global migration. Part I, "Migration and Social Justice," explored the human dimension, particularly in relation to the human experience of migrants on the margins. This part of the book, first, interrogated the gifts and challenges of contemporary migration's intersections with globalization, especially as seen from the plight of the (irregular) unskilled worker. This is followed by an exploration of the experience of migrant women and the challenges of the gendered dimension of such experience. Part I then concluded with a critical discussion of Catholic Social Teaching (CST) with a view to articulating a possible Christian ethical contribution toward the reform of migration policies.

Part II, "Migration and Religious Experience," explored the religious dimension of the experience of migrants. This part of the book, first, examined the character of religion (in general) and mission in the context of migration. This is followed by a critical discussion on how inculturation takes place in the context of migration as well as the problems and prospects that it faces. An interrogation of the ways in which migrants' way of life provides clues in understanding the Christian spiritual life then completes this part.

Contemporary global migration, as discussed in this book, drives home the point enshrined in a song sung at Eucharistic celebrations titled "one bread, one body, one people," and I argue that the three phrases in the song's title could serve as the key principle in the task of articulating a theology of migration from a Christian perspective. It is this concluding point that I now turn to discuss.

One Bread

As reflected in this book, particularly in Part 1, contemporary global migration highlights the fact that people move in search of a better life. For millions of desperate people on the move, indeed, mobility is usually about the search for the bare necessities in life. It is, in other words, a search for bread.[1] We live in only one world; we share in only one planet with limited and dwindling resources. The physical, material, or economic motivation for people on the move, in a world that is turning more and more into one global village, reinforces the Christian idea that we share, and ought to share, one bread.

If we factor the Christian ethical teaching of the universal destination of the earth's goods or, as the CST calls it, the common good, the idea of "one bread" becomes clearer. In Christian thought the legitimate right of individuals and groups to seek their own advantage has to be balanced against the common welfare of all. In fact within the right to private property lies a primordial sense that private property is under a social mortgage: "All that God gives is a product of grace. We cannot earn what God gives us; we cannot deserve it; what God gives is given out of the goodness of God's heart; what God gives us is not pay, but a gift; not a reward, but a product of love."[2] The Evangelical Free Church of America eloquently puts the idea of migration as sharing in one bread:

Similarly, as aliens and strangers in the world, the material resources of the world do not belong to us. We have what we have because God, as host, has distributed material resources to us, His guests. As recipients of God's graciousness and generosity, we need to guard against selfishness and possessiveness which would cloud our attitude toward immigrants.[3]

The movement of millions of migrants and refugees, as highlighted in Part 1, shows us that the search for a better life knows no borders. Thus, migration serves as a challenge to share the earth, share our resources, and, in the process, share the bread. Bread is a global symbol for survival. It is, however, also very much a religious symbol. The Christian tradition itself is rich with images of bread and sharing the bread as a symbol not just of physical and spiritual nourishment but also of discipleship. The story of Israel receiving manna or "bread from heaven" in the wilderness is not only a potent reminder that we all need nourishment (Exod. 16: 1–21). The story is also a stark reminder of how we must all equally share in God's providence.[4] In the Acts of the Apostles, Luke refers several times to the practice of breaking of the bread in the Christian community in Jerusalem mentioning how "they went as a body to the Temple every day but met in their houses for the breaking of bread; they shared their food gladly and generously" (Acts 2:46). Paul's rebuke of the Corinthian community for their abuse of the communal meal also highlights the social and spiritual significance of equal access to and sharing of the bread. The wealthy members arrived at the communal meal before the others (because they didn't have to work); by the time the working-class members arrived, the food and drink had been consumed.[5]

Jesus himself did not only present himself as the "bread of life" (John 6:35); many of his significant works during his ministry have to do with eating and/or the breaking of the bread, for example, feeding of the 5,000 (Matthew 14:13–21). Even his last act before he was arrested was the breaking of the bread with his disciples, that is, Last Supper. Today, the commemoration of that last act through the sacrament of the Eucharist is considered as the source and summit of Christian worship.

One Body

Contemporary global migration not only highlights the Christian idea of sharing (in) one bread but also that of being one body. As 1 Cor. 10:17 says, "because there is one bread, we who are many are one body." Because of the dramatic shrinking of spaces and the innovations in transport and communication technology brought by globalization, more and more people are able to move, making the world more interconnected than ever before. What happens in Africa will have repercussions in Asia and the rest of the world just as what happens in Wall Street will reverberate in Main Street.

Today's movement of people across borders, especially south-to-north migration, underscores the Christian idea of human beings as one body whereby if there is something wrong with one part all the other parts feel it or suffer as well. As 1 Cor. 12:12 reminds us, "the body is a unit, though it is made up of many parts; and though all its parts are many, they form one body." From a Christian perspective, every part or member of the body is important, and special attention or consideration is given to the weaker ones. If one is ill, all the other parts or members suffer. As Martin Luther King Jr. enthuses, "injustice anywhere is a threat to justice everywhere." In the same manner, migrants are part of this one body and they—as icons of the poor in the modern globalized world—deserve special attention. What follows 1 Cor. 12:12 is an eloquent description of the significance of seeing and caring for one another as one body that I quote most of the text here:

For we were all baptized by one Spirit into one body-whether Jews or Greeks, slave or free-and we were all given the one Spirit to drink. Now the body is not made up of one part but of many. If the foot should say, "Because I am not a hand, I do not belong to the body," it would not for that reason cease to be part of the body. And if the ear should say, "Because I am not an eye, I do not belong to the body," it would not for that reason cease to be part of the body. If the whole body were an eye, where would the sense of hearing be? If the whole body were an ear, where would the sense of smell be? But in fact God has arranged the parts in the body, every one of them, just as he wanted them to be. If they were all one part, where would the body be? As it is, there are many parts, but one body. The eye cannot say to the hand, "I don't need you!" And the head cannot say to the feet, "I don't need you!" On the contrary, those parts of the body that seem to be weaker are indispensable, and the parts that we think are less honorable we treat with special honor. And the parts that are unpresentable are treated with special modesty, while our presentable parts need no special treatment. But God has combined the members of the body and has given greater honor to the parts that lacked it, so that there should be no division in the body, but that its parts should have equal concern for each other. If one part suffers, every part suffers with it; if one part is honored, every part rejoices with it (1 Cor. 12:13–26).[6]

Contemporary migration, especially as explored in Part 1, points to the fact that the body, that is, God's people, is not well. So just as "the eye cannot say to the hand, 'I don't need you!' and the head cannot say to the feet, 'I don't need you!'" we cannot turn our back to the other members of the body, in this case the migrants. As illustrated in Part 2, however, neither should the body parts that are weaker be underestimated for they are vital to the overall health of the body. Though coming from a more vulnerable position, for example, migrants offer a lot not just to the cultural as well as economic health and vitality of destination countries.[7] They are not only an indispensable part of the functioning of households, families, nation-states worldwide. As shown in Part 2, particularly in chapters 4 and 5, their religious faith and practice are also providing means and pathways in the building of the Church (or at least their churches) as the body of God. Anselm Min explains what it means to be one body in the context of migration:

All the central Christian doctrines have to do with the common destiny of all humanity: their common subjection to the sovereignty of the one Creator and the saving providence of the triune God, their fundamental equality as creatures before God, their common redemption through the one mediator, Jesus Christ, their common eschatological call to share in the communion of the triune God as members of the Body of Christ, their social interdependence with one another in sin and grace.... The "Body of Christ" is not only a category of ecclesiology but also that of theological anthropology pertaining to all humanity.[8]

Thus, Min says:

It is fitting to teach the faithful that we are, by virtue of our membership of the Body of Christ, sons and daughters of the same heavenly Father; but it is also imperative to teach the corollary, that we are, therefore, brothers and sisters of one another in the triune God, and to draw the political conclusion that our global human solidarity in God should determine all our political priorities and concrete choices.[9]

Indeed, the greatest gift and challenge of being a Christian is not only in the experience of connection with, but in our sense of responsibility for, the other, especially the weaker members of the body of Christ. Contemporary global migration teaches us that in God's great economy of salvation there is bread, a room, and a place for everyone. Hence, a Christian theology of migration is one that involves xenophilia, not xenophobia.[10] Sharing the bread, making room, and providing a place for everyone, especially those in need like migrants, is part and parcel of building and being one body and forming one people.

One People

Flowing from and, at the same time, expanding the idea of migration as highlighting the Christian belief in one body sharing in one bread is the idea of one people. Migration, particularly as illustrated in Part II, draws attention to the image of being one people. The injustices it lays bare and, at the same time, the intercultural societies and churches it bears help develop a compelling sense of a common humanity with a shared destiny across the alienating and separating boundaries. It sets the stage and provides resources to more fully respect and nurture constructive and enriching differences among human beings and, at the same time, sublate these into a recognition of our more fundamental solidarity as human beings. Migration, in other words, provides a way of rediscovering and recovering a sense of universal humanity based on mutual dependence and common destiny as citizens of a single world.[11]

We are, as the title of a US National Conference of Catholic Bishops' Committee on Migration statement indicates, "*One Family Under God*" and relationality is our fundamental call as children of God. Relationship is constitutive of who we are and what we can become. Relationality is decisive for our humanity for relationship makes us or breaks us.[12] Our neighbor (without any exception) is "another self" and that it is our

inescapable duty to make ourselves the neighbor of every individual, without exception, and to take positive steps to help a neighbor whom we encounter, whether that neighbor be an elderly person abandoned by everyone, a foreign worker who suffers the injustice of being despised, a refugee . . . or a starving human being who awakens our conscience. (GS, 27)

Benedict XVI's *Caritas in Veritate*, particularly Chapter 5 ("The Cooperation of the Human Family"), accentuates the relational and collective dimension of the human quest for well-being. Benedict argues in the encyclical that "the development of peoples depends, above all, on a recognition that the human race is a single family working together in true communion, not simply a group of subjects who happen to live side by side" (CV, 53). Benedict explains this by saying:

As a spiritual being, the human creature is defined through interpersonal relations. The more authentically he or she lives these relations, the more his or her own personal identity matures. It is not by isolation that man establishes his worth, but by placing himself in relation with others and with God. Hence these relations take on fundamental importance. (CV, 53)

Benedict's point is highly relevant here because one could make a case that the discrimination and exclusion that migrants experience is rooted in a failure to recognize that migrants are part of our bigger family, that is, the human family. The idea of being one people, one human family, is the very same reason why Benedict insists on international cooperation and the collaborative nature of responses or solutions to problems brought by contemporary migration (CV, 62).

Benedict raises other points on the idea of the human family that are relevant to the idea of "one people" in the context of migration.[13] Benedict notes that "the unity of the human family does not submerge the identities of individuals, peoples and cultures, but makes them more transparent to each other and links them more closely in their legitimate diversity" (CV, 53). Such an idea aligns with the significance of inculturation and interculturality as Christian praxis in the context of multicultural and multireligious societies.

In the Christian tradition no other image more powerfully drives home the point about relationality and being "a family" than that of the Trinity.[14] The Trinity is absolute unity insofar as the three divine Persons are pure relationality. The reciprocal transparency among the divine Persons is total and the bond between each of them complete, since they constitute a unique and absolute unity. Thus, in the light of the revealed mystery of the Trinity, true openness does not mean loss of individual identity but profound interpenetration (CV, 54). This foundational role of unity in Christian life is highlighted, as well, in Jesus' prayer at the Last Supper where he prayed that "all may be one" (Jn. 17:21) and in Paul's exhortation that even in this world baptized Christians are to live in such a way that "there is no longer Jew or Greek, there is no longer slave or free, there is no longer male or female; for all of you are one in Christ Jesus" (Gal. 3:28).

Theologically, the idea of "one people" also fits well into the mark of the Church as "catholic." First of all, the true meaning of the "catholicity" of the Church lies in being an effective sign or sacrament of universal solidarity.[15] Robert Schreiter, for example, argues for catholicity as a framework for addressing migration.[16] In the context of migration I would say this is about witnessing a practical catholicity that gives evidence of the one human family to which we all belong. As Kristin Heyer argues, the subversive hospitality invited by a migrant God demands not only a reorientation of operative frameworks but also a concrete praxis of kinship with the displaced.[17]

In the context of the divisive dimensions of migration, one could also point to Eph. 2:19, which reminds us that we "are no longer foreigners and aliens, but fellow citizens with God's people and members of God's household," or Philippians 3:20–21, which tells us that "our citizenship is in heaven." As the migrant spirituality described in Chapter 6 shows, we are a pilgrim people. Min himself argues that this eschatological reality is the deepest identity of human beings. All other identities based on empirical contingencies such as nationality, status, class, gender, culture, and religion are temporal and transient. This teaching about the common origin, dignity, solidarity, and destiny of all human beings has been the most enduring constants of the most orthodox Christian tradition of the past 2,000 years and that nothing has been more unchristian than any sort of idolatry of class, nation, sect, empire, or gender. It is precisely to this teaching so central, so original, so enduring, and so essential to the Christian faith that we are compelled to return to by the crying needs of our time, of a world in the process of globalization with all its alienating and degrading contradictions best exemplified in the figure of people on the move.

Global solidarity, or being one people, may be the most important virtue, individually and collectively, in our time.[18] This is because, ultimately, our eschatological destiny has an incarnational dimension. It is there not only in the need to recognize the irreducible dignity of the other but also in the imperative to listen to the historically concrete word of God, in this case contemporary global migration, without which God would be reduced to silence and irrelevance.

The tension between the ideal and the real, as reflected in the idea of one bread, one body, one people in the context of migration, is an existential condition that confronts the Christian. It is a dynamic tension that does not paralyze but rather stimulates the Christian to devise a rich strategy of specific responses for the concrete situations that history presents. The world is on the move; "the whole creation has been groaning as in the pains of childbirth right up to the present time" (Romans 8:22). The magnitude of the movement and the collective pain and sorrow, joys and hopes, tragedies, and triumphs that accompany it evokes images of a world in childbirth.[19] Juxtaposing grace with sin, and combining Part 1 and Part 2 of the book, one could posit that migration could very well be not only the source of a renewed Christianity but also the birthplace of a new humanity.[20]

Indeed, migration is not just about the experience of shifting from place to place, it is also linked to the ability to imagine an alternative, individually and collectively. The dreams for a better life and the nightmares of loss that are inherent in migration are also very much a part of the stories of those of us who stay or receive migrants in our midst. The Christian revelation of the unity of the human race presupposes a metaphysical interpretation of the "humanum" in which relationality is an essential element. Ultimately, then, the challenge is to recognize ourselves and our lives in the other, that is, the migrant. As the philosopher Gabriel Marcel says, we human beings are *homo viator*. We are all pilgrims and, like the migrant, the metaphor of the journey, the figure of the stranger, and the experience of displacement are part of the fabric of our lives as human beings. Ultimately, to be human and to be Christian is to be always "on the way."

Notes

Introduction

1. See Stephen Castles and Mark J. Miller, *The Age of Migration: International Population Movements in the Modern World* 4th edition (New York: The Guilford Press, 2009). See also Andrés Solimano, *International Migration in the Age of Crisis and Globalization: Historical and Recent Experiences* (Cambridge: Cambridge University Press, 2010). Whereas other previous great migrations have been largely based on and described according to ethnic or regional groups, migration today, that is, in the age of globalization, literally has the "the world on the move." John Haywood, *The Great Migrations: From the Earliest Humans to the Age of Globalization* (London: Quercus, 2009), 244–249.

2. International Organization for Migration, *World Migration Report 2010: The Future of Migration: Building Capacities for Change* (Geneva: IOM, 2010), 3. The 2011report still puts the number of migrants worldwide to 214 million. This is still significant, IOM maintains, because the total number of migrants has not fallen despite the global economic crisis. International Organization for Migration, *World Migration Report 2011: Communicating Effectively About Migration* (Geneva: IOM, 2011), 49.

3. The book will focus on international migrants since they represent the majority of people on the move today. Moreover, the book will use the term "migrants" to include refugees and asylum-seekers on the basis of the fact that they share in the fundamental characteristics of migrants that this book employs, that is, people on the move in search of a better life or better living conditions.

4. At times this generic description of migrants is made more specific by including a more definite time frame for residence in another country, that is, for one year or more. In view of ministry, however, the Catholic Church has a broader and evolving understanding of migrants. *De Pastorali Migratorum Cura*, for instance, defines migrant people as "all those who live outside their homeland or their own ethnic community and need special attention because of real necessity" (DPCM, no. 15). In the circular letter "Church and Human Mobility" the parameters were widened to include not just

immigrants, migrant workers, exiles and refugees but also sailors, travelers by air, airport personnel, nomadic peoples and tourists (CHM, 2). The Pontifical Council for the Pastoral Care of Migrants and Itinerant People then added the following categories to the list: displaced people, fishermen, circus and fairground people, travelers for reasons of piety and study, land transport workers and other similar categories. As cited in Fabio Baggio, "The Migrant Ministry: A Constant Concern for the Catholic Church," *Asian Christian Review* Vol. 4, No. 2 (Winter 2010): 47.

5. It must be noted here that the complexities of contemporary migration is such that migrants also shift between categories over a period of time so someone who enters a country as a transient or sojourner like a student may subsequently overstay or seek permanent residence and eventually become a naturalized citizen.

6. "Emigrants" is related with the designation "immigrants." The former is deployed as a category (for migrants) from the perspective of the country of origin while the latter is a classification often used by the country of destination.

7. Those who move but remain within the same national borders, in the meantime, are known as internally displaced persons (IDPs) as has been the case in Darfur, Sudan.

8. These rights or privileges also include those laid out in the 1951 Geneva Convention and its 1967 Protocol as well as international humanitarian law based on the Geneva Conventions 1949 and the 1977 Protocols. Elspeth Guild, *Security and Migration in the 21st Century* (Cambridge: Polity Press, 2009), 71–72.

9. Moreover, New Zealand has already agreed to accept the 11,600 inhabitants of the low-lying Pacific island state Tuvalu if rising sea levels swamp the country. David Adam, "50M Environmental Refugees by the End of Decade, UN Warns," <http://www.guardian.co.uk/environment/2005/oct/12/naturaldisasters.climatechange1> accessed January 24, 2013.

10. John Allen, *The Future Church: How Ten Trends Are Revolutionizing the Catholic Church* (New York: Doubleday, 2009), 274.

11. See, for example, Dianne Scullion, "Gender Perspectives on Child Trafficking: A Case Study of Child Domestic Workers," in *Gender and Migration in 21st Century Europe*, ed. Helen Stalford, Samantha Currie and Samantha Velucci (Surrey: Ashgate, 2009): 45–60.

12. Germany is, in fact, known for this with its *gasterbeiter*. David Bacon, *Illegal People: How Globalization Creates Migration and Criminalizes Immigrants* (Boston: Beacon Press, 2008), 238–243.

13. Not surprisingly, the program is much criticized. Justin Akers Chacón and Mike Davis, *No One Is Illegal* (Chicago: Haymarket Books, 2006), 139–147, for example, considers the *bracero* program as "a twentieth-century caste system."

14. "STEP OUT" is an acronym which stands for Scientific, Technical, and Educated Professionals Out of Underdeveloped Territories. It is a new term proposed in Michelle R. Pistone and John J. Hoeffner, *Stepping Out of the Brain Drain: Applying Catholic Social Teaching in a New Era of Migration* (Lanham, MD: Lexington Books, 2007), 3.

15. The Global Hunger Index Report released in 2010 maintains that more than a billion people go hungry in 29 countries. As one could very well imagine hunger knows no borders. See Ania Lichtarowicz, "Hunger Index Shows One Billion Without Enough Food," <http://www.bbc.co.uk/news/science-environment-11503845> accessed January 21, 2013.

16. In 2007, for example, foreigners in America sent home $275 million dollars using the 2,625 money agents, mostly through grocers, bakers and other small immigrant shops. New York alone has 500 of these small-time money agents. "Special Report on Migration," *The Economist* (January 5, 2008): 10–11.

17. Samuel Munzele Maimbo, et al. *Migrant Labor Remittances in South Asia* (Washington, DC: The World Bank, 2005), 4. The authors also attribute the increased attention on the impact of remittances on economic development in the development debate in migration literature to the steady decline in the volume of overseas development assistance (ODA). Dilip Ratha, Sanket Mohapatra and Ani Silwal, "World Bank: Migration and Development Brief No. 10," <http://siteresources.worldbank.org/INTPROSPECTS/Resources/334934-1110315015165/Migration&DevelopmentBrief10.pdf > accessed January 9, 2013.

18. David Bacon, *Illegal People*, 23–26. See also Pav Jordan, "Mexican Farmers See Death Sentence in NAFTA," <http://www.commondreams.org/headlines02/1228-07.htm> accessed January 24, 2013.

19. A "coyote" is a guide who takes migrants across international borders in exchange for money.

20. David Grant, "Deportations of Illegal Immigrants in 2012 Reach New US Record," <http://www.csmonitor.com/USA/2012/1224/Deportations-of-illegal-immigrants-in-2012-reach-new-US-record> accessed January 23, 2013.

21. Neomi De Anda, "Border Cuentos: Sources for Reflections on Migration," *New Theology Review* Vol. 20, No. 3 (August 2007): 28, for instance, talks about the case of a pregnant woman who does not receive proper nutrition resulting to her unborn child being underweight according to her doctors.

22. As quoted in Allen, *The Future Church*, 164–165.

23. Unless indicated otherwise all Vatican II documents and other official documents of the Catholic Church are based on the Vatican website <http://www.vatican.va/>

24. Carmem Lussi explicitly points this out in "Human Mobility as a The-ological Consideration" in *Migration in a Global World*, ed. Solange Lefebvre and Luis Carlos Susin, Concilium (London: SCM Press, 2008/5): 50. One could speak of migration, in other words, as a "signs of the times" or those events of history through which God continues to speak to us and summon us to respond for the sake of the reign of God's love and justice throughout the whole of cre-ation. Richard P. McBrien, *Catholicism* (New York: HarperCollins, 1994), 95.

25. See Timothy Smith, "Religion and Ethnicity in America," *American Historical Review* 83: 1155–1185 as quoted in Helen Rose Ebaugh and Janet Saltzman Chafetz, "Introduction" in *Religion and the New Immigrants: Continuities and Adaptations in Immigrant Congrega-tions*, ed. Helen Rose Ebaugh and Janet Saltman Chafetz (Walnut Creek, CA: Altamira Press, 2000): 18.

26. Jon Sobrino, *Witnesses of the Kingdom: The Martyrs of El Salvador and the Crucified Peoples* (New York: Orbis, 2003), 13.

27. Anselm Min, "Migration and Christian Hope," in *Faith on the Move: Towards a Theology of Migration in Asia*, ed. Fabio Baggio and Agnes Brazal (Quezon City, Phils: Ateneo de Manila University Press, 2008): 187.

28. One could see this lack or dearth of attention to migration from a religious or theological perspective in a supposedly interdisciplinary book on migration. See James Hollifield and Caroline Brettell, eds. *Migration Theory: Talking Across Disciplines* (New York: Routledge, 2000). There are essays from the discipline of history, demography, economics, law, politics, sociology and anthropology but not a single essay on theology, not even religious studies. As of this writing there is one book that explicitly tackles migration from a Christian system-atic theological perspective, that of Daniel Groody and Gioacchino Campese, eds. *A Promised Land, A Perilous Journey: Theological Per-spectives on Migration* (Notre Dame, Ind.: University of Notre Dame Press, 2008) while there are a few that engage the issue from an ethical perspective such as Kristin Heyer, *Kinship Across Borders: A Christian Ethic of Immigration* (Washington, DC: Georgetown University Press, 2012); Sussana Snyder, *Asylum-Seeking, Migration and Church* (Burlington, VT: Ashgate, 2012); Arsene Brice Bado, *Dignity Across Borders: Forced Migration and Christian Social Ethics* (Denver, CO: Outskirts Press, 2011) and; David Hollenbach, S.J., ed. *Driven from Home: Protecting the Rights of Forced Migrants* (Washington, D.C.: Georgetown University Press, 2010). Other related books include Glenda Tibe Bonifacio and Vivienne S.M. Angeles, eds. *Gender, Religion and Migration: Pathways to Integra-tion* (Lanham, MD: Lexington Books, 2010); Donald Kerwin and Jill Marie Gerschutz, *And You Welcomed Me: Migration and Catholic*

Social Teaching (Lanham, MD: Lexington Books, 2009); Pierette Hondagneu-Sotelo, *God's Heart Has No Borders: How Religious Activists Are Working for Immigrant Rights* (Berkeley: University of California Press, 2008); Michele Pistone and John Hoeffner, *Stepping Out of the Brain Drain: Applying Catholic Social Teaching in a New Era of Migration* (Lanham, MD: Lexington Books, 2007); Gioacchino Campese and Pietro Ciallella, eds. *Migration, Religious Experience and Globalization* (New York: Center for Migration Studies, 2003) and; Daniel G. Groody, *Border of Death, Valley of Life: An Immigrant Journey of Heart and Spirit* (Lanham, MD: Rowman and Littlefield, 2002). Special issues of reputable journals on migration are also noteworthy to be mentioned here. These include Solange Lefebvre and Luis Carlos Susin, eds. *Migration in a Global World* (London: SCM Press, 2008) and Dietmar Mieth and Lisa Sowle Cahill, eds. *Migrants and Refugees* Concilium 1993/4, (London: SCM Press, 1993). Daniel Groody calls this theological lacuna the "migration-theology divide," which does not only need to be filled but, first and foremost, crossed and bridged. In fact Groody identifies this gap as the first divide that needs to be crossed toward the articulation and systematic development of a theology on migration. Daniel Groody, "Crossing the Divide: Foundations of a Theology of Migration and Refugees," *Theological Studies* Vol. 70, No. 3 (September 2009): 640–642.

29. For a more detailed discussion on the attention that migration has gotten, so far, in the field of theology see Gioacchino Campese, "The Irruption of Migrants: Theology of Migration in the 21st Century," *Theological Studies* Vol. 73, No. 1 (March 2012): 3–32.

CHAPTER 1

1. For instance, the notion of the "global village," which popularized the idea of identity with the global community, was already part of the discourse in the 1960s. See Roland Robertson, *Globalization: Social Theory and Global Culture* (London: Sage Publications, 1992).

2. While historical discussions on globalization have often been associated with Europe and what European colonialism has done in Asia, Africa, and Latin America, similar globalization patterns could also be seen in the Arab world through the conquest of Arab and North African countries by Europeans such as the French conquest of Tunisia and Algeria, the British conquest of Egypt, and the treaties signed by the British with the rulers of Bahrain, Oman, and what is now known as the United Arab Emirates to keep the route to India safe and open. The mobility of Arab merchants themselves centuries before European colonialism also offers us a glimpse of old routes of economic and religious globalization as these merchants not only brought commerce

but also Islam. Islam, for example, was brought to the southern part of the Philippines by Muslim traders, primarily from the Persian Gulf, in the late thirteenth and early fourteenth centuries, at least 200 years before Spain brought Christianity. See William Roger Louis, *The British Empire in the Middle East, 1945–1951: Arab Nationalism, the United States and Postwar Imperialism* (New York: Oxford University Press, 1984) and Peter G. Gowing, *Understanding Islam and Muslims in the Philippines* (Manila: New Day Publishers, 1988).

3. Pieter C. Emmer, " 'We Are Here, Because You Were There': European Colonialism and Intercontinental Migration," in *Migrants and Refugees*, ed. Dietmar Mieth and Lisa Sowle Cahill, Concilium 1993/4 (New York: Orbis 1993): 43–44.

4. The Spanish *conquistadors*, for example, connected the Spanish empire in Latin America with the Asian market via the Philippines. Gold bullions were extracted by the Spaniards in Latin America and exchanged for silk, spices, and tea from Asia using the *galleon* trade, which utilized indentured labor from its colonies like Mexico and the Philippines.

5. Examples of these legislations include the Chinese Exclusion Act in 1882, the so-called Gentlemen's Agreement in 1907, which put a moratorium on Japanese immigration, the Johnson-Reed Act of 1924—also known as Japanese Exclusion Act—which banned immigration of Japanese laborers and, last but not the least, Executive Order 9066, which authorized the exclusion of those with "foreign family ancestry" from certain military areas, especially in the West Coast, resulting in the herding of some 120,000 Japanese into internment camps. Peter Phan, "Where We Come From, Where We Are, and Where We Are Going: Asian and Pacific Catholics in the United States," *American Catholic Studies* Vol. 118, No. 3 (2007): 5–6. See also Justin Akers Chacón and Mike Davis, *No One Is Illegal*, 27–42, on this and related forms of problems encountered by other immigrants in the United States.

6. The social challenges of caring for a geriatric population are such that even churches are compelled to provide some form of care to its elderly members. About 20 percent of American parishes in 2009, for example, already has a nurse in its staff and, as the baby boomers age, a substantial number of parishes that currently do not have a parish nurse will feel the need to have one. Allen, *The Future Church*, 147, 158–159.

7. Italy, for example, resorted to declaring a state of emergency after 5,000 Tunisians fleeing their riot-torn country arrived in Lampedusa in just a matter of five days. See Nick Pisa, "Italy Declares State of Emergency Over Influx of 5,000 Tunisian Immigrants," <http://www.telegraph.co.uk/news/

worldnews/europe/italy/8321427/Italy-declares-state-of-emergen
cy-over-influx-of-5000-Tunisian-immigrants.html> accessed July 23,
2012.

8. These transmigrants are people who claim and are claimed by two or more nation-states into which they are incorporated as social actors, one of which is widely acknowledged to be their state of origin. Alejandro Portes, "Immigration Theory for a New Century: Some Problems and Opportunities," in *The Handbook of International Migration: The American Experience*, ed. Charles Hirschman, Philip Kasinitz, and Josh deWind (New York: Russell Sage Foundation, 1999): 29.

9. See Tony Anghie and Wayne McCormack, "The Rights of Aliens: Legal Regimes and Historical Perspectives," in *Migration in the 21st Century*, ed. Thomas N. Maloney and Kim Korinek (London: Routledge, 2011): 23–53.

10. See United Nations Department of Economic and Social Affairs, "International Migrants by Age," *Population Facts No. 2010/6* <http://www.un.org/esa/population/publications/popfacts/pop facts_2010-6.pdf> accessed July 23, 2012.

11. Dennis Müller "A Homeland for Transients: Towards an Ethic of Migrations," in *Migrants and Refugees*, 132.

12. The 2012 UN Millennium Development Goals Report paints a stark picture of this: more than 15 percent of the world population lives in slum conditions, 1.4 billion people live on less than $1.25 a day, and vulnerable employment accounts for 58 percent of all employment in developing regions. United Nations, *The Millennium Development Goals Report 2012* (New York, NY: United Nations, 2012), 4–5.

13. Multilateral institutions like the IMF and the World Bank, and various creditor banks from the eight most industrialized countries, for example, impose Structural Adjustment Programs (hereinafter SAP) in exchange for new loans to be given to numerous Third World countries already mired in debt. SAP component policies like trade liberalization; cutback on government spending and government subsidies; privatization and price controls, which give rise to new taxes; higher public utility rates; wage freezes; and credit squeezes consequently diminish the power of national governments and their ability to deliver basic social services.

14. The case of the Philippines, which started government-sanctioned labor migration as early as the 1970s, is noteworthy to mention here, especially since the 1 million mark has already been breached (without counting irregular migrants). This means that starting in 2006, 1 million Filipinos are deployed overseas on a yearly basis. Maruja Asis, "Philippines," *Asian and Pacific Migration Journal* Vol. 17, Nos. 3–4 (2008): 367.

15. See, for example, Grace Chang, *Disposable Domestics: Immigrant Women Workers in the Global Economy* (Cambridge, MA: South End Press, 2000) and Amnesty International, *South Korea: Disposable Labor, Rights of Migrant Workers in South Korea* (London: Amnesty International, 2009).

16. See Graziano Battistella, "The Poor in Motion: Reflections on Unauthorized Migration," *Asian Christian Review* Vol. 4, No. 2 (Winter 2010): 70–81.

17. For the US context, see Patricia Fernandez-Kelly, "Facts and Fictions of Unauthorized Immigration to the US," in *Migration in the 21st Century*, 192–201.

18. Out of the 2 million workers that Malaysia legally accepted in 2006, for instance, 1.9 million were unskilled. Jerold W. Huguet, "Towards a Migration Information System in Asia: Statistics and the Public Discourse on International Migration," *Asian and Pacific Migration Journal* Vol. 17, Nos. 3–4 (2008): 248.

19. The Middle East reflects this demand for unskilled migrant workers and wage discrimination of foreign workers. In the mid-1980s, buoyed by the revenues from their investments in industrialized countries, Middle Eastern countries' foreign labor pool expanded but started to be dominated by women domestic workers, hotel workers, mechanics, personal drivers, sanitation, and farm workers. There has also been a progressively larger number of professional and managerial-level Asians working in the Gulf region, most of whom were actually hired to replace Westerners and non-national Arabs because these Asians were willing to work for much less. Manolo Abella and Lin Lean Lim, "The Movement of People in Asia: Internal, Intra-regional and International Migration," in Christian Conference of Asia, *Uprooted People in Asia* (Hong Kong: CCA, 1995): 18–19.

20. Foreign (mostly Asian) domestic workers in Hong Kong, for instance, have been victimized a number of times already through wage cuts or wage freezes that the HK government imposed on foreign domestic helpers' wages to alleviate Hong Kong's economic woes. After failing to impose its proposed 20 percent wage cut (the employers wanted 35 percent) in 1998, the HK government reduced foreign domestic helpers' (FDHs) minimum wage by 5 percent during the economic crisis in 1999. Because of growing budget deficit, it (the HK government) implemented another (and higher) wage cut for contracts signed after April 1, 2003, bringing the HK$ 3,670 a month minimum wage of the already lowest-paid Hong Kong workers to HK$ 3, 270. Between 2003 and 2009 the FDHs' minimum wage increased to HK$ 3,580. Due to the global economic crisis, however, they were again targeted for a wage freeze in August 2009. See Jerome Aning, "Pinoys, Asians Protest Low

HK Wage for Maids," <http://services.inquirer.net/print/print.php?article_id=20090907–223983> accessed June 16, 2012.

21. Stephen Castles maintain that destination countries in Asia have three dominant attitudes with regard to migrants: (1) immigrants should not be allowed to settle, (2) foreign residents should not be offered citizenship except in exceptional cases, and (3) national culture and identity should not be modified in response to external influences. Stephen Castles, *The Myth of the Controllability of Difference: Labour Migration, Transnational Communities and State Strategies in East Asia.* See <http://www.unesco.org/most/apmrcast.htm> accessed June 16, 2012.

22. Consider the following living conditions of migrants who work in the fishing industry in Taiwan: Before they are picked up by bigger boats, which take them to their fishing grounds, they are made to live in barracks in 50-ton old, worn-out, broken boats with plastic roofing that sometimes do not have light or water. Men fill every nook and cranny of the boat. All their daily life and activities are done inside the boat. Their food is provided in plastic bags without spoon or chopsticks. Some receive a salary that does not conform to the original agreement; sometimes they do not receive it for almost half a year. See "Case Studies: Migrant Workers and the Fishermen's Service Center, Presbyterian Church of Taiwan," in Christian Conference of Asia, *Uprooted People in Asia* (Hong Kong: CCA, 1995): 131–132.

23. See, for example, Grace Chang, *Disposable Domestics: Immigrant Women Workers in the Global Economy* (Cambridge, MA: South End Press, 2000).

24. The cheap labor of these men, who are predominantly from India and Pakistan, has powered the rise of the Gulf countries' skyscrapers. They are among the 15 million foreigners working in the Gulf Cooperation Council countries of Saudi Arabia, Kuwait, Bahrain, Oman, and Qatar whose economies are heavily dependent on migrant labor. Tim Hume, "Photographer Captures 'new slaves' of the Gulf," <http://edition.cnn.com/2011/11/11/world/meast/emirates-workers-art/index.html> accessed July 3, 2012.

25. Nikos Papastergiadis, *The Turbulence of Migration* (Cambridge: Polity Press, 2000), 40.

26. Lou Aldrich, S.J., "A Critical Evaluation of the Migrant Workers' Situation in Taiwan in Light of the Catholic Social Tradition," in *Faith on the Move: Toward a Theology of Migration in Asia*, ed. Fabio Baggio and Agnes Brazal (Manila, Philippines: Ateneo de Manila University Press, 2008): 50–51.

27. The *khafel* system is a sponsorship system for recruitment, a form of franchise to import foreign labor granted to loyal subjects, which thrives on bringing in ever-increasing numbers of foreign workers willing to pay money for their jobs.

28. Graziano Battistela, "Irregular Migration: Issues from the Asian Experience," in Pontifical Council for the Pastoral Care of Migrants and Itinerant People, *Migration at the Threshold of the Third Millennium: Proceedings of the IV World Congress on the Pastoral Care of Migrants and Refugees*, Vatican, 5–10 October 1998: pp. 149, 150–151.

29. Veronica Uy, "International Labor Organization: 40M Illegal Migrants Prop up Economies," <http://newsinfo.inquirer.net/topstories/topstories/view/20081027-168750/40M-illegal-migrants-prop-up-economics> accessed June 26, 2012.

30. See Aviva Chomsky, *They Take Our Jobs!: and 20 Other Myths About Immigration* (Boston: Beacon Press, 2007): 1–49 and Patricia Fernandez-Kelly, "Facts and Fictions of Unauthorized Immigration to the US," 196–200.

31. Wetback is a derogatory label for migrants who came to the United States by swimming through the Rio Grande. It is reminiscent, in some ways, of the label "fresh off the boat" (FOB), which Asians, particularly Vietnamese refugees, got branded with at the height of the Asian immigration to the United States.

32. The term or status "illegal," for example, is often unfairly imposed on Mexicans, especially non-white Mexican workers. See Justin Akers Chacón and Mike Davis, *No One Is Illegal*, 191–195, for a discussion on the social construction of the "illegal" Mexican worker.

33. The case of Mexican immigrant Luis Ramirez illustrates this. See Associated Press, "Immigrant Beaten to Death in Pennsylvania," <http://www.msnbc.msn.com/id/25739051/ > accessed July 6, 2012.

34. The lure of social benefits and privileges, for example, better or free health care that come with permanent residency or citizenship in developed countries, is said to account for the growing maternity tourism in the United States, whereby rich foreign women, especially those from China, Mexico, South Korea, and Turkey, avail of tourism packages that allow them to give birth in the United States and, consequently, have so-called anchor babies who get citizenship by virtue of the 14th Amendment, which gives automatic citizenship to any baby born in the United States. At age 21 these babies would be able to petition the US government to grant their parents permanent residence status. Hence, they serve as their parents' ticket to better quality of life in the United States should they need to move, especially in their old age. Jennifer Medina, "Arriving as Pregnant Tourists, Leaving with American Babies," <http://www.nytimes.com/2011/03/29/us/29babies.html> accessed June 30, 2012.

35. See Catherine R. Cooper and Rebecca Burciaga, "Pathways to College, to the Professoriate, and to a Green Card: Linking Research, Policy, and Practice on Immigrant Latino Youth," in *Migration in the 21st Century*, 177–191.

36. Chain migration is the process whereby migrants facilitate the migration of a number of family members (nuclear and extended). A study of Filipino women migrant workers in Italy, for example, showed that in Barangay Sta. Rosa in Alaminos, Laguna, there are clans that have as much as 300 members working in Padova, Italy. See Mai Dizon Anōnuevo, "Revisiting Migrant Women's Lives: Stories of Struggles, Failures and Successes," in *Coming Home: Women, Migration and Reintegration*, ed. Estrella Dizon Anōnuevo and Augustus T. Anōnuevo (Quezon City, Philippines: Balikbayani Foundation, 2002): 20. See also Rosanna Luz F. Valerio, "Iisang Pisa: Clans in Chain Migration," in *Coming Home*, 30–37.

37. Allen, *The Future Church*, 157. See also Patricia Fernandez-Kelly, "Facts and Fictions of Unauthorized Immigration to the US," 196.

38. R. Puentes, "Towards an Assessment of Migration, Development and Human Rights Links: Conceptual Framework and New Strategic Indicators." Paper presented at Peoples' Global Action on Migration, Development and Human Rights, IV Global Forum, Mexico City, November 2010, p. 24, as cited in International Organization for Migration, *World Migration Report 2011*, 29.

39. International Organization for Migration, *World Migration Report 2011*, 11.

40. A study in the United States, which shows that natives clearly get or benefit much more for their taxes in terms of social services than do migrants, disputes this line of thinking. See the graph in R. Puentes, "Towards an Assessment of Migration, Development and Human Rights Links," 25, as cited in International Organization for Migration, *World Migration Report 2011*, 29.

41. Several Arab governments, for example, have recognized that emigration can help alleviate pressure on the domestic labor market. As early as the 1960s and 1970s, Algeria, Egypt, Jordan, Morocco, and Tunisia began actively facilitating the international mobility of their nationals, albeit mostly those in lower skilled categories.

42. Michelle R. Pistone and John J. Hoeffner, *Stepping Out of the Brain Drain: Applying Catholic Social Teaching in a New Era of Migration* (Lanham, MD: Lexington Books, 2007), 129–174.

43. For an examination on the use of migrant remittances to encourage small-business development, see Sidney Weintraub and Sergio Diaz-Briquets, *Migration, Remittances, and Small Business Development: Mexico and Carribean Basin Countries* (Boulder, CO: Westview Press, 1991).

44. International Organization for Migration, *World Migration Report 2011*, 30.

45. "Special Report on Migration," *The Economist* (January 5, 2008): 11.

46. In terms of official remittances (those sent through banks or government agencies) in 2006, the Philippines actually ranked fourth. India

topped the list with $24.5 billion, followed by Mexico at $24.2 billion and China at $21.0 billion.

47. Pistone and Hoeffner, *Stepping Out of the Brain Drain*, 129–130. See also Peggy Levitt, *The Transnational Villagers* (Berkeley: University of California Press, 2001), 54–55; 180–197.

48. This claim has greater traction in the case of villages or small towns because socioeconomic interventions are clearly more evident and strategic at the community level. Jeremiah Opiniano describes an example in the case of *Barangay* (village) Sta. Rosa in Laguna in the Philippines, where 85 percent of families are dependent on remittances from the 2,500 migrant workers in Italy, Spain, and the United States. See Jeremiah Opiniano, "Social Capital and the Development Potential of Migration in Barangay Sta. Rosa," in *Coming Home*, 152–164. See also May-an Villalba, "Migrant Workers Challenge Globalization," *In God's Image* Vol. 19, No. 1 (2000): 30–34.

49. See Francis Schüssler Fiorenza, "Redemption," in *The New Dictionary of Theology*, ed. Joseph A. Komonchak, Mary Collins and Dermot A Lane (Dublin: Gill and Macmillan, 1987): 836–851.

50. Anselm Min, *Dialectic of Salvation: Issues in Theology of Liberation* (Albany, NY: State University of New York Press, 1989), 79.

51. Leslie J. Hoppe, "Israel and Egypt: Relationships and Memory," *The Bible Today* Vol. 45 (July/August 2007): 209, as quoted in vanThanh Nguyen, SVD, "Asia in Motion: A Biblical Reflection on Migration," *Asian Christian Review* Vol. 4, No. 2 (Winter 2010): 22.

52. Nguyen himself gives an interesting summary of the Bible from the perspective of migration. He writes: "The Bible is loaded with stories written by, for, and about strangers, migrants and refugees. It begins with the first human parents being exiled from Paradise and ends with the prophet John in exile on the island of Patmos. Encapsulated between these two bookends namely Genesis and Revelation are stories of God's people constantly being purified and transformed as they struggled to find their way home to be with their creator." Nguyen, "Asia in Motion," 21–22.

53. The experience and theme of displacement is also very much a part of Christian experience in Late Antiquity. See Bronwen Neil and Pauline Allen, "Displaced Peoples: Reflections from Late Antiquity on a Contemporary Crisis," *Pacifica* Vol. 24 (February 2011): 29–42.

54. Silvano Tomasi, "The Prophetic Mission of the Churches: Theological Perspectives," in *The Prophetic Mission of the Churches in Response to Forced Displacement of Peoples*, report of a global ecumenical consultation, Addis Ababa, November 6–11, 1995 (Geneva: World Council of Churches, 1996): 41.

55. P. Giacomo Danesi, "Towards a Theology of Migration," in *The Prophetic Mission of Churches in Response to Forced Displacement of People*, 35.

56. Bobby Byrd and Susannah Byrd, eds. *The Late Great Mexican Border* (El Paso, TX: Cinco Puntos Press, 1998), viii, quoted in Daisy Machado, "The Unnamed Woman: Justice, Feminists, and the Undocumented Woman," in *Religion and Justice: A Reader in Latina Feminist Theology*, ed. Maria Pilar Aquino et al. (Austin: University of Texas Press, 2002): 169.

57. Machado, "The Unnamed Woman," 169.

58. See Jerry H. Gill, *Borderland Theology* (Washington, DC: EPICA, 2003).

59. Justin Akers Chacón and Mike Davis, *No One Is Illegal*, 201. A thoughtful treatment of this idea in the case of the US-Mexico border is done in Néstor P. Rodríguez, "The Social Construction of the US-Mexico Border," in *Immigrants Out! The New Nativism and the Anti-Immigrant Impulse in the United States*, ed. Juan F. Perea (New York: New York University Press, 1997): 223–243.

60. Battistella, "The Poor in Motion," 81.

61. Ada María Isasi-Díaz, "A Hispanic Garden in a Foreign Land," in *Inheriting Our Mothers' Gardens*, ed. Letty Russell et al. (Philadelphia: Westminster Press, 1988): 92. This is, in a way, reflective of the anthropologist Victor Turner's description of the state of liminality, whereby some dwell in two worlds, or more precisely, betwixt and between two worlds, in the place where the two worlds intersect and often collide, belonging to neither fully but belonging to both. They form a mixture, a *mestizaje*, of two cultural worlds, creating hyphenated identities and cultural hybrids.

62. Virgilio Elizondo, " 'Transformation of Borders': Border Separation or New Identity," in *Theology: Expanding the Borders*, ed. Maria Pilar Aquino and Roberto S. Goizueta (Mystic, CT: Twenty-Third Publications, 1998), 29.

63. Julia Kristeva, *Strangers to Ourselves*. Trans. Leon S. Roudiez (New York: Columbia University Press, 1991), 1.

64. The Incarnation, as described by Peter Phan, reflects this. Phan posits that in the divine crossing over to the human, the border between the divine nature and the human nature of Jesus functions as markers constituting the distinct identity of each. The one is not transmuted into the other, nor is confused with it; rather, the two natures are to be acknowledged. Thus, in the Incarnation as border crossing, the boundaries are preserved as identity markers, but, at the same time, they are overcome as barriers and transformed into frontiers from which a totally new reality emerges. Phan, "Where We Come From, Where We Are, and Where We Are Going," 24.

65. Justo L. González, *Santa Biblia: The Bible through Hispanic Eyes* (Nashville: Abingdon, 1996), 86–87.

66. Melanie May, *A Body Knows: Theopoetics of Death and Resurrection* (New York: Continuum, 1995), 90–91.

67. Nelle Morton, *The Journey Is Home* (Boston: Beacon Press, 1985), xix, quoted in Letty Russell, *Household of Freedom: Authority in Feminist Theology* (Philadelphia: The Westminster Press, 1987), 67.

68. See Aida Besancon Spencer, "Being a Stranger in a Time of Xenophobia," *Theology Today* Vol. 54 (April 1997–January 1998): 464–469 and "God the Stranger: An Intercultural Hispanic American Perspective," 89–103. See also A. Lacocque, "The Stranger in the Old Testament," in *World Council of Churches and Migration: WCC Fifth Assembly Dossier No. 13* (Geneva: WCC Migration Secretariat, 1981): 49–59 and Frank Crusemann, " 'You Know the Heart of the Stranger' (Exodus 23:9): A Recollection of the Torah in the Face of New Nationalism and Xenophobia," *Concilium* Vol. 4 (1993): 95–109 for a more detailed discussion on this.

69. For a comprehensive discussion on hospitality in the Christian tradition, see Christine Pohl, "Responding to Strangers: Insights from the Christian Tradition," *Studies in Christian Ethics* Vol. 19, No. 1 (2006): 81–101. See also John Koenig, *New Testament Hospitality: Partnership with Strangers as Promise and Mission* (Philadelphia: Fortress Press, 1985); Thomas Ogletree, *Hospitality to the Stranger: Dimensions of Moral Understanding* (Philadelphia: Fortress Press, 1985); and Christine Pohl, *Making Room: Recovering Hospitality as a Christian Tradition* (Grand Rapids, MI: Wm B. Eerdmans Publishing Company, 1999).

70. James William Brodman contends that Christian bishops and monasteries played a central role in the emergence and proliferation of the ancestor of the modern hospital. James William Brodman, *Charity and Religion in Medieval Europe* (Washington, DC: Catholic University of America Press, 2009): 45–88.

71. Jerome, who is well known for the Latin translation of the Bible, migrated to Bethlehem, where he established several monasteries always ready to offer hospitality to two kinds of migrants: the devout pilgrims to the Holy Land and the asylum seekers coming from the territories occupied by the barbarians. Fabio Baggio, "The Migrant Ministry: A Constant Concern for the Catholic Church," *Asian Christian Review* Vol. 4, No. 2 (Winter 2010): 47–69.

72. Carmen Nanko Fernandez, *Theologizing en Spanglish* (Maryknoll, NY: Orbis Books, 2010), 119.

73. See, for example, Graziano Battistela, "Human Rights of Migrants: A Pastoral Challenge," in *Migration, Religious Experience and Globalization*, ed. Gioacchino Campese and Pietro Ciallella(New York: Center for Migration Studies, 2003): 76–102.

74. It has to be noted, here, however, that even if the usual biblical stranger has laws in place for him/her, s/he is more significantly constrained and is still very much at the mercy of his/her host or his/her host community (cf. Gen. 19:1–11) compared to migrants today.

75. Bram Lancee's study of immigrants in the Netherlands, for example, draws attention to how bonding (dense network, especially with family) and bridging (crosscutting network, especially along inter-ethnic boundaries) become significant positive factors with both employment and income. See Bram Lancee, "The Economic Returns of Immigrants' Bonding and Bridging Social Capital: The Case of the Netherlands," *International Migration Review* Vol. 44, No. 1 (Spring 2010): 202–226.

76. A. Lacocque, "The Stranger in the Old Testament," 50–51, says the Old Testament stranger, particularly the *ger*—the most common term used to refer to the stranger—has no other choice than to accept the religious and cultic obligations of the house of Israel. In fact, the *gerim* were required to submit themselves to circumcision to enjoy all the rights of sharing fully in the house of Israel. While Crusemann, " 'You Know the Heart of the Stranger' (Exod. 23:9)," 104, says somewhat otherwise, the significant degree of religious assimilation of the *gerim* still stands in stark contrast to contemporary migrants' greater freedom and assertion to practice their religion.

77. Jon Sobrino, "Redeeming Globalization Through Its Victims," in *Globalization and Its Victims*, ed. Jon Sobrino and Felix Wilfred *Concilium* 2001/5 (London: SCM Press): 106. Coleman "Making the Connections," 13, offers a stark picture of this inequality on a global scale. Coleman writes that 40 percent of Latin Americans still cannot read or write and less than 1 percent of Africans have ever used the internet while Tokyo has more telephones than all of Africa.

78. For a comprehensive treatment of globalization in relation to the mission of the Church, see Neil Ormerod and Shane Clifton, *Globalization and the Mission of the Church* (New York: T & T Clark, 2010). See also T. Howland Sanks, "Globalization and the Church's Social Mission," *Theological Studies* Vol. 60, No. 4 (December 1999): 625–651.

79. David Bacon, *Illegal People*, 105–118.

80. And while the 2008 global economic crisis reduced irregular migration flows temporarily, the IOM reports that irregular migrant stocks increased as laid-off workers stayed on in destination countries without authorization, rather than leaving the country at the risk of not being able to return after the recovery from the recession.

81. Silvano Tomasi, "Migration and Catholicism in a Global Context," in *Migration in a Global World*, 25. And as Teresa Okure points out, particularly in the case of Africa, the historical dimension of the injustices that propel or force people to move must not be forgotten. Okure says that Africa as a continent itself is a big refugee camp due, in part, to its colonial experience. Teresa Okure, "Africa: A Refugee Camp Experience," in *Migrants and Refugees*, 15–18.

82. Daniel D. Groody, "Jesus and the Undocumented Immigrant: A Spiritual Geography of a Crucified People," *Theological Studies* Vol. 70 (2009): 307–316.

83. International Organization for Migration, *World Migration Report 2010* <http://publications.iom.int/bookstore/free/WMR_2010_ENGLISH.pdf > accessed July 21, 2012. There is actually a kind of international safety net for migrants through the International Convention on the Protection of the Rights of All Migrant Workers and Their Families, which was enforced in 2003 and is primarily aimed at discouraging or ending unauthorized recruitment and trafficking of migrant workers. The convention also provides a set of binding international standards to address the treatment, welfare, and human rights of migrants, as well as the obligations and responsibilities on the part of countries of origin and countries of destination. However, not all countries are signatory to the convention. Moreover, even those who signed the convention have not always enforced it.

84. Like the majority of Christian theologians, this does not mean that Gutierrez is completely against globalization. In Gutierrez's words, "to be against globalization as such is like being against electricity." Gustavo Gutierrez, "Memory and Prophecy," in *The Option for the Poor in Christian Theology*, ed. Daniel G. Groody (Notre Dame, IN: University of Notre Dame Press, 2007): 32.

85. *Economic Justice for All, no. 13.* See United States Conference of Catholic Bishops, *Economic Justice for All* <http://www.usccb.org/upload/economic_justice_for_all.pdf> accessed July 24, 2012.

86. Gill, *Borderland Theology*, 117.

87. See Daniel J. Harrington, *The Gospel of Matthew*. Sacra Pagina 1. (Collegeville, MN: Liturgical Press, 1991) and Jose David Rodriguez, "The Parable of the Affirmative Action Employer," *Apuntes* Vol. 15, No. 5 (1988): 418–424, as cited in Jean Pierre Ruiz, "The Bible and People on the Move: Another Look at Matthew's Parable of the Day Laborers," *New Theology Review* Vol. 20, No. 3 (August 2007): 17–18.

88. Ruiz bolsters this argument by focusing on the workers' complaint, the owner's singling out of one of the workers and calling him by using the condescending term *hetaire* rather than the term used for a social equal, *phile*, and the owner's rhetorical question, "Am I not free to do as I wish with my own money?," which, Ruiz posits, reflects a capricious and impulsive conscience. Ruiz, "The Bible and People on the Move," 22.

89. Daniel Groody, "Jesus and the Undocumented Immigrant: A Spiritual Geography of a Crucified People," *Theological Studies* Vol. 70, No. 2 (June 2009): 341–316. The idea of the "crucified peoples" will be elaborated in Chapter 6.

90. Pope Benedict XVI, "Address to the General Assembly of the United Nations Organization," New York, April 18, 2008, as quoted in Silvano Tomasi, "Human Rights as a Framework for Advocacy on Behalf of the Displaced: The Approach of the Catholic Church," in *Driven from Home: Protecting the Rights of Forced Migrants*, ed. David Hollenbach, S.J. (Washington, DC: Georgetown University Press, 2010): 65.

Chapter 2

1. This is reflected in the 2012 UN Millennium Development Goals Report, which notes how gender inequality persists. United Nations, *The Millennium Development Goals Report 2012*, 4–5.

2. The work of Sasskia Sassen, particularly *Globalization and Its Discontents*, is often considered critical in this field. In that book, Sassen analyzes the relationship between globalization, gender, and social change in general and the relationship between the globalization of labor flows and the new dynamics of inequality in particular. Sassen's work shows not only how mainstream accounts of globalization focus on abstract economic dynamics and proceed as if those dynamics are inevitably gender neutral but also how to contribute to a feminist analytics that allows for the re-reading and reconceptualization of major features of today's global economy in a manner that captures strategic instantiations of gendering as well as formal and operational openings that make women visible and lead to greater presence and participation. Sasskia Sassen, *Globalization and Its Discontents* (New York: Columbia University Press, 1998), 82.

3. Ann Brooks, *Gendered Work in Asian Cities: The New Economy and Changing Labour Markets* (Hampshire: Ashgate, 2006), 2–3.

4. See Pamela Brubaker, "Reforming Global Economic Policies," in *Justice in a Global Economy: Strategies for Home, Community and World*, ed. Pamela K. Brubaker, Rebecca Todd Peters and Laura A. Stivers (Louisville, KY: WJK Press, 2006): 127–128.

5. Maria Arcelia Gonzales-Butron, "The Effects of Free-market Globalization on Women's Lives," in *Globalization and its Victims*, ed. Jon Sobrino and Felix Wilfred, Concilium 2001/5 (London: SCM Press), 44–45.

6. But the jobs generated by migration, like most female jobs, are also undermined by economic recession since women's quality of employment often suffers first in times of economic restructuring and flexibility. As a UN study says, women generally continue to be the last to benefit from job expansion and the first to suffer from job contraction. See Valentine M. Moghadam, "Gender Aspects of Employment and Unemployment in a Global Perspective," in *Global Employment: An*

International Investigation into the Future of Work, ed. Mihaly Simai, Valentine M. Moghadam, and Arvo Kuddo (London and Tokyo: Zed Books and UNU Press, 1995), 111.

7. Consequently, an estimated 80 percent of refugees are women and children. Allen, *The Future Church*, 277.

8. "Gender" as an analytical category largely informs this chapter, so a clarification of the term is in order here. The study of gender looks at social roles based on biological sex. It assumes that sex is a given but gender is socially constructed. Thus, gender theorists consider the roles of men and women in the light of other categories of power and difference. This also means that the dynamics of race and class, and the manner in which they intersect with gender relations, inform much of the critical study of gender. Elaine Graham, "Gender," in *An A–Z of Feminist Theology*, ed. Lisa Isherwood and Dorothea McEwan (Sheffield: Sheffield Academic Press, 1996): 78.

9. See Mirjana Morokvasic, "Birds of Passage Are Also Women," *International Migration Review* Vol. 18, No. 4 (Winter 1984): 886–907.

10. This is buttressed by a UN report that states that women account for 49 percent of all international migrants. Women even predominate (57 percent) among older international migrants, particularly those aged 65 or above. See United Nations Department of Economic and Social Affairs, "International Migrants by Age," *Population Facts* No. 2010/6 <http://www.un.org/esa/population/publications/popfacts/popfacts_2010-6.pdf> accessed September 23, 2012.

11. In 2007, for instance, 67 percent of overseas Filipino workers were women.

12. Amy Sim, "Introduction: Women, Mobilities, Immobilities, and Empowerment," *Asian and Pacific Migration Journal* Vol. 18, No. 1 (2009): 4.

13. Nikos Papastergiadis, *The Turbulence of Migration: Globalization, Deterritorialization, and Hybridity* (Cambridge: Polity Press, 2000), 10.

14. Allen, *The Future Church*, 274.

15. See Ebonne Ruffins, "Rescuing Girls from Sex Slavery," <http://www.cnn.com/2010/LIVING/04/29/cnnheroes.koirala.nepal/index.html> accessed August 30, 2012.

16. Gustavo Capdevilla, "IOM Report: Filipinas, Russians trafficked for US military bases in Korea," *OFW Journalism Consortium Eleventh News Packet* (November 13, 2002): 15. For a more global perspective on the forced migration of women, see Sharon Pickering, *Women, Borders and Violence: Current Issues in Asylum, Forced Migration and Trafficking* (New York: Springer, 2010).

17. Today, health care is quickly developing into a major employment sector for women migrants. This is not surprising given the care-based nature of jobs in health care. The United Kingdom,

for example, suffers an estimated shortfall of 20,000 nurses annually; the United States 200,000. Rita Monteiro, "Global Mom: Migrant Mom," <http://www.nationalcatholicreporter.org/globalpers/gp050703.htm> accessed August 19, 2012.

18. Amy Sim, "Women Versus the State: Organizing Resistance and Contesting Exploitation in Indonesian Labor Migration to Hong Kong," *Asian and Pacific Migration Journal* Vol. 18, No. 1 (2009): 55–56.

19. Keiko Osaki, "Economic Interactions of Migrants and their Household of Origin: Are Women More Reliable Supporters," *Asian and Pacific Migration Journal* Vol. 8, No. 4 (1999): 447–471.

20. Daniel G. Groody, "Fruit of the Vine and Work of Human Hands: Immigration and the Eucharist," in *A Promised Land, A Perilous Journey*, 307.

21. See Deidre McKay, "Filipinas in Canada: Deskilling as a Push toward Marriage," in *Wife or Worker: Asian Women and Migration*, ed. Nicola Piper and Mina Roces (Lanham, MA: Rowman and Littlefield, 2003): 23–52. See also Tomoku Nakamatsu, "International Marriage though Introduction Agencies: Social and Legal Realities of 'Asian' Wives of Japanese Men," in *Wife or Worker*, 181–202.

22. See Maruja M.B. Asis, "Caring for the World: Filipino Domestic Workers Gone Global," in *Asian Women as Transnational Domestic Workers*, ed. Shirlena Huang, Brenda S. Yeoh and Noor Abdul Rahman (Singapore: Marshall Cavendish, 2005): 21–53; Deirdre McKay, "Success Stories?: Filipina Migrant Domestic Workers in Canada," in *Asian Women as Transnational Domestic Workers*, ed. Shirlena Huang, Brenda S. Yeoh and Noor Abdul Rahman (Singapore: Marshall Cavendish, 2005): 305–340 and; Nobue Suzuki, "Gendered Surveillance and Sexual Violence in Filipino Pre-migration Experiences to Japan," in *Gender Politics in the Asia Pacific Region*, ed. Brenda S. Yeoh, P. Teo and S. Huang (London and New York: Routledge, 2002): 99–116.

23. See Ninna Nyberg Sorensen and Luis Guarnizo, "Transnational Family Life Across the Atlantic: The Experience of Colombian and Dominican Migrants in Europe," in *Living Across Worlds: Diaspora, Development and Transnational Engagement*, ed. Ninna Nyberg Sorensen (Geneva: IOM, 2008): 151–176.

24. The case of the "picture brides" or migrant wives selected via matchmakers by immigrant workers (primarily from Japan and Korea) in Hawaii and the West Coast in the early twentieth century illustrates this. The women were known as "picture brides" as the immigrant men choose a bride from their native countries through photographs. While some of the women did it out of obligation to their families, most did it for economic mobility while others did it to gain freedoms denied to them in Japan or Korea and to escape familial duties, particularly filial piety that comes with traditional marriage. See Kei Tanaka,

"Japanese Picture Marriage and the Image of Immigrant Women in Early Twentieth-century California," *The Japanese Journal of American Studies* No. 15 (2004): 115–138. See also Alice Yun Chai, "Women's History in Public: 'picture brides' of Hawaii," *Women's Studies Quarterly*, Vol. 16, Nos. 1–2 (Spring-Summer 1988): 51–62.

25. I have discussed this elsewhere. See Gemma Tulud Cruz, *An Intercultural Theology of Migration: Pilgrims in the Wilderness* (Leiden: Brill, 2010), 39–40. Various factors account for the difficulty to find a potential good boyfriend or husband. These include the women's race or ethnicity, occupation, and, sometimes, the migration profile of the women's racial or ethnic group. The Filipino women domestic workers in Hong Kong illustrate this. Because Filipino migrants in Hong Kong are predominantly women and they are domestic workers, the chances of finding a Filipino man or a man who will see beyond a potential subservient wife and a maid or homemaker are diminished.

26. It turns out that one of the reasons why the wife refuses to come home is that Nestor is a jobless, lazy, and, most of all, abusive husband. See Susan K., "More Gripes from Husbands of OFWs," <http://globalnation.inquirer.net/27225/more-gripes-from-husbands-of-ofws> accessed August 4, 2012.

27. Pierette Hondagneu-Sotelo and Ernestine Avila, " 'I'm Here, But I'm There': The Meaning of Latina Transnational Motherhood," *Gender and Society* Vol. 11, No. 5 (1997): 562.

28. Rhacel Salazar Parreñas, "The Gender Paradox in the Transnational Families of Filipino Migrant Women," *Asian and Pacific Migration Journal* Vol. 14, No. 3 (2005): 256.

29. Parreñas "The Gender Paradox in the Transnational Families of Filipino Migrant Women," *Asian and Pacific Migration Journal* Vol. 14, No. 3 (2005): 256–257. A more vivid description of the need or pressure to do transnational mothering is outlined in Patricia Ringen, "Parenting Tips for Overseas Working Moms," <http://globalnation.inquirer.net/11589/parenting-tips-for-overseas-working-moms> accessed October 19, 2012.

30. See, for example, E. Mulong, "Mothers Once Again" *TNT Hong Kong* Vol. 6, No. 4 (June–July 2000): 4–5 and "When Children Become Parent Carers," *TNT Hong Kong* Vol. 7, No. 1 (February–March 2001): 9.

31. Parreñas, "The Gender Paradox," 265.

32. Maia Jachimowicz and Deborah W. Meyers, "Executive Summary," in *Women Immigrants in the United States Conference Proceedings*, ed. Philippa Strum and Danielle Tarantolo (Washington, DC: Woodrow Wilson International Center for Scholars, 2002): 1–6.

33. Kathleen Valtonen, "East Meets North: The Finnish-Vietnamese Community," *Asian and Pacific Migration Review* Vol. 5, No. 4

(1996): 481–482. Valtonen also makes a good point about the growing literature as to whether migration leads to a loss or gain in the
status of women as a result of changes in the distribution of power
within the family. She contends that the answers vary according to the
immigrant context and cultural background. She elaborates by saying
that in some situations new economics and social responsibilities have
been the basis of a woman's increasing importance within the family.
In other cases, in the meantime, the woman's role in the family has
been undermined, especially for nonworking women, isolated from
an extended family network, who find themselves dependent on their
children.

34. Yaghoob Foroutan, "Migration and Gender Roles: The Typical Work
Pattern of the MENA Women," *International Migration Review*
Vol. 43, No. 4 (Winter 2009): 987. Tanu Priya Uteng also challenges
the idea of home/host dichotomy, which states that the home country
equals oppression and the host country equals freedom for immigrant
women. In Uteng's case, however, she highlights the disadvantage
and discrimination angle between immigrant women and Western
women. See Tanu Priya Uteng, "Gendered Mobility: A Case Study of
Non-Western Immigrant Women in Norway," in *Ethics of Mobilities*,
ed. Sigurd Bergmann and Tore Sager (Hampshire: Ashgate, 2008):
73–101, esp.98.

35. See Helen Rose Ebaugh and Janet Saltzman Chafetz, *Religion and
the New Immigrants: Continuities and Adaptations in Immigrant
Congregations* (Walnut Creek, CA: Altamira Press, 2000), especially
Chapters 4, 6, and 8.

36. Olivia Ruiz Marrujo, "The Gender of Risk: Sexual Violence against
Undocumented Women," in *A Promised Land, A Perilous Journey*,
229. See also Groody, *Border of Death, Valley of Life*, 22.

37. Binaifer Nowrojee, "Sexual Violence, Gender Roles and Displacement" in *Refugee Rights: Ethics, Advocacy, and Africa*, ed. David
Hollenbach (Washington, DC: Georgetown University Press, 2008):
126.

38. See Amnesty International, "Refugee Women in Chad Face High
Levels of Rape Despite UN Presence," <http://www.unhcr.org/
refworld/docid/4ac483011e.html> accessed August 30, 2012.

39. Maryanne Loughry, "The Experience of Displacement by Conflict:
The Plight of Iraqi Refugees," in *Driven from Home*, 177, cites this
experience of rape by Iraqi women refugees on top of forced prostitution, trafficking, forced marriage, economic, and sexual exploitation as
well as domestic violence. Loughry mentions that some Iraqi women
and girls are reported to have resorted to commercial sex work in
order to provide funds for their families.

40. A picture of the global extent of the problem is sketched
in Elizabeth Stannard Gromisch, "Refugees and the Risk of

Rape," <http://www.thewip.net/contributors/2009/07/refugees_and_the_risk_of_rape.html> accessed August 28, 2012.

41. RELA (*Ikatan Relawan Rakyat Malaysia* or Volunteers of Malaysian People) is a paramilitary civil volunteer corps formed by the Malaysian government to check the immigration documents of foreigners in Malaysia to reduce the increasing rate of illegal immigrants in Malaysia. They are authorized to interrogate, even detain, people; they can conduct raids on streets, factories, restaurants, hotels, and even churches.

42. Tenaganita, *The Revolving Door: Modern Day Slavery Refugees* (Kuala Lumpur, Malaysia: Tenaganita, 2008), 58–59.

43. Jachimowicz and Meyers, "Executive Summary," 2–3.

44. See Daffyd Roderick, "Making the Poor Even Poorer," <http://www.time.com/time/magazine/article/0,9171,189810,00.html> accessed August 28, 2012.

45. See related report: "Maternity Benefits for Maids Opposed" *Philippine Daily Inquirer* (July 4, 1997): 3; Nicole Constable, *Maid to Order in Hong Kong: Stories of Filipina Workers* (Ithaca, NY: Cornell University Press, 1997), 72, cites a similar violation of the domestic workers' reproductive right whereby the domestic worker was given an abortion without her knowledge when her employer brought her for physical exam and pregnancy test.

46. Permanent residency status will make a big difference in these women's lives as it will grant them additional rights and access to government services. Evangeline Vallejos, the maid who took the HK government to court on the issue, initially won the legal battle when the High Court ruled in her favor. The Court of Appeals overturned the decision and Vallejos appealed the decision in Hong Kong's Final Court of Appeal but she lost. See Simon Lee and Fox Hu, "Hong Kong Maids Lose Final Appeal for Residence Rights," <http://www.bloomberg.com/news/2013-03-25/hong-kong-court-rejects-residency-appeal-by-domestic-helper.html> accessed August 20, 2013.

47. Constable, *Maid to Order in Hong Kong*, 60–82 gives a more comprehensive discussion on this.

48. James Tyner, "The Web-Based Recruitment of Female Foreign Domestic Workers in Asia," *Singapore Journal of Tropical Geography* Vol. 20, No. 2 (1999): 199–201. Some agencies in Tyner's research include information on marital status and family size on the assumption that women who have children are more experienced and a family life could mean that the applicant is less likely to party or seek a "social life" in the host country. Women who are impoverished or have significant family responsibilities are also presented as more willing to put in long hours.

49. Tyner, "The Web-Based Recruitment of Female Foreign Domestic Workers in Asia," 199–204.
50. Constable, *Maid to Order in Hong Kong*, 61.
51. Lisa Sowle Cahill, "Justice, Gender, and the Market," in *Outside the Market No Salvation*, ed. Dietmar Mieth and Marciano Vidal, Concilium 1997/2 (London: SCM Press): 133–142.
52. Monteiro, "Global Mom: Migrant Mom," <http://www.national catholicreporter.org/globalpers/gp050703.htm> accessed August 19, 2012.
53. Elisabeth Schüssler-Fiorenza, "The Endless Day: Introduction," in *Women, Work, and Poverty*, ed. Elisabeth Schüssler-Fiorenza and Anne Carr, *Concilium* 194 (London: SCM Press, 1987): xviii–xix.
54. Shawn Copeland, "Interaction of Racism, Sexism and Classism in Women's Exploitation," in *Women, Work, and Poverty*, 24.
55. First World countries or territories, for example, could more easily hire the labor or services of women from Third World countries, rich women employers can transfer their domestic responsibilities to poor migrant women workers, and poor migrant women workers do the same over poorer women whom they employ back home to be their own maid or babysitter.
56. Elina Vuola, *Limits of Liberation: Feminist Theology and the Ethics of Poverty and Reproduction* (New York: Sheffield Academic Press, 2002) gives an eloquent critique on this.
57. Vuola, *Limits of Liberation* 141–155, gives a comprehensive list and discussion of feminist theologians, particularly Latina feminist theologians, who tackle this issue.
58. Maria Pilar Aquino, "The Feminist Option for Poor and Oppressed in the Context of Globalization," in *The Option for the Poor in Christian Theology*, ed. Daniel Groody (Notre Dame, IN: University of Notre Dame Press, 2007): 191–215. See also Mary Catherine Hilkert, "The Option for the Poor in the Context of Globalization: A Feminist Vision," in *The Option for the Poor in Christian Theology*, 228–237.
59. Fiorenza. "The Endless Day," xx, for instance, cites an example of a discriminatory pay-scale in the New Testament, particularly in 1 Tim. 5:3–16, which stipulates that the widow/elder should receive only half of the payment or honor that is due to the male presiding elder. While male elders and officers of the community should be remunerated independently of their family status and income, widows/elders should only receive financial support from the community when they are absolutely without family support.
60. Monteiro, "Global Mom: Migrant Mom," <http://www.national catholicreporter.org/globalpers/gp050703.htm> accessed August 19, 2012.
61. W. Anne Joh, "Relating to Household Labor Justly," in *Justice in a Global Economy: Strategies for Home, Community and the World*,

ed. Pamela K. Brubaker, Rebecca Todd Peters and Laura Stivers (Louisville, KY: 2006): 29–39.

62. For a general discussion on the areas of productive and reproductive work, see Carol S. Robb, "Principles for a Woman-Friendly Economy," *Journal of Feminist Studies in Religion* Vol. 9, Nos. 1–2 (Spring/Fall 1993): 147–160.

63. Margaret Farley, *Just Love: A Framework for Christian Sexual Ethics* (New York: Continuum, 2010).

64. Isabel Carter Heyward, *The Redemption of God: A Theology of Mutual Relation* (New York: University Press of America, 1982), 18.

65. Min, "Migration and Christian Hope," 195.

66. It is nearly always classified along masculine and feminine lines, often formulated as a "nuptial hermeneutics" (in terms of bridegroom and bride) and in terms of an "ontological complementarity" whereby men and women, though fundamentally equal and complete in themselves, are incomplete as a couple. Todd Salzmann and Michael Lawler, "Catholic Sexual Ethics: Complementarity and the Truly Human," *Theological Studies* Vol. 67, No. 3 (September 2006): 627–628.

67. See, for example, Carter Heyward, *The Redemption of God: A Theology of Mutual Relation*; Lisa Isherwood and Dorothea McEwan, *Introducing Feminist Theology* (Sheffield: Sheffield Academic Press, 2001); and Rosemary Radford Ruether and Eugene Bianchi, *From Machismo to Mutuality: Essays on Sexism and Woman-Man Liberation* (Mahwah, NJ: Paulist Press, 1976).

68. Brenda S.A. Yeoh, Elspeth Graham, and Paul J. Boyle, "Migrations and Family Relations in the Asia-Pacific Region," *Asian and Pacific Migration Journal* Vol. 11, No. 1 (2002): 1.

69. For purposes of a clearer and more manageable focus, this section will primarily tackle the transnational family, particularly with women-away transnational families. This is to also align the current section with the previous one, which dealt primarily with situations where it is only the female member, especially the mother, who is away. For specific theological reflections on immigrant families, see Elizabeth Conde Frazier, *Listen to the Children: Conversations with Immigrant Families* (Valley Forge, PA: Judson Press, 2011); Jin Sook Kwon, *Contemplating Connection: A Feminist Pastoral Theology of Connection for Korean Christian Immigrant Parent-Child Relationships*, unpublished PhD dissertation, Claremont School of Theology, September 2011.

70. Michelle Gamburd, *The Kitchen Spoon's Handle: Transnationalism and Sri Lanka's Migrant Housemaids* (Ithaca, NY: Cornell University Press, 2000), 241.

71. Episcopal Commission for the Pastoral Care of Migrants and Itinerant People, *Migration 2002: Situationer and Impact, Biblical Inspiration, Pastoral Challenges* (Manila, Philippines: ECMI-CBCP, 2002): 19,

21–23, offers a glimpse of the maintenance of patriarchal practices and expectations by saying that when the wife migrates the husband is less responsible at home, freer to yield to temptations of gambling or womanizing, and may relegate the children's education task to relatives/others. The authors also argue that when it comes to children's social development, the absence of the mother is felt more than that of fathers and that children whose mothers are abroad receive less awards in school.

72. Rhacel Salazar Parreñas, "The Gender Paradox in the Transnational Families of Filipino Migrant Women," *Asian and Pacific Migration Journal* Vol. 14, No. 3 (2005): 244.

73. For example, transnational family life in the age of feminization of migration challenges dominant discourses, which generally frame gender relations within households or families and ignore how state policies and programs influence family-level-gender politics and the political economy of emotions. In Indonesia, for instance, aspiring women migrant workers are required to get permission from the male head of their households before their papers can be processed for overseas employment. As cited in Sim, "Introduction: Women, Mobilities, Immobilities, and Empowerment," 8.

74. Among Filipino migrant workers, for example, there is a phenomenon called BSA or *Biyuda/Biyudo Sa Abroad* (Widow/Widower When Abroad). What happens is that when married migrants become attracted to someone overseas, instead of introducing themselves as single or unmarried (probably because they do not look the part), they introduce themselves as *biyudo* (widower) and *biyuda* (widow) even when the spouse is very much alive. See cases on this phenomenon as it plays out in Taiwan in Susan K. "The Tragic Sagas of BSAs in Taiwan," <http://globalnation.inquirer.net/25033/the-tragic-sagas-of-bsas-in-taiwan> accessed February 5, 2012.

75. See, for example, Susan K., "On OFW Family Problems: Readers Talk Back," <http://globalnation.inquirer.net/27831/on-ofw-family-problems-readers-talk-back> accessed August 11, 2012. It is doubly hard for the children, especially for those who were born to migrant parents not recognized in host countries. This phenomenon of "stateless children" is noticeable, for example, in the Middle East, where there are as many as 6,000 stateless children. Jerome Aning, "Filipino Woman Runs for Seat in South Korean Parliament," <http://globalnation.inquirer.net/31289/filipino-woman-runs-for-seat-on-south-korean-parliament> accessed August 1, 2012.

76. The challenges posed by migration to the family is the subject of an essay by Archbishop Agostino Marchetto, former secretary of the Pontifical Council for the Pastoral Care of Migrants and Itinerant People. See Archbishop Agostino Marchetto, "The Migrant

Family: Challenges Today and the Way Forward for the Church," in *The Migrant Family in Asia: Reaching Out and Touching Them*, ed. Anthony Rogers, FSC (Manila, Philippines: Office for Human Development, 2007): 13–27. The essay, however, focused more on the issue or the need for (re)unification of families.

77. See Joanne Heaney-Hunter, "Domestic Church: Guiding Beliefs and Daily Practices," in *Christian Marriage: Contemporary Theological and Pastoral Perspectives*, ed. Michael G. Lawler and William P. Roberts (Collegeville: Liturgical Press, 1996): 59–78.

78. These include Julie Hanlon Rubio, David Matzko Mc-Carthy, Florence Caffrey Bourg and Richard Gaillardetz. Lisa Cahill, "Marriage: Developments in Catholic Theology and Ethics," *Theological Studies* Vol. 64, No. 1 (March 2003): 97.

79. Even older generation of theological ethicists see some elements for reconsideration. Kenneth Himes and James Coriden explore the reasons for such reconsideration in "The Indissolubility of Marriage: Reasons to Reconsider." Himes and Coriden think that indissolubility of a *ratum et consummatum* marriage is a doctrinal teaching open to revision by the *magisterium*, and that existing arguments are not sufficient to reject all proposals for alteration of the teaching. Issues raised by Himes and Coriden to explore the reasons for reconsideration include consent, consummation, the meaning of the bond, the reality of the bond, and marital commitment. At the heart of Himes and Coriden's argument is the question: "What does it mean to say a marriage perdures even though the marital relationship has totally disintegrated? See Kenneth Himes and James Coriden, "The Indissolubility of Marriage: Reasons to Reconsider," *Theological Studies* Vol. 65, No. 3 (September 2004): 480, 482–490.

80. With regard to the argument on the basis of sociological diversity, Atkinson contends there must be some boundaries and that when diversity is of such a nature that it attacks the constitutive structure of an entity, it cannot then be said to participate properly in that reality. Joseph Atkinson, "Family as Domestic Church: Developmental Trajectory, Legitimacy and Problems of Appropriation," *Theological Studies* Vol. 66, No. 3 (September 2005): 602–603.

81. K. Soin, "Challenges for Women and Men in a Changing Environment," in *A Gender Agenda: Asia-Europe Dialogue*, ed. D. Colome, Y. Meguro and T. Yamamoto (Singapore: Japan Centre for International Exchange): 6, as quoted in Brooks, *Gendered Work in Asian Cities*, 3.

82. Hope S. Antone, "Asian Women and the Globalization of Labor," *The Journal of Theologies and Cultures in Asia* Vol. 2 (2003): 102.

83. Moreover, in the process of detraditionalization, voice is displaced from established sources to the self. Anthony Giddens, *The Runaway World: How Globalization Is Shaping Our Lives* (London: Routledge, 2000) offers a more substantial discussion on this.

84. Joan Chittister, *The Story of Ruth: Twelve Moments in Every Woman's Life* (Ottawa: Novalis, 2000).

85. Walter Burghardt, *Justice: A Global Adventure* (New York: Orbis, 2004), 6.

CHAPTER 3

1. Graham Kelly and John Hooper, "Grim Toll of African Refugee Mounts on Spanish Beaches," <http://www.guardian.co.uk/world/2008/jul/13/spain > accessed November 20, 2012.

2. Alan Cowell and Elisabetta Povoledo, "UN Urges Ships to Help Migrants in Mediterranean," <http://www.nytimes.com/2011/05/10/world/africa/10migrants.html?_r=0> accessed November 18, 2012.

3. This is also increasingly the case in the United States because of highly militarized land borders. See "Immigrants Turn to the Sea to Enter US Illegally," <http://www.cbsnews.com/2100-201_162-6807922.html> accessed September 21, 2012.

4. The journey via the sea is often fatal for many African migrants not only because the boats they use are makeshift and overcrowded but also because these boats are often not equipped with (nor are the migrants knowledgeable of) navigation devices. Consequently, a considerable number of migrants die from hunger, thirst, and even exhaustion. Graham Kelly and John Hooper, "Grim Toll of African Refugee Mounts on Spanish Beaches," <http://www.guardian.co.uk/world/2008/jul/13/spain> accessed November 20, 2012.

5. See Frank Brennan, "Human Rights as a Challenge to National Policies That Exclude Refugees: Two Case Studies from Southeast Asia," in *Driven* from *Home*, 97–114. See also Joe Kelly and James Massola, "Government Reveals Rioting, Mass Breakout of Detainees," <http://www.theaustralian.com.au/news/nation/government-reveals-rioting-mass-breakouts-of-detainees/story-e6frg6nf-1226021185013> accessed July 21, 2012.

6. At that time the public rhetoric of the political establishment was that the policy was intended to discourage migrants from coming through the southern border and help federal agents gain better control of the borders. By militarizing the border through installing state-of-the-art surveillance technologies and doubling the number of Border Patrol agents stationed along the southwest border, however, what political leaders more explicitly intended was to push migrants out into the desert where Border Patrol agents could more easily apprehend them. See Robin Hoover, "The Story of Humane Borders," in *A Promised Land, A Perilous Journey*, 160–173.

7. The number would be even higher if one takes into account the claim of human rights groups that for every migrant found dead, at least

ten others are missing in the desert. The figure is also conservative primarily because, as human rights groups in the United States say, agencies typically undercount deaths because of inconsistent classification standards. For example, the statistics, which are usually those given by the Border Patrol to the Department of Homeland Security, often does not count or include those deaths that are reported first to local authorities. See Spencer Hsu, "Border Deaths Are Increasing," <http://www.washingtonpost.com/wp-dyn/content/article/2009/09/29/AR2009092903212.html> accessed August 20, 2012.

8. Randal C. Archibold, "Arizona Enacts Stringent Law on Immigration," <http://www.nytimes.com/2010/04/24/us/politics/24immig.html> accessed July 22, 2012.

9. The Senate bill anchors the provision of a path to citizenship on tough border security provisions that must be in place before the immigrants can gain legal status. See Ashley Parker and Jonathan Martin, "Senate, 68 to 32, Passes Overhaul for Immigration," <http://www.nytimes.com/2013/06/28/us/politics/immigration-bill-clears-final-hurdle-to-senate-approval.html?pagewanted=all&_r=0> accessed August 18, 2013.

10. John Rawls, *Political Liberalism* (New York, NY: Columbia University Press, 1993): 181.

11. Contrary to common belief that immigrants, especially "illegal" immigrants, are economic burden, there is reputable information that say otherwise. See, for example, Veronica Uy, "International Labor Organization: 40M Illegal Migrants Prop Up Economies, <http://services.inquirer.net> accessed June 26, 2012.

12. Graziano Battistella, "Migration and Human Dignity," in *A Promised Land, A Perilous Journey*, 186–187.

13. Peter Kivisto and Thomas Faist, *Beyond a Border: The Causes and Consequences of Contemporary Immigration* (Thousand Oaks, CA: Pine Forge Press, 2010), 171–172, further sheds light on liberal perspectives on integration.

14. Bridget Kratz, "Libertarianism and Catholic Social Teaching on Immigration," *Journal of Markets and Morality* Vol. 15, No. 1 (Spring 2012): 29.

15. Battistella, "Migration and Human Dignity," 186.

16. For streamlining purposes this chapter focuses primarily on modern CST, that is, from *Rerum Novarum* (1891) onward. Kenneth Himes, O.F.M., "Introduction," in *Modern Catholic Social Teaching: Commentaries and Interpretations*, ed. Kenneth Himes, O.F.M. (Washington, DC: Georgetown University Press, 2004): 2–3, provides an explanation on what constitutes *modern* CST.

17. Kenneth Himes, "Globalization with a Human Face: Catholic Social Teaching and Globalization," *Theological Studies* Vol. 69, No. 2 (June 2008): 274–280. Dennis McCann echoes this position by arguing

that CST's theological understanding of the human person could serve as an important resource for business ethics. McCann elaborates by pointing at how CST understands finance capital as socially embedded. Dennis McCann, "Catholic Social Teaching in an Era of Economic Globalization," *Business Ethics Quarterly* Vol. 7, No. 2 (1997): 69.

18. *Rerum Novarum*, no. 45. John Paul II, in his message for World Migrants Day in 1998, affirms this by saying the migrant is to be considered not merely as an instrument of production but a subject endowed with full human dignity.

19. *Gaudium et Spes*, no. 66.

20. In May 2008, in one of the biggest single-site immigration raids in the US history, dozens of immigration agents swooped down on Agriprocessors—the largest processor of kosher meat in the United States—where the agents detained 389 undocumented male and female workers, most of whom come from Guatemala. The handcuffed workers were subsequently loaded into Homeland Security buses and were sent to prisons throughout the country, where they would spend five months before they got deported to Guatemala. Maggie Jones, "Postville, Iowa Is Up for Grabs," <http://www.nytimes.com/2012/07/15/magazine/postville-iowa-is-up-for-grabs.html?pagewanted=all> accessed August 18, 2013.

21. Brennan Hill, *The Ongoing Renewal of Catholicism* (Winnona, MN: St. Mary's Press, 2008), 262–263.

22. John Paul II's successor Benedict XVI affirms this centrality and enduring power of human rights in building a better and safer world in an address to the United Nations, where he reiterates that "the promotion of human rights remains the most effective strategy for eliminating inequalities between countries and social groups, and for increasing security." As quoted in Silvano Tomasi, "Human Rights as a Framework for Advocacy on Behalf of the Displaced: The Approach of the Catholic Church," in *Driven from Home*, 64.

23. Graziano Battistella, "The Human Rights of Migrants: A Pastoral Challenge," in *Migration, Religious Experience and Globalization*, 95–96. *Pacem in Terris*, no. 106, makes this right more explicit: "Among man's personal rights we must include his right to enter a country in which he hopes to be able to provide more fittingly for himself and his dependents." The apostolic exhortation by John Paul II titled *Familiaris Consortio* also affirms this by pointing out "the right to emigrate as family in search of better life" (FC, no. 46).

24. Such stance is articulated as early as 1891 in *Rerum Novarum*, no. 13, which insists that "men would cling to the country in which they were born, for no one would exchange his country for a foreign land if his own afforded him the means of living a decent and happy life [*sic*]."

25. Graziano Battistella, "The Human Rights of Migrants," in *Migration, Religious Experience and Globalization*, 95.

26. Michael Blume, S.V.D., "Migration and the Social Doctrine of the Church," in *Migration, Religious Experience and Globalization*, 70. Blume points out as well the need to change language that already carries with it a judgment, particularly the word "illegal". Others, in the meantime, also still find the more commonly used term "undocumented" as problematic and it is in this context that Carmen Nanko-Fernadez suggests using the term "alternately documented." See Carmen Nanko Fernandez, "Preference for the Young" *Vital Theology* Vol. 4, No. 2–3 (April/May 2007): 13.

27. See paragraph 3 of USCCB, "A Resolution by the National Conference of Catholic Bishops," <http://www.usccb.org/mrs/reform. shtml> accessed October 26, 2012.

28. Catholic Bishops of Mexico and the United States, *Strangers No Longer: Together on the Journey of Hope: A Pastoral Letter Concerning Migration from the Catholic Bishops of Mexico and the United States*. See <http://www.usccb.org/mrs/stranger.shtml> accessed October 26, 2012.

29. Tomasi, "Human Rights as a Framework for Advocacy on Behalf of the Displaced," 64.

30. See John Paul II, "Address to Officials and Advocates of the Tribunal of the Roman Rota," (February 17, 1979), 4 and Code of Canon Law, canons 208–223, as quoted in Pontifical Council for Justice and Peace, *Compendium of the Social Doctrine of the Church*, no. 159.

31. The synodal document *Justice in the World*, no. 6, reflects this: "Action on behalf of justice and participation in the transformation of the world fully appear to us as a constitutive dimension of the preaching of the Gospel, or, in other words, of the Church's mission for the redemption of the human race and its liberation from every oppressive situation." As posted on <http://www.osjspm.org/ majordoc_justicia_in_mundo_offical_test.aspx> accessed October 26, 2012.

32. *Mater et Magistra*, no. 65, defines common good as the sum total of "all those social conditions which favor the full development of human personality."

33. See *Redemptor Hominis*, no. 17, and *Octogesima Adveniens*, no. 23, as quoted in Pontifical Council for Justice and Peace, *Compendium of the Social Doctrine of the Church*, no. 158.

34. A similar measure has been passed and struck down by courts in Hazelton, Pennsylvania, and Farmers Branch, Texas. See Ed Hornick, "Nebraska City's Controversial Immigration Rule Passes," <http://edition.cnn.com/2010/POLITICS/06/22/ fremont.immigration.ballot/> accessed September 20, 2012.

35. Steven Bouma-Prediger in "Environmental Racism," for example, points to a study that concluded that although socioeconomic status plays an important role, race is the best predictor in identifying communities most likely to be the best location for toxic waste sites. Steven Bouma-Prediger, "Environmental Racism," in *Handbook of U.S. Theologies of Liberation*, ed. Miguel de la Torre (St. Louis, MO: Chalice Press, 2004): 283.

36. As the Catechism of the Catholic Church states: "Political authorities, for the sake of the common good for which they are responsible, may make the exercise of the right to immigrate subject to various juridical conditions, especially with regard to the immigrants' duties toward their country of adoption," *Catechism of the Catholic Church*, no. 2241.

37. Battistella, "Migration and Human Dignity," 188.

38. The global commerce in weapons, which usually end up harming and killing civilians or noncombatants, has often been criticized for exacerbating the movement of refugees. Allen, *The Future Church*, 273.

39. Olivia Ruiz Marrujo, "Immigrants at Risk, Immigrants as Risk: Two Paradigms of Globalization," in *Migration, Religious Experience and Globalization*, 19.

40. Marrujo, "Immigrants at Risk, Immigrants as Risk," 19.

41. As quoted in Pistone and Hoeffner, *Stepping Out of the Brain Drain*, 5.

42. National Conference of Catholic Bishops Committee on Priestly Formation, *People on the Move: A Compendium of Church Documents on the Pastoral Care for Migrants and Refugees* (Washington, DC: United States Catholic Conference, 1988), 65, 85 as quoted in Pistone and Hoeffner, *Stepping Out of the Brain Drain*, 5. Some scholars such as Pistone and Hoeffner argue the migration of professionals tends to benefit more than harm the world's poorest population. However, there are understandable moral concerns, especially when it comes to the overall and long-term effects. A recent study on the migration of health workers gives voice to these concerns by concluding that the purported benefits of migration, indeed, exist but that they are unlikely to be sufficient to compensate for the costs. See Pistone and Hoeffner, *Stepping Out of the Brain Drain*, xviii–xix, and Corinne Packers, Vivien Runnels and Ronald Labonté, "Does the Migration of Health Workers Bring Benefits to the Countries They Leave Behind?" in *The International Migration of Health Workers*, ed. Rebecca S. Shah (London: Palgrave, 2010): 44–61 respectively.

43. Pontifical Council for Justice and Peace, *Compendium of the Social Doctrine of the Church*, 192.

44. Italics in original text. Pontifical Council for Justice and Peace, *Compendium of the Social Doctrine of the Church*, no. 193.

45. See *Gaudium et Spes*, nos. 26, 29, 38.

46. Christopher Llanos, S.J. "Refugees or Economic Migrants: Catholic Thought on the Moral Roots of the Distinction" in *Driven from Home*, 255.

47. Pope John Paul II, "Message: World Migration Day 2001," as cited in Battistella, "Migration and Human Dignity," 189.

48. Ada Maria Isasi Diaz, "Solidarity: Love of Neighbor in the 1980s," in *Feminist Theological Ethics: A Reader*, ed. Lois K. Daly (Louisville, KY: WJK Press, 1994): 78–85.

49. Pontifical Council for Justice and Peace, *Compendium of the Social Doctrine of the Church*, no. 193.

50. For example, trafficked women and children have prompted a coalition of women religious that has compelled governments to take notice of this problem and enact legal provisions. See Tomasi, "Human Rights as a Framework for Advocacy on Behalf of the Displaced," 65.

51. Gustavo Gutierrez, "Poverty, Migration, and the Option for the Poor," in *A Promised Land, A Perilous Journey*, 76–86.

52. Dennis Müller, "A Homeland for Transients: Towards and Ethic of Migrations," in *Migrants and Refugees*, 130–147, elaborates on this, particularly in the context of Europe.

53. As quoted in Pontifical Council for Justice and Peace, *Compendium of the Social Doctrine of the Church*, no. 193.

54. Sharon Welch, *A Feminist Ethic of Risk* (Minneapolis: Fortress Press, 2000), 68. The concept of "sheer holy boldness" is attributed by Welch to Toni Cade Bambara, *The Salt-Eaters* (New York: Vintage Books, 1981), 265.

55. Welch, *A Feminist Ethic of Risk*, 48.

56. *Rerum Novarum*, no. 20, for example, states "Women...are not suited to certain trades; for a woman is by nature fitted for homework, and it is that which is best adapted at once to preserve her modesty and to promote the good upbringing of children and the well-being of the family."

57. *Quadragesimo Anno*, no. 71, in the meantime, reinforces the role of women as economically dependent on the male workforce by saying, "the wage paid to the workingman should be sufficient for the support of himself and his family....It is wrong to abuse the tender years of children or the weakness of women." See Lisa Cahill, "Family and Catholic Social Teaching," in *Change in Official Catholic Moral Teaching: Readings in Moral Theology No. 13*, ed. Charles E. Curran (New York: Paulist, 2003): 255. See a related critique on the CST's idea of the "family wage" vis-a-vis women and children's economic dependency on men in Maria Riley, "Reception of Catholic Social Teaching Among Christian Feminists," in *Rerum Novarum: One Hundred Years of Catholic Social Teaching*, ed. John

Coleman and Gregory Baum, Concilium 119/5 (London: SCM Press): 110.

58. The CST ensures this stand with teachings such as those found in *Pacem in Terris*, no. 19, which says, "Women have the right to working conditions **in accordance with their requirements and their duties as wives and mothers** (emphasis mine)." As quoted in Maria Riley, *Trouble and Beauty: Women Encounter Catholic Social Teaching* (Washington DC: Center for Concern, 1992), 15–16. Lisa Cahill makes a similar observation in relation to the closing homily of John Paul II for the Synod on the Family in 1980. Lisa Cahill, "Commentary on *Familiaris Consortio*," in *Modern Catholic Social Teaching*, 374.

59. Christine Gudorf, "Encountering the Other: The Modern Papacy on Women," in *Change in Official Catholic Moral Teaching*, 273.

60. Riley, *Trouble and Beauty*, 13.

61. Cahill, "Family and Catholic Social Teaching," 264, makes this observation since the Letter presents the family as constituted by, and beginning in, marriage and especially in the sexual relations of the couple, in which love is expressed and a child conceived.

62. For a discussion on the Roman roots of the Christian understanding of the family, see Rosemary Radford Ruether, *Christianity and Social Systems: Historical Constructions and Ethical Challenges* (Lanham, MD: Rowman and Littlefield, 2009), 31–34.

63. Riley, "Reception of Catholic Social Teaching among Christian Feminists," 110.

64. Salzmann and Lawler, "Catholic Sexual Ethics," 627–628.

65. Quotation from *Letter to Families*, no. 16 (italics added), as cited in Cahill, "Family and Catholic Social Teaching," 264.

66. Cahill, "Family and Catholic Social Teaching," 254, 261, contends that this defence of gender equality should not be received with a wholly uncritical attitude as it tends to devolve in practice to less socially valued role for women, with a smaller sphere of freedom, self-determination, and social leadership than is allotted to men.

67. As quoted in Cahill, "Commentary on *Familiaris Consortio*," 374. It must be pointed out here, however, that FC actually presents a much more egalitarian picture of gender roles than previous official sources. John Paul II's *Letter to Women* also reflect some of this ambivalent or complementary approach to gender equality. On the one hand, John Paul denounces abuses such as sexual violence against women (LW, no. 5) and upholds "real equality in every area" as well as "equality of spouses with regard to family rights" (LW, no. 4) when referring to process of women's liberation. On the other hand, the pope praises the "genius of women" and argues that women's vocation is to give of themselves, since "more than men" women "see persons with their hearts" (LW, no. 12). Moreover, he points out that

men and women have different roles, considered of equal value, in the economy of salvation (LW, no. 11). All quotations from John Paul II, "Letter to Women," *Origins* 25/9 (27 July 1995) as cited in Cahill, "Family and Catholic Social Teaching," 263–264.

68. Riley, "Reception of Catholic Social Teaching Among Christian Feminists," 110. Riley cites, as an example, what the council fathers note in *Gaudium et Spes* that "there is an ever-increasing number of men and women who are conscious that they themselves are the artisans and the authors of the culture of their community" and that "women are now employed in almost every area of life"; the document also maintains that "it is appropriate that they [women] should be able to assume their full proper role in accordance with their own nature" (GS, nos. 55, 60).

69. Cahill cites, as an example, *Casti Connubi* as advocating the idea that the primary function of women are to be wives and mothers and that the socioeconomic status of women is dependent on that of their male family members, especially their husbands. Cahill, "Commentary on *Familiaris Consortio*," 373.

70. Christine Firer-Hinze's critique on the social encyclicals' deal of a "family living wage" is an example here. Firer-Hinze contends that while it seems to benefit women and children within the family unit, the CST's idea of "family living wage" concedes too much to a market economic model and fails to register the many contributions adults make to the common good through a variety of activities outside the current structure of wage labor. See Christine Firer-Hinze, "Bridge Discourse on Wage Justice: Roman Catholic and Feminist Perspectives on the Family Living Wage," in *Feminist Ethics and the Catholic Moral Tradition* ed. Charles Curran, Margaret Farley and Richard McCormick (New York: Paulist, 1996): 511–540 as cited in Cahill, "Commentary on *Familiaris Consortio*," 377.

71. Cahill, "Commentary on *Familiaris Consortio*," 377.

72. Katherine E. Zappone, "Women's 'Special Nature': A Different Horizon for Theological Anthropology" in *The Special Nature of Women?* ed. Anne Carr and Elisabeth Sch?ssler Fiorenza, Concilium 1991/6 (London: SCM Press): 87. Zappone concurs with Judith Plaskow's theory of the content of women's experience through an analysis of what the culture expects and how women live in relation to these expectations. Like Plaskow, Zappone thinks that based on such an analysis, women's sin could more aptly be described as self-negation (rather than self-assertion) and self-realization (rather than selfless love) is her grace-filled process. See Judith Plaskow, *Sex, Sin and Grace: Women's Experience and the Theologies of Reinhold Niebuhr and Paul Tillich* (Washington, DC: University Press of America, 1980) as cited in Zapone, "Women's 'Special Nature,' "89.

73. Zapone, "Women's 'Special Nature,' " 87. The problem, in other words, is the dualistic anthropology that informs the CST. *Octogesima*

Adveniens, for example, notes that "in many countries a charter for women which would put an end to an actual discrimination and would establish relationships of equality in rights and of respect for their dignity is the object of study and at times of lively demands" (*OA,* no. 13). But the text goes on to say: "We do not have in mind that false equality which would deny the distinctions laid down by the Creator himself and which would be in contradiction with woman's **proper role,** which is of such capital importance, at the heart of the family as well as within society. Development in legislation should on the contrary be directed to protecting her **proper vocation** and at the same time recognizing her independence as a person, and her equal rights to participate in cultural, economic, social and political life."

74. Gudorf, "Encountering the Other," 269.
75. The papal view of marriage, Gudorf observes, is distinctly clerical. It is based on children's experience of marriage as revolving around them and their needs, rather than on spouses' experience of marriage. Gudorf, "Encountering the Other," 279.
76. Charles Curran, *Catholic Social Teaching 1891–Present: A Historical, Theological and Ethical Analysis* (Washington, DC: Georgetown University Press, 2002), 94.
77. Curran, *Catholic Social Teaching 1891–Present,* 120.
78. *Erga Migrantes Caritas Christi,* no. 5.
79. As quoted and emphasized in Johann Ketelers, "Migrants to and from Asia, and Their Families: Responses to New Challenges in Advocacy," in *The Migrant Family in Asia: Reaching Out and Touching Them,* ed. Anthony Rogers, FSC (Manila: Office for Human Development, 2007): 127.
80. Kenneth Himes, "Globalization with a Human Face: Catholic Social Teaching and Globalization," *Theological Studies* Vol. 69, No. 2 (June 2008): 274.
81. Maria Pilar Aquino, *Our Cry for Life: Feminist Theology from Latin America* (New York: Orbis, 1993), 94.
82. Heinrich Bedford-Strohm, "Responding to the Challenges of Migration and Flight from a Perspective of Theological Ethics," in Churches' Commission for Migrants in Europe, *Theological Reflections on Migration: A CCME Reader* (Brussels: CCME, 2008): 38.
83. Tomasi, "Human Rights as a Framework for Advocacy on Behalf of the Displaced," 64. Using the acronym A GOD OF LIFE, Groody offers a matrix for understanding CST, which could serve as a synthesis of the ethical framework that could be provided by CST. See Daniel G. Groody, *Globalization, Spirituality, and Justice: Navigating the Path to Peace* (Maryknoll, NY: Orbis, 2007), 102–117.
84. William, R., O'Neill, S.J. and William C. Spohn, "Rights of Passage: The Ethics of Immigration and Refugee Policy," *Theological Studies* Vol. 59, No. 1 (1998): 84–106, illustrates this approach.

85. Thomas Massaro, *Living Justice: Catholic Social Teaching in Action* (Lanham, MD: Rowman and Littlefield, 2012), 125.

CHAPTER 4

1. See Will Herberg, *Protestant-Catholic-Jew: An Essay in American Religious Sociology* (Garden City, NY: Doubleday, 1960), as quoted in Ebaugh and Chafetz, "Introduction" in *Religion and the New Immigrants*, 17 18.
2. See Diana Eck, *A New Religious America: How a "Christian Country" Has Become the World's Most Religiously-Diverse Nation* (HarperOne: San Francisco, 2002).
3. Robert Schreiter summarizes contemporary migration's challenges to religious identity in three categories: (1) the new religious configurations within countries; (2) forms of religiosity and related practices that had been thought to be part of the past, that is, popular religiosity; and (3) the creation of new hybrid forms of religiosity. Robert Schreiter, "Catholicity as Framework for Addressing Migration," in *Migration in a Global World*, 32–33.
4. William Portier, *Tradition and Incarnation* (New York, NY: Paulist Press, 1993), 9.
5. Allen, *The Future Church*, 98.
6. The growing literature on the intersection of religion and migration is proof of this. Aside from the texts that are directly used in this book, particularly in this chapter, see Paul Johnson, *Diaspora Conversions: Black Carib Religion and the Recovery of Africa* (Berkeley: University of California Press, 2007); Jacob Olupona and Regina Gemignani, *African Immigrant Religions in America* (New York: New York University Press, 2007); Jenna Weissman Joselit, *A Parade of Faiths: Immigration and American Religion* (New York: Oxford University Press, 2007); Helen Rose Ebaugh and Janet Saltman Chafetz, *Religion Across Borders: Transnational Religious Networks* (Walnut Creek, CA: Altamira Press, 2002); Thomas Tweed and Stephen Prothero, *Asian Religions in America: A Documentary History* (New York: Oxford University Press, 1998); Steven Vertovec and Ceri Peach, ed. *Islam in Europe: The Politics of Religion and Community* (London: Palgrave, 1997); Susan Wiley Hardwick, *Russian Refuge: Religion, Migration and Settlement on the North American Pacific Rim* (Chicago: University of Chicago Press, 1993); and Frank van Tubergen, "Religious Affiliation and Attendance Among Immigrants in Eight Western Countries: Individual and Contextual Effects," *Journal for the Scientific Study of Religion* Vol. 45, No. 1 (2006): 1–22.
7. Jacqueline Maria Hagan, *Migration Miracle: Faith, Hope and Meaning on the Undocumented Journey* (Cambridge, MA: Harvard

University Press, 2008), 2. Bishop Alvaro Ramazzini of Guatemala, for example, has not only opened a hospitality center for immigrants deported from Mexico and the United States. He also developed a sister relationship with the Diocese of Wilmington in Delaware, where many of his parishioners—displaced by the coffee crisis—ended up laboring in poultry packing plants. Jerry H. Gill, *Borderland Theology* (Washington, DC: EPICA, 2003), 111.

8. See Jacqueline Maria Hagan, "The Church vs. the State: Borders, Migrants, and Human Rights," 96–101, and Cecilia Menjivar, "Serving Christ in the Borderlands: Faith Workers Respond to Border Violence," 110–115 in *Religion and Social Justice for Immigrants*, ed. Pierrette Hondagneu-Sotelo (New Brunswick, NJ: Rutgers University Press, 2007).

9. Not surprisingly, the increasing mobility worldwide has also made more possible the migration of religious groups and organizations themselves. See Donald M. Lewis, ed. *Christianity Reborn: The Global Expansion of Evangelicalism in the Twentieth Century* (Grand Rapids, Michigan: Eerdmans, 2004).

10. Some like Border Angels go beyond providing water but food and clothing as well. Pierette Hondagneu-Sotelo, *God's Heart Has No Borders: How Religious Activists Are Working for Immigrant Rights* (Berkeley, CA: University of California Press, 2008), 141–143.

11. Cruz, *An Intercultural Theology of Migration*, 96–98, provides a more exhaustive description.

12. Fenggang Yang, "Chinese Gospel Church: The Sinization of Christianity," in *Religion and the New Immigrants*, 89, 97–98, 101–102.

13. A concise treatment of this role based on the experience of the Catholic Church could be found in Kevin Appleby, "The Role of the Catholic Church in Immigrant Integration," *The Review of Faith and International Affairs* Vol. 9, No. 1 (Spring 2011): 69. On a more general Christian perspective, see Jenny Yang, "A Christian Perspective on Immigrant Integration," *The Review of Faith and International Affairs* Vol. 9, No. 1 (Spring 2011): 80–83.

14. For example, altar boys and girls who never learned the language memorize Ukrainian liturgy. Janet Mancini Billson, *Keepers of the Culture: The Power of Tradition in Women's Lives* (New York: Lexington Books, 1995), 345, 368.

15. Kathleen Sullivan, "St. Mary's Catholic Church: Celebrating Domestic Religion," in *Religion and the New Immigrants*, 130. See also Nancy J. Wellmeier, "Santa Eulalia's People in Exile: Maya Religion, Culture and Identity in Los Angeles," in *Gatherings in Diaspora: Religious Communities and the New Immigration*, ed. R. Stephen Warner and Judith Wittner (Philadelphia: Temple University Press, 1998): 97–122.

16. Sullivan, "St. Mary's Catholic Church," 130.

17. Hondagneu-Sotelo, *God's Heart Has No Borders*, 143.

18. The Christian idea of "sanctuary" could be traced to the Hebrew concept of sanctuary, which is rooted in the tradition of the cities of refuge (Exod. 21:13; Num. 35: 9–11). These "cities" were holy or sanctified places, often a temple, where God and the people of Israel protected those who sought refuge (Deut. 19:7–10). The provision was usually intended to protect those who were guilty of involuntary murder and extended not only to the Israelites but also to any "resident or transient alien among them" (Num. 35:15). Letty Russell, *Just Hospitality: God's Welcome in a World of Difference* (Louisville, KY: WJK Press, 2009), 86–87.

19. For a similar movement in Canada, see Mary Jo Leddy, "When the Stranger Summons: Spiritual and Theological Considerations for Ministry," *New Theology Review* Vol. 20, No. 3 (August 2007):10–12.

20. Renny Golden and Michael McConnell, *Sanctuary: The New Underground Railroad* (New York: Orbis, 1986), 46, as quoted in Hondagneu-Sotelo, *God's Heart Has No Borders*, 145.

21. Julia Preston, "Obama to Push Immigration Bill as One Priority," <http://www.nytimes.com/2009/04/09/us/politics/09immig.html> accessed August 26, 2012.

22. Fenggang Yang and Helen Rose Ebaugh, "Religion and Ethnicity Among New Immigrants: The Impact of Majority/Minority Status in Home and Host Countries," *Journal for the Scientific Study of Religion* Vol. 40, No. 3 (2001): 374.

23. Simon Jacob and Pallavi Thakur, "Jyothi Hindu Temple: One Religion, Many Practices," in *Religion and the New Immigrants*, 153.

24. See The Pew Forum on Religion and Public Life, "Public Remains Conflicted Over Islam," <http://www.pewforum.org/Muslim/Public-Remains-Conflicted-Over-Islam.aspx> accessed August 14, 2012.

25. After the death of Osama bin Laden, for instance, a mosque in Maine was vandalized while the doors of a Louisiana mosque was smeared with pork. See Liz Goodwin, "Muslim Americans Still Find Acceptance Elusive in the Wake of bin Laden's Death," <http://news.yahoo.com/s/yblog_thelookout/20110511/us_yblog_thelookout/muslim-americans-still-find-acceptance-elusive-in-the-wake-of-bin-ladens-death> accessed August 12, 2012.

26. The dramatic killing of Dutch filmmaker Theo van Gogh in 2004 by a Dutch Muslim jihadist, primarily on account of a film by van Gogh (*Submission*) that is critical on the condition and treatment of women in Islamic societies, reflects this increased tension with regard to religio-cultural worldviews between immigrant and receiving societies, particularly in relation to Islam.

27. Jomar Canlas, "Riyadh Nabs 14 OFWs for Practicing Religion," *The Manila Times* (October 7, 2010), 3.

28. Sullivan, "St. Mary's Catholic Church," 126. For concrete struggles involved in forging multiethnic churches, see Warren St. John, "The World Comes to Georgia, and an Old Church Adapts," <http://www.nytimes.com> accessed August 3, 2012.

29. This is based on a study of 13 immigrant religious congregations in Houston, Texas. See Fenggang Yang and Helen Rose Ebaugh, "Transformations in New Immigrant Religions and Their Global Implications," *American Sociological Review* Vol. 66, No. 2 (April 2001): 269–288.

30. Yang and Ebaugh, "Transformations in New Immigrant Religions and Their Global Implications," 273–276.

31. Yang and Ebaugh, "Transformations in New Immigrant Religions and Their Global Implications," 276–278.

32. See Gertrud Húwelmeier, "Female Believers on the Move: Vietnamese Pentecostal Networks in Germany" in *Gender, Religion and Migration*, 115–131.

33. Nearly all of the women members are non-permanent residents, most of whom are single mothers who are dependent on German welfare.

34. Problems with the female leader include a highly traditional approach to marriage and dress codes in church. Húwelmeier, however, primarily credits the split and the maintenance of the group to how Pentecostalism enhances women's autonomy by providing a place where women find support for problems in their family and kinship relations and, in particular, by a less androcentric understanding of charismatic authority, which makes it more possible for women to take on leadership positions. Húwelmeier, "Female Believers on the Move," 115–116.

35. See Thomas J. Douglas, "Changing Religious Practices Among Cambodian Immigrants in Long Beach and Seattle," in *Immigrant Faiths: Transforming Religious Life in America*, ed. Karen Leonard et al. (Lanham, MD: Altamira Press, 2005), 134–137.

36. She is not the only church member who does this. Other members of her Catholic church are Catholic on Saturday nights and equally Pentecostal, Methodist, or Baptist on Sunday mornings. Sullivan, "St. Mary's Catholic Church," 201.

37. Kathleen Sullivan, "St. Catherine's Catholic Church: One Church, Parallel Congregations," in *Religion and the New Immigrants*, 259.

38. Yang and Ebaugh, "Transformations in New Immigrant Religions and Their Global Implications," 274.

39. Islam Sithi Hawwa, "Religious Conversion of Filipina Domestic Helpers in Hong Kong," *ISIM Newsletter* Vol. 4 (1999): 10.

40. Stephen Bevans, "Mission *among* Migrants, Mission *of* Migrants," in *A Promised Land, A Perilous Journey*, 99–102, elucidates on this.

41. Jehu Hanciles, *Beyond Christendom: Globalization, African Migration and the Transformation of the West* (New York: Orbis, 2008), 277–278.

42. Hanciles points out, for example, how the strong immigrant ethos coupled with the ingrained proclivity for voluntary association has helped American society develop a greater capacity for religious pluralism than any other country in the Western world. Hanciles, *Beyond Christendom*, 278.

43. Hanciles, *Beyond Christendom*, 283.

44. "Filipino Migrant Workers in Hong Kong," *Asian Migrant* Vol. 7, No. 1 (January–March 1994): 6–7. Such missionary effect is often felt more strongly in receiving countries where churches are experiencing significant losses in membership as well as decline in religious practice, making migrants important in the survival or flourishing of the Christian faith. As Philip Jenkins contends, southern-derived immigrant communities play a critical role in the future face of Christianity, especially in Western countries. See Philip Jenkins, *The Next Christendom: The Coming of Global Christianity* (Oxford: Oxford University Press, 2003).

45. Hanciles writes that by the time the first European missionary arrived in Jamaica, George Liele (1750–1825), America's first overseas missionary, already had a church of more than 500 members. Hanciles, *Beyond Christendom*, 283–285.

46. Yang, "Chinese Gospel Church," 90–92, 101–103.

47. Sullivan, "St. Mary's Catholic Church,"127.

48. Gerrie ter Haar, *Halfway to Paradise: African Christians in Europe* (Cardiff: Cardiff Academic Press, 1998), 92.

49. Jehu J. Hanciles, "Migration and Mission: Some Implications for the Twenty-first Century Church," *International Bulletin of Missionary Research* Vol. 27, No. 4 (October 2003): 150; 152

50. Jehu Hanciles, *Beyond Christendom: Globalization*, 204.

51. Avery Dulles, *The Catholicity of the Church* (Oxford: The Clarendon Press, 1985) as quoted in Robert J. Schreiter, *The New Catholicity: Theology Between the Global and the Local* (New York: Orbis Books, 1997), 128.

52. Miroslav Volf, *Exclusion and Embrace: A Theological Exploration of Identity, Otherness and Reconciliation* (Nashville, TN: Abingdon Press, 1996), 51.

53. I take "*kin*dom" from Ada Maria Isasi-Diaz, who uses it instead of the usual word "kingdom" for two reasons: First, she argues "kingdom" is a sexist word. Second, she reckons that, today, the concept of kingdom—as is the word "reign"—is both hierarchical and elitist. *Kin*dom, on the other hand, makes it clear that when the fullness of God becomes a day-to-day reality in the world at large, we will be sisters and brothers—kin to each other—and will,

indeed, be the family of God. See endnote no. 8 in Ada Maria Isasi-Diaz, "Solidarity: Love of Neighbor in the 21st Century," in *Lift Every Voice: Constructing Christian Theologies from the Underside*, ed. Susan Brooks Thislethwaite and Mary Potter Engel (New York: Orbis Books, 2004): 36.

54. Christine Pohl, *Making Room: Recovering Hospitality as a Christian Tradition* (Grand Rapids, Michigan: Wm B. Eerdmans Publishing Company, 1999), 61–62.

55. Mike Purcell, "Christ the Stranger: The Ethical Originality of Homelessness," in *Migration in a Global World*, 66.

56. Kristin Heyer tackles this perspective using the category of social sin in Kristin Heyer, "Social Sin and Immigration: Good Fences Make Bad Neighbors," *Theological Studies* Vol. 71, No. 2 (June 2010): 410–436.

57. For more substantive treatment on hospitality or welcome to the stranger from a biblical perspective, see Matthew Soerens and Jenny Hwang, *Welcoming the Stranger: Justice, Compassion and Truth in the Immigration Debate* (Downers Grove, IL: Intervarsity Press, 2009): 82–92.

58. Parker Palmer, *The Company of Strangers: Christians and the Renewal of America's Public Life* (New York: Crossroad, 1981), 70, quoted in John Koenig, *New Testament Hospitality: Partnership with Strangers as Promise and Mission* (Philadelphia: Fortress Press, 1985), 145.

59. The Orthodox icon of the Trinity even identifies the divine communion between the Father, the Son, and the Spirit with the communion of three strangers who were received and fed by Abraham in the spirit of genuine hospitality (Gen. 18 and Hebrews 13:2). World Council of Churches, *A Moment to Choose: Risking to Be With Uprooted People* (Geneva: WCC, 1996), 15.

60. Linh Hoang, "Crossing and Dwelling: Hospitality in a Theology of Migration," *Asian Christian Review* Vol. 4, No. 2 (Winter 2010): 88.

61. Elisabeth Schüssler-Fiorenza speaks of the *ekklesia* as the assembly/movement of free citizens who determine their own and their children's communal, political, and spiritual well-being. See Elisabeth Schüssler-Fiorenza, *Discipleship of Equals: A Critical Feminist Ekklesia-Logy of Liberation* (New York: Crossroad, 1993), for an elaboration on this.

62. Russell contends that the doctrine of election has been tainted in the Christian tradition with the influences of messianic and imperialistic universalism. Russell points, in particular, to the nineteenth-century partnership between Christianity and European imperialism that wiped out others' cultures, religions, and political systems to establish uniformity through enforcement of Christianity and new economic systems. In ways reflective of some of the dilemma and struggle by contemporary immigrants, Russell recalls that in order

to be counted as "one of the elect" colonized people were forced to assimilate, to be *saved* from their savage ways of living. Of course, on the part of today's immigrants the reasons for assimilation go beyond the meta-narrative of cultural superiority. Assimilation becomes, for immigrants, a strategic political and economic decision as it often becomes the best way, if not the only way, to survive or thrive in the receiving country. Russell, *Just Hospitality*, 38–42.

63. Linbert Spencer, *Building a Multi-ethnic Church* (London: SPCK, 2007), 20–32, chronicles how this plays out in the case of the United Kingdom.

64. Russell, *Just Hospitality*, 43.

65. Felix Wilfred, "Towards a Better Understanding of Asian Theology," *Vidyajyoti Journal of Theological Reflection* Vol. 62, No. 12 (1998): 890–915.

66. Peter Phan, "Where We Come From, Where We Are, and Where We Are Going: Asian and Pacific Catholics in the United States," *American Catholic Studies* Vol. 118, No. 3 (2007): 22.

67. Michael Amaladoss, "The Church and Pluralism in the Asia of the 1990s," in *FABC Papers No. 57e* (Hong Kong: FABC, 1990), 12.

68. Peter Phan, "Multiple Religious Belonging: Opportunities and Challenges for Theology and Church," *Theological Studies* Vol. 64, No. 3 (September 2003): 504.

69. John Hick, *God and the Universe of Faiths: Essays in the Philosophy of Religion* (London: Macmillan Press, 1973), 120–132.

70. Jeanine Hill Fletcher, *Monopoly on Salvation?: A Feminist Approach to Religious Pluralism* (New York: Continuum, 2005), 57, cites, as an example, the passage in 1 Timothy 2:4–5: "[God our Savior] desires everyone to be saved and to come to the knowledge of truth. For there is one God, there is also one mediator between God and humankind, Christ Jesus."

71. Eck, *A New Religious America*, 309. See also Jacques Dupuis, S.J., *Christianity and the Religions: From Confrontation to Dialogue* (New York: Orbis, 2001), 117, 119, which give examples of quotes on God by Christian personalities like Blaise Pascal and Walbert Bühlmann that, Dupuis says, actually has Christian underpinnings.

72. Fletcher submits that while we may not have the same religious affiliation with our neighbor, we might share other features that could serve as points of connection for conversation. The conversation partners could either be of the same gender, race, ethnicity, or political ideology or simply share a passion for justice. Fletcher says that in the process of finding and engaging these commonalities, we might have the opportunity to glimpse the incomprehensible mystery as it is seen through the others' eyes. Fletcher, *Monopoly on Salvation?*, 134. See also Jeanine Hill Fletcher, "Religious Pluralism in an Era of Globalization: The Making of Modern Religious Identity," *Theological Studies*

Vol. 69, No. 8 (June 2008): 394–411, for more on Hill Fletcher's thesis on hybridity as a heuristic lens for theologically making sense of religious plurality.

73. James Kroeger, "Living Faith in a Strange Land: Migration and Interreligious Dialogue," in *Faith on the Move*, 225–245.

74. On why this is the case, see Hanciles, *Beyond Christendom*, 177–179.

75. Oftentimes such an attitude is rooted in view of what migrants perceive as the diminished Christian condition of Western countries. Hanciles, *Beyond Christendom*, 298. On reverse mission see Allen, *The Future Church*, 44–47.

76. Afe Adogame, "Contesting the Ambivalences of Modernity in a Global Context: The Redeemed Christian Church of God, North America," *Studies in World Christianity* Vol. 10, No. 1 (2005): 29, as quoted in Hanciles, *Beyond Christendom*, 300.

77. William LaRousse, M.M., "Migration and Mission," in *Faith on the Move*, 169.

78. Hanciles, *Beyond Christendom*, 295.

79. Sullivan, "St. Mary's Catholic Church," 132.

80. As could be seen in the previous section on the need for a Christian theology of religious pluralism, this dialogical attitude or mission as dialogue is also important in relation to non-Christian religions.

81. More than 50 percent of Hispanic Catholics, for instance, identify themselves as charismatics who, like Pentecostals, emphasize recurrent spiritual renewal, the infilling of the Holy Spirit, divine healings, prophecies, speaking in tongues, and divine revelation in addition to the traditional Catholic teachings. Like Pentecostals their rituals are often marked by a spontaneous and joyous form of worship. They are, however, part of a group that is growing within Catholicism worldwide (especially in the churches in the global south) known as Catholic Charismatics. Allen argues that the Catholic Charismatic movement could actually be regarded as the Catholic response or counterpart to the world's fastest growing religion, that is, Pentecostalism. Allen, *The Future Church*, 186, 384–386.

82. On the so-called world church or the shift of global Christian demographics from the North to the South, see Allen, *The Future Church*, 13–53.

83. This urban character of mission by immigrant congregation constitutes an enhanced if not unique feature of mission in the context of contemporary migration. This is partly fueled by the fact that the majority of the world's population now lives in the cities (by 2030 some 3.3 billion people will be crowding the cities). In view of these developments Allen talks about the emergence as well as the need for an urban ministry in the swelling urban centers, which puts an emphasis on forming community as an antidote to the breakdown

204   NOTES

of traditional rural social networks. Allen, *The Future Church*, 334–336.

84. Hanciles, *Beyond Christendom*, 298.

CHAPTER 5

1. In the West, as well, this is true not just in major cities but even in smaller towns and cities. Take the case of the midwestern city that I mentioned above. A few weeks after my encounter with the Vietnamese-American community I went inside a smaller Protestant church nearby which literally has numerous flags of various countries adorning its walls. A church leader proudly told me that the flags represent their church members' home countries. Moreover, a sizeable Korean-American community is very active in the church. The Sunday I dropped by the church, for example, the Korean-Americans were in the church's foyer getting ready for their own service.

2. James H. Kroeger, M.M., "The Faith-Culture Dialogue in Asia: Ten FABC Insights on Inculturation," *East Asian Pastoral Review* Vol. 45, No. 3 (2008): 242.

3. See also Robert Schreiter, "Globalization, Postmodernity and the New Catholicity," in *For All People: Global Theologies in Contexts* ed. Else Marie Wiberg Pedersen, Holger Law and Peter Lodberg (Grand Rapids, MI: WmB. Eerdmans, 2002): 27.

4. Aylward Shorter, *Toward a Theology of Inculturation* (Eugene, OR: Wipf and Stock, 2006), 11.

5. Anscar Chupungco, "Liturgical Inculturation," *Handbook for Liturgical Studies II: Fundamental Liturgy* (Collegeville: Liturgical Press, 1998), 339 as quoted in Mark R. Francis, C.S.V., "Hispanic Liturgy in the U.S.: Toward a New Inculturation," *Journal of Hispanic/Latino Theology* Vol. 8, No. 2 (2000): 38.

6. terr Haar, *Halfway to Paradise*, 92.

7. Emphasis mine. Randy David, *Public Lives: Essays on Selfhood and Social Solidarity* (Pasig City: Anvil Publishing, 1998), 50–51.

8. It also includes other actions of the Church such as the daily prayer of the Liturgy of the Hours, the rites of Christian burial, and the rites for the dedication of a church or for those making religious profession. See USCCB, *Popular Devotional Practices: Basic Questions and Answers* <http://www.nccbuscc.org/bishops/devprac.shtml> accessed September 9, 2012.

9. Citing *Sacrosantum Concilium*, no. 37 Dan Groody points out that insofar as inculturation deals with how the unique qualities of various races and nations enrich our understanding of God's action in the world hymnody gives us a unique, poetic window into the spirituality and theology of a people. Groody, *Globalization, Spirituality and Justice*, 216.

10. This is supposed to represent the couple's desire to serve the needy as part of the marital covenant. See Bishops' Committee for Pastoral Research and Practice, National Conference of Catholic Bishops, *Planning Your Wedding Ceremony* (Washington, D.C.: United States Catholic Conference, 1990) 11–13 as cited in Timothy Matovina, "Marriage Celebrations in Mexican-American Communities," in *Mestizo Worship: A Pastoral Approach to Liturgical Ministry* ed.Virgilio P. Elizondo and Timothy Matovina (Collegeville: Liturgical Press, 1998): 93.

11. When marriage is celebrated outside the Mass the commentary is done before the final blessing. Matovina, "Marriage Celebrations in Mexican-American Communities," 94.

12. Other elements in Mexican-American marriage rites include the *padrino* (godparents), the *cojines* (cushions), the *libro y rosario* (prayer book or Bible and rosary), and the *velo* (veil). See Timothy Matovina, "Marriage Celebrations in Mexican-American Communities," 94–99 for further description, historical explanation and contemporary interpretations of these symbols and practices, some of which are also practiced by Filipino-Americans (e.g. *arras, velo*, and *padrino*) based on the *Tagalog* Rite approved by the Vatican in 1983.

13. Language is critical for immigrants such that some have been known to join other churches because these had people who could preach in their languages. As far as Asian and Pacific Catholics are concerned see Phan, "Where We Come From, Where We Are, and Where We Are Going," 8.

14. See "Asian and Pacific U.S. Catholics Will Celebrate Heritage, Tenth Anniversary of Bishops' Pastoral Statement *Harmony in Faith*" <http://www.usccb.org/comm/archives/2011/11-090.shtml> accessed August 11, 2012. At a Mass held by Vietnamese-Americans to celebrate the Vietnamese New Year, for example, there was even a dragon dance complete with drums and the crackling of firecrackers in the church right before the Mass. And like most cultural groups' gatherings the Mass was immediately followed by a hearty meal consisting mainly of native dishes.

15. Popular piety is often used interchangeably with popular religion/religiosity or folk religion/religiosity.

16. Mercado puts a biblical basis to his argument by pointing at how the woman who was bleeding for 12 years (Luke 8:43–48) thought she will become well if she touches the clothes of Jesus (and she did get well) or how the Acts of the Apostles (19:11–12) mention that the handkerchiefs that touched the skin of St. Paul were used for curing the sick and expelling evil spirits. Leonardo Mercado, *Filipino Popular Devotions: The Interior Dialogue Between Traditional Religion and Christianity* (Manila, Phils: Logos, 2000), 70.

17. Luis Maldonado, "Popular Religion: Its Dimensions, Levels and Types," in *Popular Religion*, ed. Norbert Greinacher and Norbert Mette, Concilium 186 (London: T &T Clark, 1986): 4.

18. This is, of course, most identified with Mexican-Americans. See, for example, Jeanette Rodriguez, "Devotion to Our Lady of Guadalupe Among Mexican-Americans," in *Many Faces, One Church: Cultural Diversity and the American Catholic Experience*, ed. Peter Phan and Diana Hayes (Lanham, MD: Rowman and Littlefield, 2004): 83–97 and Michael E. Engh, S.J. "Companion to Immigrants: Devotion to Our Lady of Guadalupe among Mexicans in the Los Angeles Area, 1900–1940," *Journal of Hispanic/Latino Theology* Vol. 5, No. 1 (1997): 37–47.

19. A *posada*—a reenactment of the journey of Joseph and Mary from Nazareth to Bethlehem—is a kind of Advent novena that combines prayers, songs and games. The *Via Crucis, Siete Palabras* and *pésame a la Virgen* are Holy Week rituals which are primarily done on Good Friday. Virgilio Elizondo "Living Faith: Resistance and Survival," in *Mestizo Worship: A Pastoral Approach to Liturgical Ministry*, ed.Virgilio P. Elizondo and Timothy Matovina (Collegeville, MN: Liturgical Press, 1998): 7–11, 15–17.

20. *Simbang Gabi* refers to the nine-day novena Masses held from December 16–24 in connection with Christmas while *Visita Iglesia* is a practice of visiting more or less seven churches on Holy Thursday and *salubong* is an Easter Sunday pre-dawn ritual that reenacts the Risen Christ's meeting with His mother. However, the realities of life in the United States have led to some changes in these rituals. Whereas *Simbang Gabi* in the Philippines is usually held at dawn (or at least before six o'clock in the morning)—a practice rooted in the agrarian history and rural lifestyle in the Philippines—it is held in the evening in the United States to accommodate the more urban and industrial American culture, especially when it comes to waking up. Based on my experience in Chicago the nine Masses are also held in nine different churches (to involve as many Filipino-Americans as possible) compared to the Philippines where every church will hold the nine day novena Masses. The *salubong*, which is usually performed in churchyards in the Philippines, is also done mostly inside the church, a change which, I surmise, is attributed to the American culture of greater sensitivity and/or criticism toward public displays of religion. The confinement of religious rituals to churches due to the enforcement of the separation of church and state, coupled with local laws, also put a limit when it comes to space and creativity for forms of popular piety. At a Holy Week gathering of Asian and Pacific-American lay leaders, for instance, a suggested ritual of burning personal notes by the participants was not allowed due to the fact that the parking lot is the only available space for such an activity and it cannot also be done

in the parking lot not just because of the cars but also because of a city ordinance.

21. Sullivan, "St. Mary's Catholic Church," 129.

22. Other parish organizations include mutual aid societies such as *Sociedad Mutualista de San José* and pious associations such as *El Santísimo, El Apostolado de la Oración, Hijas de Maria, Damas de Caridad* etc. Engh, "Companion of the Immigrants," 45–46.

23. Rachel Bundang, "May You Storm Heaven with Your Prayers: Devotions to Mary and Jesus in Filipino-American Catholic Life," in *Off the Menu: Asian and Asian North American Women's Religion and Theology*, ed. Rita Nakashima Brock etal. (Louisville: WJK Press, 2007): 89, 91.These prayer circles are usually set up by first-generation immigrant women wherever a minimum critical mass of Filipino—American population is reached. These devotions are often centered on a "Filipino" Mary, e.g. *Birhen ng Antipolo* (Our Lady of Peace and Good Voyage), Jesus, especially *Santo Niño* (Infant Jesus of Prague), or a saint. The coordinator of the novena circuit, oftentimes an older pious woman, escorts the current host and the statue to the home of the next sponsoring family. The prayers, which are recited in various languages and often lasting an hour, include a full rosary, various litanies as well as prayers to different images of Jesus and Mary and a couple of saints, e.g. St. Francis and St. Michael the Archangel. See also Glenda Tibe-Bonifacio and Vivienne SM.Angeles, "Building Communities through Faith: Filipino Catholics in Philadelphia and Alberta," in *Gender, Religion and Migration*, 262 and Helen Rose Ebaugh and Janet Chafetz, "Reproducing Ethnicity," in *Religion and the New Immigrants*, 392 for a similar home-based practice of "the visiting Mary" among Filipino women in Philadelphia and Texas respectively. The latter text also mentions the Mexican-American counterpart of this practice (in this case Our Lady of Guadalupe) which is organized by the women's group called *Guadalupanos.*

24. Keith Pecklers, S.J., "The Liturgical Year and Popular Piety," in *Directory on Popular Piety and the Liturgy: A Commentary*, ed. Peter Phan (Collegeville, MN: Liturgical Press, 2002): 87.The clergy takes its cue, of course, from the Church's official stance on popular piety, especially in relation to the Liturgy. The *Directory on Popular Piety and the Liturgy*, for example, asserts "the preeminence of the Liturgy over any other possible form of legitimate Christian prayer" as well as "the objective superiority of the Liturgy over all other forms of piety". See Congregation for Divine Worship and the Discipline of the Sacraments, *Directory on Popular Piety and the Liturgy*, no. 11, 46 <http://www.vatican.va/roman_curia/congregations/ccdds/documents/rc_con_ccdds_doc_20020513_vers-direttorio_en.html> accessed August 9, 2012.

25. See also Elizabeth McAlister, "The Madonna of 115th Street Revisited: Vodou and Haitian Catholicism in the Age of Trasnationalism," in *Gatherings in Diaspora: Religious Communities and the New Immigration*, ed. R. Stephen Warner and Judith Wittner (Philadelphia: Temple University Press, 1998): 123–160.

26. An *orisha* is a spirit or deity that reflects one of the manifestations of *Olodumare* (God in the Yoruba tradition). *Ochún*, in the meantime, is a Yoruba goddess seen in *Santería* as the patroness of Cuba. In the narrative used to counter the mainstream Catholic narrative on Our Lady of Charity as the patroness of Cuba *Ochún* is presented as the goddess who followed her African children taken to Cuba as slaves, in the process making her hair a little straighter and her skin lighter so that all Cubans, regardless of their color, could worship her. She is also often confused with Our Lady of Charity because of shared symbols e.g. water, the color yellow, sweets, money and love. What makes the shrine a magnet for *Santería* followers and Cuban Catholics who dabble in *Santería* is that the shrine is by the water (Biscayne Bay), it is facing Cuba, and yellow rose bushes and painted yellow stones encircle the left exterior of the shrine. Like *Ochún* the Virgin is also associated with fertility and love as evidenced by prayer cards in the shrine asking the Virgin for a successful pregnancy. See Thomas Tweed, "Identity and Authority at a Cuban Shrine in Miami: *Santería*, Catholicism, and Struggles for Religious Identity," *Journal of Hispanic/Latino Theology* Vol. 4, No. 1 (1996): 37–39.

27. These are especially directed to the significant number of parishioners and pilgrims who dabble in *Santería*, e.g. those who sporadically visit the *santero* (*Santería* minister) looking for good luck, health, protection or for fortune telling. See Agustin Roman, *The Popular Piety of the Cuban People* Unpublished M.A. Thesis, Barry University, 1976 as cited in Tweed, "Identity and Authority at a Cuban Shrine in Miami," 35.

28. Raul R. Gómez, "Beyond *Sarapes* and *Maracas*: Liturgical Theology in a Hispanic/Latino Context," *Journal of Hispanic Theology* Vol. 8, No. 2 (2000): 56, 58 illustrates this tendency toward superficiality as he laments how, too often, liturgy with a Hispanic/Latino dimension is approached as if all it involved was the placement of a *sarape* on the altar or the addition of *maracas* to the choir. Gomez notes that a meaningful liturgical inculturation entails the appropriation and integration of the Church's prayer by specific cultures in culturally appropriate ways.

29. While Shorter's definition of inculturation, for example, does say "culture or cultures" many definition of inculturation still reflect an understanding of inculturation as if the faith is encountering only one culture or only one group that is homogenous. Right below his definition of inculturation, for instance, Shorter quotes Pedro

NOTES   209

Arrupe's definition of inculturation which still talks of "the incarnation of Christian life and of the Christian message in **a particular cultural context...**" (emphasis mine). Pedro Arrupe, S.J., "Letter to the Whole Society on Inculturation" *Aixala* Vol. 3 (1978): 172 as quoted in Shorter, *Toward a Theology of Inculturation*, 11.

30. The case of the Italians in a Brooklyn parish illustrates this. When the procession to St. Cono in Our Lady of Mount Carmel Church in Brooklyn was revived by recent immigrants in 1973 (the procession died after World War II after the attempt by the clergy to control community celebrations) the American-born Teggianesi and the Italian-speaking devotees had problems not only with which language to use during society meetings but also with membership. At that time society membership was open only to those who could trace their roots to Teggiano, despite the fact that devotion to St. Cono had become popular among non-Teggianesi. The American St. Cono Society, which was founded in 1988, complicated relationships by opening its membership to non-Italians. Joseph Sciorra "We Go Where the Italians Live: Religious Processions as Ethnic and Territorial Markers in a Multi-Ethnic Brooklyn Neighborhood," in *Gods of the City: Religion and the American Urban Landscape*, ed. Robert Orsi (Bloomington, IN: Indiana University Press, 1999): 326.

31. Phan, "Where We Come From, Where We Are, and Where We Are Going," 9.

32. See "Filipino Migrant Workers in Hong Kong," *Asian Migrant* Vol. 7, No. 1 (January–March 1994): 7

33. See Sullivan, "St. Catherine's Catholic Church", 264.

34. Phan, "Where We Come From, Where We Are, and Where We Are Going," 15–16.

35. Phan, "Where We Come From, Where We Are, and Where We Are Going," 15–16.

36. While this may make the task look challenging one could find comfort in the fact that different cultures are not isolated but intertwined with one another. This much is true not just due to colonialism and the cultural hegemony of the West but more so because of the global cultural integration that is happening side by side with the globalization of religion, politics, and economics. Kwok Pui-Lan, "Feminist Theology as Intercultural Discourse," in *The Cambridge Companion to Feminist Theology*, ed. Susan Frank Parsons (Cambridge: Cambridge University Press, 2002): 24–25.

37. Francis, "Hispanic Liturgy in the U.S," 38.

38. Shorter, *Toward a Theology of Inculturation*, 13–16 does talk about the idea of an "interculturation" (a term coined by Bishop Joseph Blomjous in 1980). "Interculturation" would have been a good term for what I am trying to propose here. Unfortunately "interculturation" as described by Shorter and Blomjous is not exactly

the idea I am arguing for insofar as their understanding of the term only corrects the problematic impressions the term "inculturation" carries, e.g. the suggestion of a mere transfer of faith from one culture to another or the simple insertion of the Christian message into a given culture. Moreover, while Shorter does make references to "culturally heterogeneous churches" or to inculturation as "an intercultural activity with intercultural benefits" these references do not have migrant churches or the idea of an inculturation that takes into account intercultural relations.

39. Roberto Goizueta, "Reflecting on America as a Single Entity: Catholicism and U.S. Latinos," in *Many Faces, One Church: Cultural Diversity and the American Catholic Experience*, ed. Peter Phan and Diana Hayes (Lanham, MD: Sheed and Ward, 2004): 73.

40. These are the words used in Justo Gonzalez, "Hispanic Worship: An Introduction," in *Alabadle!Hispanic Christian Worship*, ed. Justo L. Gonzalez (Nashville: Abingdon Press, 1996): 20–22 to describe and explain the *fiesta* spirit of Latino worship.

41. For theology this has to do with how, for a long time, popular piety has been associated with the unlettered masses, magic, superstition, and religious ignorance which had somehow not been "christianised." For example, Ernest Henau, "Popular Religiosity and Christian Faith," in *Popular Religion*, 79 says that as a religion that is (1) lived and experienced; (2) not expressed in formulae and; (3) transmitted by means of other forms, popular religiosity leads to insights and intuitions which cannot be adequately contained within the framework of formulated logic. It can, therefore, be easily dismissed as subjective and emotive, attributes that are downplayed in mainstream theology which is highly rational and logical.

42. Virgilio Elizondo, "Popular Religion as Support of Identity based on the Mexican-American Experience in the U.S.A.," in *Spirituality of the Third World*, ed. K.C. Abraham and Bernadette Mbuy-Beya (New York: Orbis, 1994): 55–63 illustrates this.

43. As the Puebla document maintains because it is subject to sociohistorical conditions popular religion can be ambivalent. Moreover, because it is tied up with individual and collective identity it can also be the cause of the most profound alienation and oppression. It can hold people in the grip of irreversible regression and can have pathological and destructive effects. As such, Christian theology must grapple with it by judging it on its own merits. It must expose and point out the various mechanisms of oppression in Church and society, which have penetrated it, and critically distinguish the various ways of dealing with it so that its liberating potential can be surfaced. Ultimately, popular religion can give coherence and a sense of direction to life; it is a central factor in creating and maintaining individual and collective identity and could even be an expression of discipleship. Puebla

450 as cited in Norbert Greinacher and Norbert Mette, "Editorial," in *Popular Religion*, ix–x.

44. On a more focused treatment of popular religion in relation to suffering see Orlando Espin, "Popular Religion as an Epistemology (of Suffering)," *Journal of Hispanic/Latino Theology* Vol. 2, No. 2 (1994): 55–78.

45. As Cristian Parker argues it could serve as a protest against the official culture and religion and at the same time contribute to the symbolic resolution of real-life contradictions. Through it, unsatisfied longings of hope or people's deepest hopes and aspirations find expression making it a means of comfort and, at the same time, a means of protest or resistance. See Cristian Parker, "Popular Religion and Protest Against Oppression: The Chilean Example," in *Popular Religion*, 28–35.

46. Orlando Espin, *The Faith of the People: Theological Reflections on Popular Catholicism* (New York: Orbis, 1997): 92. Espin acknowledges, of course, its problematic tendencies by engaging it from a perspective of alienation and hope.

47. Ricardo Ramirez, "Liturgy from the Mexican-American Perspective," *Worship* 51 (July 1977): 296 as quoted in Matovina, "Marriage Celebrations in Mexican-American Communities," 99.

48. See Karen Mary Davalos, "The Real Way of Praying: The *Via Crucis*, Mexicano Sacred Space, and the Architecture of Domination," in *Horizons of the Sacred: Mexican Traditions in U.S. Catholicism*, ed. Timothy Matovina and Gary Riebe-Estrella (New York: Cornell University Press, 2002): 42.

49. Emphasis mine. "That moment" here naturally refers to suffering. Davalos, "The Real Way of Praying," 41.

50. This practice, as studied by Ashley in 1989–1990, emerged months after the 1988 anti-gentrification protest in the area. See Wayne Ashley, "The Stations of the Cross: Christ, Politics and Processions on New York City's Lower East Side," in *Gods of the City: Religion and the American Urban Landscape*, ed. Robert Orsi (Bloomington, IN: Indiana University Press, 1999): 341–342.

51. The emergence of an image of God which is not common in the Philippines, that is, God as a host or God of strangers offers a similar, albeit more social-psychological example. The DHs are discovering and embracing this God image in an apparent resistance to their alienation in their host society. Cruz, *An Intercultural Theology of Migration*, 99–100.

52. At DePaul University, for example, a young participant spoke about being told to study hard only to find out he cannot attend college because no government financial aid can go to undocumented students. See Michelle Martin, "Posada Draws Attention to Immigration Reform," <http://ncronline.org/news/immigration-and-church/posada-draws-attention-immigration-reform> accessed April 3, 2012.

53. Campese cites the *El Día de los Muertos* (All Souls Day), *Posada sin Fronteras* (Posada Without Borders) and *Via Crucis del Migrante* (Way of the Cross of the Migrant) that human rights and religious activists have organized and staged at the border to denounce the senseless death of so many migrants. Gioacchino Campese, "¿*Cuantos Mas*?: The Crucified Peoples at the U.S. Mexico Border," in *A Promised Land, A Perilous Journey*, 272.

54. Schreiter, "Globalization, Postmodernity and the New Catholicity," 27.

55. Emphasis mine. Michael Pasquier, "Our Lady of Prompt Succor: The Search for an American Marian Cult in New Orleans," in *Saints and Their Cults in the Atlantic World*, ed. Margaret Cormack (Columbia, S.C.: University of South Carolina Press, 2007): 129.

56. Ashley, "The Stations of the Cross," 345.

57. Francis cites as an example the suppression of local initiatives for liturgical inculturation such as the insistence that in addition to a review of the texts, decisions about translations, including punctuation and typesetting, be made by curial officials in Rome rather than on the more local levels of church that are in intimate contact with cultures. Francis, "Hispanic Liturgy in the U.S.," 52.

58. This happened in the 1940s and 1950s but the effects could still be seen today in how representatives of Mount Carmel Church, on the one hand, and of the lay society in honor of the Madonna, on the other, would skillfully avoid crossing paths as they march in two rival processions on July 16. Joseph Sciorra, "We Go Where the Italians Live: Religious Processions as Ethnic and Territorial Markers in a Multi-Ethnic Brooklyn Neighborhood," in *Gods of the City*, 326.

59. My priest friend in Georgia, for instance, shared how some of his white parishioners take issue with the accent of a fellow foreign priest, a problem my friend encountered when he was new in the parish and his English still had a heavy foreign accent.

60. Allen, *The Future Church*, 45.

61. The identifiable ethnic communities include Mexican, Peruvian, Colombian, Nigerian, Creole, African-American, Filipino, Vietnamese, Indian, Middle Eastern, Czech, and German. There are three Masses in Vietnamese, one in Spanish, and six in English. Sullivan, "St. Catherine's Catholic Church," 255.

62. Schreiter, "Globalization, Postmodernity and the New Catholicity," 24–31.

63. Schreiter cautions, however, that a new catholicity does not simply exult in a return of religion, but tries to understand the different approaches within secularity. This is worth noting here, especially in view of what may amount to an overestimation of migrants' rejuvenation of Christianity in their host countries to the point of remaining

complacent and not bothering to reach out to or engage secularists or the secular world.

64. What is arguably at the heart of these intergenerational tensions and conflicts are the serious difficulties immigrant youth experience in adjusting to American culture which often lead to identity problems. At home and in the church, authorities try to inculcate traditional ethnic values whereas society (and their "American" peers) presents a quite different set of norms and behaviors.

65. For a Protestant experience, perspective and approach see Karen Chai, "Competing for the Second Generation: English-Language Ministry at a Korean Protestant Church," in *Gatherings in Diaspora*, 295–331.

66. Phan, "Where We Come From, Where We Are, and Where We Are Going," 24.

67. Sullivan, "St. Mary's Catholic Church," 128.

68. Bundang, "May You Storm Heaven with Your Prayers," 101.

69. The conflict took its toll with the exodus of adults from the church in the late 1980s and early 1990s, particularly those associated with the traditional devotional societies. Ashley, "The Stations of the Cross," 346–347.

70. The new music included songs such as "The Age of Aquarius" from the musical *Hair*. I imagine, however, that such vociferous resistance to modern music is probably less likely (as long as it's not heavy metal or rock and roll music I guess) among the older generation in today's migrant churches. I was pleasantly surprised, for example, at hearing the congregation sing with gusto Josh Groban's pop hit "You Raise Me Up" as a communion song at a Mass in a church in Jakarta, Indonesia. Many of those in the church were expatriates or migrant workers.

71. Sociologists Rodney Stark and Alan Miller theorize that there is a "religious gender gap" whereby women are more religious than men by virtually every measure in virtually every culture. One could also see this deep association of women with religion today in the rise of laywomen serving as "pastoral leaders" of the growing number of priestless parishes, especially in the Catholic Church. See David Gibson, *The Coming Catholic Church: How the Faithful are Shaping a New American Catholicism* (New York: Harper Collins, 2003).

72. Upon the invitation of a female Sri Lankan Methodist pastor and friend of mine I attended the Sunday service of a congregation of Caribbean migrants in the Netherlands. In the homily the female pastor literally pointed out the predominantly female make-up not only of her congregation but of the Christian Church in general and how Christianity, especially migrant Christianity's future, depends a lot on women.

73. Billson's study focused on the Ukrainian women in Saskatoon, Saskatchewan. Billson also notes that some Ukrainian women see the

church as a virtual extension of the family and as another way of keeping the culture and keeping the family at the same time. Billson, *Keepers of the Culture*, 358–359.

74. Other women, in the meantime, are simply forced to conform to traditional gender roles for the sake of continuing to experience the advantages of being a member of a church. In their fieldwork with "at-risk" teenage and college-age Hispanic females involved in youth-based religious groups and activities in Protestant evangelical ministries in the Chicago area, for example, Janet S. Armitage and Rhonda E. Dugan, "Marginalized Experiences of Hispanic Females in Youth-Based Religious Groups," *Journal for the Scientific Study of Religion* Vol. 45, No. 2 (2006): 217–231 maintain that these churches simultaneously promote traditional gender roles that foster feelings of oppression. Consequently, young Latina members are forced into a difficult position to either conform and maintain connectedness to the ministry, or resist the traditional expectations and forfeit what the youth group provides to at-risk youth.

75. For example, Greek immigrant women are expected to keep the holidays as they are practiced in Greece by sticking to a specific roster of foods: roast lamb, red eggs and traditional soup for Easter, fish for Palm Sunday, *vasilopita* for New Year's Day, *prasforo* bread for Sundays after services, and *koliva* to honor the deceased. Ebaugh and Chafetz, "Reproducing Ethnicity," 398.

76. Ebaugh and Chafetz, "Reproducing Ethnicity," 399.

77. Not surprisingly, food could be a source of tension in multiethnic parishes. At a multi-ethnic Catholic church in Texas where the parish board is dominated by Anglos, other immigrant groups strongly resent the fact that they have been kept from providing ethnic foods for parish-wide events, where hot dogs and other "American" foods constitute the staples. Ebaugh and Chafetz, "Reproducing Ethnicity," 398.

78. Matovina, for example, offers a critique of Mexican-American marriage practices by pointing out the need to more clearly reflect the mutuality between the partners by (1) having the bride and groom exchange *arras* rather than the groom giving them and the bride receiving them; (2) presenting the *libro y rosario* to both the bride and the groom; (3) having the groom participate in the bouquet offering and; (4) incorporating the groom into the entrance procession so as to dispel the notion of the bride being "given" away. Matovina, "Marriage Celebrations in Mexican-American Communities," 100.

79. Pyong Gap Min, "Severe Underrepresentation of Women in Church Leadership in the Korean Immigrant Community in the United States," *Journal for the Scientific Study of Religion* Vol. 47, No. 2 (2008): 225–241 provides an example in this for the Korean-American community.

80. Francis, "Hispanic Liturgy in the U.S.," 51.
81. Change also happens, of course, in the faith of the migrants themselves. See Joaquin Jay Gonzalez, "Americanizing Philippine Churches and Filipinizing American Congregations," in *Religion at the Corner of Bliss and Nirvana: Politics, Identity and Faith in New Migrant Communities*, ed. Lois Ann Lorentzen et al., (Durham, NC: Duke University Press, 2009): 141–165.
82. Engh, "Companion of the Immigrants," 45.
83. See Patrick Hayes, "Massachusetts Miracles: Controlling Catholic Cures in Boston, 1929–1930," in *Saints and Their Cults in the Atlantic World*, 114–115, 119.
84. Bundang, "May You Storm Heaven with Your Prayers," 89.
85. Elizondo, "Popular Religion as Support of Identity based on the Mexican-American Experience in the U.S.A.," 62–63.

CHAPTER 6

1. Walter Principe, "Towards Defining Spirituality," *Studies in Religion* Vol. 12, No. 2 (1983): 139.
2. Sandra Schneiders, "The Study of Christian Spirituality," *Christian Spirituality Bulletin* Vol. 1, No. 1 (1998): 5–6.
3. Lawrence Cunningham and Keith Egan, *Christian Spirituality: Themes from the Tradition* (Mahwah, NJ: Paulist, 1996), 9.
4. Pew Research Center's Forum on Religion and Public Life, "Faith on the Move: The Religious Affiliation of International Migrants," <http://www.pewforum.org/Geography/Religious-Migration-exec.aspx> accessed November 29, 2012. See also Todd Johnson and Gina Bellofatto. "Migration, Religious Diasporas, and Religious Diversity: A Global Survey," *Mission Studies* Vol. 29, No. 1 (July 2012): 3–22.
5. Groody, *Border of Death, Valley of Life*, 17.
6. Rhacel Salazar Parrenas, *Servants of Globalization: Women, Migration and Domestic Work* (Stanford, CA: Stanford University Press, 2001), 44–47.
7. Groody, *Border of Death, Valley of Life*, 22.
8. Groody, *Border of Death, Valley of Life*, 23–24.
9. Groody, *Border of Death, Valley of Life*, 21.
10. See James Scott, *Domination and the Arts of Resistance* (New Haven, CT: Yale University, 1990) and *Weapons of the Weak: Everyday Forms of Peasant Resistance*. (New Haven, CT: Yale University Press, 1995). I have also discussed this elsewhere. See Gemma Tulud Cruz, "Weapons of the Weak: Cultural Forms of Resistance and their Implications for Missionary Theology and Practice," in *Mission and Culture: The Louis J. Luzbetak Lectures*, ed. Stephen Bevans (Maryknoll, NY: Orbis, 2012): 249–273.
11. James Scott, *Domination and the Arts of Resistance*, 14–15, 19.

12. Federation of Asian Bishops' Conferences-Office of Human Development, *Pilgrims of Progress??? A Primer of Filipino Migrant Workers in Asia* (Manila: FABC-OHD, 1994), 13.

13. The issue became known because the management did not only issue a notice which read as: "Washing oil or dirt off a Mercedes is OK, but not off a maid's feet." An article about it came out in the *South China Morning Post*. See "Atin-Atin Lamang," *TNT Hong Kong* Vol. 1, No. 3: 23.

14. Vicky, "Cook Yourself," *Tinig Filipino* (July 1992): 48 quoted in Constable, *Maid to Order in Hong Kong*, 177–178. Foreign domestic workers in Hong Kong, in general, exhibit such creativity in the comic book *Saya Migran* which raises awareness and educates every migrant worker on their various rights. See United for Foreign Domestic Workers' Rights, *Saya Migran: A Domestic Worker's Guide to Understanding and Asserting Our Rights* (Hong Kong: UFDWR, 2007). Available at <http://ufdwrs.blogspot.com.au/2009/06/saya-migran-comics.html> accessed August 3, 2012.

15. Ben Daniel, *Neighbor: Christian Encounters with "Illegal" Immigration* (Louisville, KY: WJK, 2010), 5.

16. Ana Maria Bidegain, "Living a Trans-national Spirituality: Latin American Catholic Families in Miami," in *Migration in a Global World*, 103–104.

17. Those who are in dire straits resort to lighting fires to signal for help. See Reuters, "GAO study Links Arizona Wildfires to Illegal Immigrants," <http://usnews.msnbc.msn.com/_news/2011/11/22/8955730-gao-study-links-arizona-wildfires-to-illegal-immigrants> accessed November 23, 2012.

18. Peter Mares writes that many German Lutherans who came to Adelaide, Australia to escape from religious persecution in Prussia and Silesia dropped German-sounding names. Peter Mares, *Borderline* (Sydney: University of New South Wales Press, 2002), 1.

19. Allen, *The Future Church*, 338.

20. See, for example, the story of Marcelino Manuel deGraca who became Charles M. Grace in Danielle Brune Sigler, "Daddy Grace: An Immigrant's Story," in *Immigrant Faiths*, 67.

21. To avoid discrimination on the basis of their religious practices, which were stigmatized as "superstition," Okinawans decided to send their children to Christian schools while some converted to Christianity because of perceived opportunities for social mobility. Ronald Nakasone and Susan Sered, "Ritual Transformations in Okinawan Immigrant Communities," in *Immigrant Faiths*, 87.

22. See, for example, Vivienne SM Angeles, "From Catholic to Muslim: Changing Perceptions of Gender Roles in the Balik-Islam Movement in the Philippines." Paper presented at the European Southeast Asian

Studies Conference (EUROSEAS), L'Orientale, University of Naples, Italy, September 12, 2007.

23. Lip stitching dates back to a protest in 2000 in a detention center in a remote area in northwestern Australia. Mares, *Borderline*, 10.

24. Marie Friedman Marquardt, "Structural and Cultural Hybrids: Religious Congregational Life and Public Participation of Mexicans in the New South," in *Immigrant Faiths*, 197.

25. David, *Public Lives*, 51.

26. Groody, "Jesus and the Undocumented Immigrant: A Spiritual Geography of a Crucified People," *Theological Studies* Vol. 70, No. 2 (June 2009): 303.

27. Daniel, *Neighbor*, 4.

28. David, *Public Lives*, 52.

29. Sullivan, "St. Mary's Catholic Church," 129.

30. The popular Minor Basilica of the Black Nazarene in Manila, for example, has introduced the online streaming of its hourly Masses following numerous requests from overseas Filipino workers. Jocelyn R. Uy, "Quiapo Faithful Abroad can hear Mass Online," <http://technology.inquirer.net/6205/quiapo-faithful-abroad-can-hear-mass-online>/accessed November 18, 2012.

31. Karen Richman, "The Protestant Ethic and the Dis-Spirit of Vodou," in *Immigrant Faiths*, 169.

32. Asian Migrant Workers Center, *Foreign Domestic Workers in Hong Kong: A Baseline Study* (Hong Kong: AMC, 1991), 67.

33. Eliseo Tellez Jr., "An Overview of Filipino Migrant Workers in Hong Kong," in Christian Conference of Asia, *Serving One Another* (Kowloon, H.K.: CCA Urban Rural Mission): 82.

34. Shu-Ju Ada Cheng, "Migrant Women Domestic Workers in Hong Kong, Singapore, and Taiwan: A Comparative Analysis," in *Asian Women in Migration*, ed. Graziano Battistela and Anthony Paganoni (Quezon City, Philippines: SMC, 1996): 119.

35. Chris Yeung, "A building that serves both God and mammon," *SCMP* (June 27, 1983) as quoted in Mission for Filipino Migrant Workers, *Filipino Workers: Off to Distant Shores*, (Hong Kong: MFMW, 1983), 66.

36. Groody, "Jesus and the Undocumented Immigrant," 305.

37. Pyong Gap Min, "Religion and Maintenance of Ethnicity among Immigrants: A Comparison of Indian Hindus and Korean Protestants," in *Immigrant Faiths*, 99–122. See also Pyong Gap Min, "The Structure and Social Functions of Korean Immigrant Churches in the United States," *International Migration Review* Vol. 27 (1992): 1370–1394.

38. Min, "Religion and Maintenance of Ethnicity among Immigrants," 117.

39. These are common to about 45 percent of the Korean Protestants interviewed by Min. See Min, "Religion and Maintenance of Ethnicity among Immigrants," 116–117.

40. Valtonen makes the claim based on the observation that the strongest and most resilient social links that Vietnamese have with native Finns were described best in terms of fictive kinship roles such as older brother or sister, aunt, grandparent, etcetera. Valtonen, "East Meets North," 476–477.

41. Marquardt, "Structural and Cultural Hybrids," 197.

42. Ebaugh and Chafetz, "Reproducing Ethnicity," 90–92 argue that the collective consumption of traditional foods, together with the use of native language, plays a central role in how migrant groups define cultural boundaries and reproduce ethnic identities and to the extent that women monopolize this role, they constitute a critical lynchpin in the reproduction of ethnicity within migrant congregations.

43. David, *Public Lives*, 52.

44. Eddie Gibbs and Ryan Bolger, *Emerging Churches: Creating Christian Community in Postmodern Cultures* (London: SPCK, 2006), 119.

45. Cunningham and Egan, *Christian Spirituality*, 184–185.

46. Valtonen, "East Meets North," 477, 484.

47. Bidegain, "Living a Trans-national Spirituality," 104.

48. John Macquarrie, *Paths in Spirituality* (New York: Harper and Row, 1972), 40, 47.

49. Jung Young Lee, *Marginality: The Key to Multicultural Theology* (Minneapolis, MN.: Fortress Press, 1995), 110–111.

50. Min, "Migration and Christian Hope," 197.

51. Groody, *Border of Death, Valley of Life*, 32–33. See also Groody, "Jesus and the Undocumented Immigrant," 311.

52. Groody, "Jesus and the Undocumented Immigrant," 312. Gioacchino Campese makes an eloquent case for such a perspective in "¿*Cuantos Mas?*: The Crucified Peoples at the U.S. Mexico Border," in *A Promised Land, A Perilous Journey*, 287–293 where he discusses the structural violence that migrants, especially those who are unauthorized, are subjected to.

53. Ignacio Ellacuria, "The Crucified People," in *Mysterium Liberationis: Fundamental Concepts of Liberation Theology*, ed. Ignacio Ellacuria and Jon Sobrino (Maryknoll, NY: Orbis, 1993): 590.

54. Jon Sobrino, *Jesus the Liberator: A Historical-Theological Reading of Jesus of Nazareth* (New York: Orbis, 1993), 255.

55. Groody, "Jesus and the Undocumented Immigrant," 311.

56. Frederick John Dalton, *The Moral Vision of Cesar Chavez* (New York: Orbis, 2003), 64 as quoted in Groody, "Jesus and the Undocumented Immigrant," 312.

57. Phan, "Where We Come From, Where We Are, and Where We Are Going," 25–26.

58. Robert Lasalle-Klein, "A Postcolonial Christ," in *Thinking of Christ: Proclamation, Explanation, Meaning*, ed. Tatha Wiley (New York: Continuum, 2003): 143.
59. Lasalle-Klein, "A Postcolonial Christ," 135–136.
60. Lydio F. Tomasi, "The Other Catholics" (Ph.D. dissertation, New York University, 1978), 301 as quoted in Groody, "Jesus and the Undocumented Immigrant," 316.
61. Jon Sobrino, *The Principle of Mercy: Taking the Crucified People from the Cross* (Maryknoll, NY: Orbis Books, 1994), 30.
62. Robert Egan, "The Mystical and the Prophetic: Dimensions of Christian Existence," *The Way* (Supplement, 2002): 92–106. See also Philip Sheldrake, "Christian Spirituality as a Way of Living Publicly: A Dialectic of the Mystical and Prophetic," *Spiritus: A Journal of Christian Spirituality* Vol. 3, No. 1 (2003): 19–37.
63. Rev. Chad M. Rimmer, "Prospects for Ecumenism in the 21st Century: Towards an Ecumenical Theology of the Wilderness," <http://www.oikoumene.org/en/programmes/the-wcc-and-the-ecumenical-movement-in-the-21st-century/relationships-with-member-churches/60th-anniversary/contest/essay-towards-an-ecumenical-theology-of-the-wilderness.html> accessed November 28, 2012. For a similar theological reflection in the context of migrant journeys along the southern border of the US see Alex Nava, "God in the Desert: Searching for the Divine in the Midst of Death," in *A Promised Land, A Perilous Journey*, 65–67.
64. Elizabeth Amoah, "A Living Spirituality Today," in *Spirituality of the Third World*, 51.
65. Ivone Gebara, "A Cry for Life from Latin America," in *Spirituality of the Third World*, 115–116.
66. Lee, *Marginality*, 110–116.
67. William Cavanaugh, *Migrations of the Holy: God, State and the Political Meaning of the Church* (Grand Rapids, MI: Eerdmans, 2011), 69–87.
68. Rev. Marga Janete Ströher, "People Are Made To Shine—Not To Suffer," in World Council of Churches, *The Prophetic Mission of Churches in Response to Forced Displacement of People*, Report of a Global Ecumenical Consultation, Addis Ababa, November 6–11, 1995 (Geneva: World Council of Churches, 1996): 50.
69. Silvano Tomasi, "The Prophetic Mission of the Churches," in *The Prophetic Mission of Churches in Response to Forced Displacement of Peoples*, 40.
70. Min, "Migration and Christian Hope," 196.
71. Groody, *Globalization, Spirituality and Justice*, 243.
72. Michael Downey, *Understanding Christian Spirituality* (Mahwah, NJ: Paulist, 1997), 14.
73. Weekends, especially Sundays in the Central District of Hong Kong, when migrant domestic workers occupy almost every nook and cranny

of the Central District illustrate this. Gillian Youngs, "Breaking patriarchal bonds: Demythologizing the public/private," in *Gender and Global Structuring: Sightings, Sites, and Resistances*, ed. Marianne H. Marchand and Anne Sisson Runyan (London: Routledge, 2003): 51, 54 even considers this successful and dramatic claim to high—profile public space as one of those rare "sightings" of gender resistance in the context of global restructuring or globalization especially in the way it represents a disruption of public/private divides.

74. Phan, "Where We Come From, Where We Are, and Where We Are Going," 25.

75. See Delores Williams, *Sisters in the Wilderness: The Challenge of Womanist God-Talk* (Maryknoll, NY: Orbis, 1993).

76. See Ada Maria Isasi-Diaz, *En la lucha (In The Struggle): Elaborating a mujerista theology* (Minneapolis, MN: Fortress Press, 1993) especially 16–22.

77. See Anthony Kelly, *Eschatology and Hope* (Maryknoll, NY: Orbis, 2006).

78. A substantial part of the encyclical is devoted to a discussion on faith-based hope. See *Spe Salvi*, nos. 2–9, 24–50.

79. See *Spe Salvi*, nos. 32–34.

80. Groody, *Globalization, Spirituality and Justice*, 249–250.

81. Frank Chikane echoes this symbiotic relationship between action and contemplation. Chikane maintains there is no spirituality outside of acts in the struggle for celebration; the acts of worship become acts of celebration, meditation and reflection on these struggles. Frank Chikane, "Spirituality of the Third World: Conversion and Commitment," in *Spirituality of the Third World*, 180.

82. Groody, *Globalization, Spirituality and Justice*, 250.

83. Phan, "Where We Come From, Where We Are, and Where We Are Going," 25–26.

84. Karl-Josef Kuschel, "The Destructive and Liberating Power of Laughter: Anthropological and Theological Aspects," *Concilium* 4 (2000): 119. See also Karl-Josef Kuschel, *Laughter. A Theological Reflection*, trans. John Bowden (London, SCM Press, 1994).

85. Jacqueline Bussie's study of what she calls "the laughter of the oppressed" as expressed in Elie Wiesel's *God's Mistake*, Shusaku Endo's *Silence*, and Toni Morrison's *Beloved* is helpful in this regard. Bussie argues that laughter increases our consciousness of faith since faith is born of the very stuff that also engenders laughter, namely contradictions, incongruity, and paradox. Bussie also contends that laughter reflects and heightens our consciousness of hope since life is a conflict between two narratives: the narrative of reason/reality and the narrative of faith, the narrative of facts and the narrative of longing. This collision can lead to despair or hope but when it leads to hope that hope is heroic but appears to many eyes as madness.

Jacqueline Bussie, *The Laughter of the Oppressed: Ethical and Theological Resistance in Wiesel, Morrison, and Endo* (New York: T & T Clark: 2007), 187.

86. Karl-Josef Kuschel, *Laughter: A Theological Reflection*, 133. Gerald Arbuckle also sheds light on the theological significance of laughter. Arbuckle maintains that although humor and laughter are non-confrontational styles of critiquing an oppressive situation they are effective as they are often able to portray fraud, hypocrisy, and injustice far more powerfully and emotively than the written word. Humor's subversive quality, for example, is its most important function according to Arbuckle as it deflates pomposity and undermines the rigidity of the status quo. When humor pokes fun at the oppressive stringencies and conventions of society people have the chance to re-imagine alternative ways of behaving. Arbuckle, *Laughing With God*, 13.

87. Cunningham and Egan, *Christian Spirituality*, 185.

88. Cunningham and Egan, *Christian Spirituality*, 12–13.

89. Thomas Aquinas, *Summa Theologiae* 3.73.2. As posted on <http://www.op.org/summa/letter/summa-IIIq73a2.pdf> accessed December 26, 2012.

90. Cunningham and Egan, *Christian Spirituality*, 14.

91. Christian spirituality in itself cannot be limited to an exclusively individualistic "care of the soul." It is found and nourished in community.

92. Philip Sheldrake, *Spirituality and History* (New York: Crossroad, 1992), 50.

93. See, for example, Peter Damian Belisle, *The Language of Silence: The Changing Face of Monastic Solitude* (Maryknoll, NY: Orbis, 2003); Columba Stewart, *Prayer and Community: The Benedictine Tradition* (Maryknoll, NY: Orbis, 1998); Jon Sobrino, *Spirituality of Liberation: Toward Political Holiness* (Maryknoll, NY: Orbis, 1988); Donald Dorr, *Integral Spirituality: Resources for Community, Justice, Peace and the Earth* (Melbourne, Australia: Collins Dove, 1990); Judith Plaskow and Carol Christ, ed., *Weaving the Visions: New Patterns in Feminist Spirituality* (New York: HarperOne, 1989) and; Chris Klassen, ed. *Feminist Spirituality: The Next Generation* (Lanham, MD: Lexington, 2009).

CONCLUSION

1. Daniel Groody, "Fruit of the Vine and Work of Human Hands: Immigration and the Eucharist," in *A Promised Land, A Perilous Journey*, 305.

2. Jose David Rodriguez, "The Parable of the Affirmative Action Employer," *Apuntes* Vol. 15, No. 5 (1988): 424.

3. *A Stranger at Our Gates: A Christian Perspective on Immigration*, Resolution adopted at a General Conference, 1996, The Evangelical Free Church of America <http://www.gum.org/download/EvangelicalFree-GeneralConferenceonImmigration-1996.pdf> accessed December 5, 2012.

4. In the story everyone was instructed to get only what one needs for the day. Those who hoarded did not benefit from their extra picking as the manna became rotten and smelly, hence inedible. Such an arrangement ensures that no one gets hungry, no one has an undue advantage by having extra food, and everyone is able to partake in the food.

5. Another story in the Bible, which highlights the importance of bread and sharing, tells of a man who goes knocking at his friend's house in the middle of the night to ask for three loaves of bread to give to a friend in need, who happens to be "on a journey" or a visitor (Luke 11:5–8).

6. This idea is echoed in Romans 12:4–5: "Just as each of us has one body with many members, and these members do not all have the same function, so in Christ we who are many form one body, and each member belongs to all the others." It is also mentioned or referred to several times in the Bible, for example, Eph. 1:22–23; Eph. 5:29–30; Col. 1:18; Col. 3:15.

7. Benedict VXI echoes this point in *Caritas in Veritate*:

> We are all witnesses of the burden of suffering, the dislocation and the aspirations that accompany the flow of migrants. The phenomenon, as everyone knows, is difficult to manage; but there is no doubt that foreign workers, despite any difficulties concerning integration, make a significant contribution to the economic development of the host country through their labor, besides that which they make to their country of origin through the money they send home. (CV, 62)

8. Min, "Migration and Christian Hope," 190–191.

9. Min, "Migration and Christian Hope," 194–195.

10. See Luis Rivera Pagan, "Xenophobia or Xenophilia: Towards a Theology of Migration," *The Ecumenical Review* Vol. 64, No. 4 (December 2012): 575–589.

11. Min, "Migration and Christian Hope," 187, 189.

12. Eleazar S. Fernandez, *Reimagining the Human: Theological Anthropology of Response to Systemic Evil* (St. Louis, MO: Chalice Press, 2004), 187–188.

13. For a more comprehensive treatment of this idea in the context of migration, see Sister Stephanie Spandl, "One Family Under God: A Theological Reflection on Serving our Immigrant Brothers and Sisters as Christian Social Workers," <http://www.nacsw.org/

Publications/Proceedings2008/SpandlSOne.pdf> accessed January 28, 2013.

14. A similar treatment of the Trinitarian dimension of migration is offered by Fabio Baggio, "Diversity in Trinitarian Communion: Pointers Toward a Theology of Migrations," in *Migration in a Global World*, 74–85.

15. Cunningham and Egan, for example, point out that the deepest meaning of Catholic spirituality is a discipleship that concerns the universal (catholic) needs of the world and that our common way of discipleship is best understood as being part of the pilgrim people of God. Cunningham and Egan, *Christian Spirituality*, 19.

16. Schreiter, "Catholicity as Framework for Addressing Migration," 41–46.

17. See Kristin Heyer, "Reframing Displacement and Membership: Ethics of Migration," *Theological Studies* Vol. 73, No. 1 (March 2012): 188–206.

18. Min, "Migration and Christian Hope," 191.

19. An eloquent representation of this idea in pictures is depicted by internationally renowned photographer Sebastião Salgado in photographs taken over seven years and across more than 35 countries. This 432-page book is a first-of-its kind pictorial survey to extensively chronicle the current global flux of humanity by documenting the epic displacement of the world's people at the close of the twentieth century. See Sebastião Salgado, *Migrations: Humanity in Transition* (New York: Aperture, 2000).

20. Anthony Rogers, FSC, "Towards Globalising Solidarity Through Faith Encounters In Asia," in *The Migrant Family in Asia: Reaching Out and Touching Them*, ed. Anthony Rogers, FSC (Manila: Office for Human Development, 2007): 68–71. Daniel Groody describes a dramatic liturgical depiction of the idea of one bread, one body of people. This is the annual Eucharistic celebration among Mexicans and Americans on the southern border on November 1. It is auspiciously the Day of the Dead for the Mexicans and liturgically the feast of All Saints. What makes the scene compelling is that a 16-foot iron fence divides the community in two (one half in Mexico and the other half in the United States) and an altar joining them in the middle. Groody, who has made a documentary on it, correctly observes that "the ritual is one of the most powerful testimonies of God's universal, undivided and unrestricted love for all people" and that "it speaks of the gift and challenge of Christian faith and the call to feed the world's hunger for peace, justice and reconciliation." Daniel Groody, "Dying to Live: The Undocumented Immigrant and the Paschal Mystery," in *Migration in a Global World*, 113.

BIBLIOGRAPHY

BOOKS AND MONOGRAPHS

Allen, John. *The Future Church: How Ten trends Are Revolutionizing the Catholic Church* (New York: Doubleday, 2009).

Amaladoss, Michael. *The Church and Pluralism in the Asia of the 1990s: FABC Papers No. 57e* (Hong Kong: FABC, 1990).

Amnesty International. *South Korea: Disposable Labor, Rights of Migrant Workers in South Korea* (London: Amnesty International, 2009).

Aquino, Maria Pilar. *Our Cry for Life: Feminist Theology from Latin America* (New York: Orbis, 1993).

Arbuckle, Gerald. *Laughing With God: Humor, Culture, and Transformation* (Collegeville, MN: Liturgical Press, 2008).

Asian Migrant Workers Center. *Foreign Domestic Workers in Hong Kong: A Baseline Study* (Hong Kong: AMC, 1991).

Bacon, David. *Illegal People: How Globalization Creates Migration and Criminalizes Immigrants* (Boston, MA: Beacon Press, 2008).

Bado, Arsene Brice. *Dignity Across Borders: Forced Migration and Christian Social Ethics* (Denver, CO: Outskirts Press, 2011).

Belisle, Peter Damian. *The Language of Silence: The Changing Face of Monastic Solitude* (Maryknoll, NY: Orbis, 2003).

Billson, Janet Mancini. *Keepers of the Culture: The Power of Tradition in Women's Lives* (New York: Lexington Books, 1995).

Brettell, Caroline and James Hollifield eds. *Migration Theory: Talking Across Disciplines* (New York: Routledge, 2000).

Brodman, James William. *Charity and Religion in Medieval Europe* (Washington, DC: Catholic University of America Press, 2009).

Brooks, Ann. *Gendered Work in Asian Cities: The New Economy and Changing Labour Markets* (Hampshire: Ashgate, 2006).

Burghardt, Walter. *Justice: A Global Adventure* (New York: Orbis, 2004).

Bussie, Jacqueline. *The Laughter of the Oppressed: Ethical and Theological Resistance in Wiesel, Morrison, and Endo* (New York: T & T Clark: 2007).

Carroll, M. Daniel. *Christians at the Border: Immigration, the Church and the Bible* (Grand Rapids, MI: Baker Academic, 2008).

Carroll, Peter N. *Puritanism and the Wilderness: The Intellectual Significance of the New England Frontier, 1629–1700* (New York: Columbia University Press, 1969).

Castles, Stephen and Mark J. Miller. *The Age of Migration: International Population Movements in the Modern World* 4th edition (New York: The Guilford Press, 2009).

Cavanaugh, William. *Migrations of the Holy: God, State and the Political Meaning of the Church* (Grand Rapids, MI: Eerdmans, 2011).

Chacón, Justin Akers and Mike Davis. *No One Is Illegal* (Chicago, IL: Haymarket Books, 2006).

Chang, Grace. *Disposable Domestics: Immigrant Women Workers in the Global Economy* (Cambridge, MA: South End Press, 2000).

Chittister, Joan. *The Story of Ruth: Twelve Moments in Every Woman's Life* (Ottawa: Novalis, 2000).

Chomsky, Aviva. *They Take Our Jobs!: and 20 Other Myths About Immigration* (Boston: Beacon Press, 2007).

Coleman, John. *Globalization and the Common Good: Present Crisis, Future Hope* (New York: Orbis, 2005).

Constable, Nicole. *Maid to Order in Hong Kong: Stories of Filipina Workers* (Ithaca, NY: Cornell University Press, 1997).

Cruz, Gemma Tulud. *An Intercultural Theology of Migration: Pilgrims in the Wilderness* (Leiden: Brill, 2010).

Cunningham, Lawrence and Keith Egan. *Christian Spirituality: Themes from the Tradition* (Mahwah, NJ: Paulist, 1996).

Curran, Charles. *Catholic Social Teaching 1891-Present: A Historical, Theological and Ethical Analysis* (Washington, D.C.: Georgetown University Press, 2002).

Daniel, Ben. *Neighbor: Christian Encounters with "Illegal" Immigration* (Louisville, KY: WJK, 2010).

David, Randy. *Public Lives: Essays on Selfhood and Social Solidarity* (Pasig City: Anvil Publishing, 1998).

Diaz, Ada Maria Isasi. *En la lucha (In the Struggle): Elaborating a Mujerista Theology* (Minneapolis: Fortress Press, 1993).

Dorr, Donald. *Integral Spirituality: Resources for Community, Justice, Peace and the Earth* (Melbourne, Australia: Collins Dove, 1990).

Downey, Michael. *Understanding Christian Spirituality* (Mahwah, NJ: Paulist, 1997).

Ebaugh, Helen Rose and Janet Saltman Chafetz. *Religion and the New Immigrants: Continuities and Adaptations in Immigrant Congregations* (Walnut Creek, CA: Altamira Press, 2000).

——. *Religion across Borders: Transnational Religious Networks* (Walnut Creek, CA: Altamira Press, 2002).

Eck, Diana. *A New Religious America: How a "Christian Country" Has Become the World's Most Religiously-Diverse Nation* (Harper One: San Francisco, 2002).

Episcopal Commission for the Pastoral Care of Migrants and Itinerant People. *Migration 2002: Situationer and Impact, Biblical Inspiration, Pastoral Challenges* (Manila, Phils.: ECMI-CBCP, 2002).

Espin, Orlando. *The Faith of the People: Theological Reflections on Popular Catholicism* (New York: Orbis, 1997).

Farley, Margaret. *Just Love: A Framework for Christian Sexual Ethics* (New York: Continuum, 2010).

Federation of Asian Bishops' Conferences-Office of Human Development. *Pilgrims of Progress??? A Primer of Filipino Migrant Workers in Asia* (Manila: FABC-OHD, 1994).

Fernandez, Carmen Nanko. *Theologizing en Spanglish* (Maryknoll, NY: Orbis Books, 2010).

Fernandez, Eleazar. *Reimagining the Human: Theological Anthropology of Response to Systemic Evil* (St. Louis, MO: Chalice Press, 2004).

Fletcher, Jeanine Hill. *Monopoly on Salvation?: A Feminist Approach to Religious Pluralism* (New York: Continuum, 2005).

Frazier, Elizabeth Conde. *Listen to the Children: Conversations with Immigrant Families* (Valley Forge, PA: Judson Press, 2011).

Gamburd, Michelle. *The Kitchen Spoon's Handle: Transnationalism and Sri Lanka's Migrant Housemaids* (Ithaca, NY: Cornell University Press, 2000).

Gibbs, Eddie and Ryan Bolger. *Emerging Churches: Creating Christian Community in Postmodern Cultures* (London: SPCK, 2006).

Gibson, David. *The Coming Catholic Church: How the Faithful are Shaping a New American Catholicism* (New York: Harper Collins, 2003).

Giddens, Anthony. *The Runaway World: How Globalization Is Shaping Our Lives* (London: Routledge, 2000).

Gill, Jerry. *Borderland Theology* (Washington, D.C.: EPICA, 2003).

González, Justo L. *Santa Biblia: The Bible through Hispanic Eyes* (Nashville: Abingdon, 1996).

Gowing, Peter G. *Understanding Islam and Muslims in the Philippines* (Manila: New Day Publishers, 1988).

Groody, Daniel. *Border of Death, Valley of Life: An Immigrant Journey of Heart and Spirit* (Lanham, MD: Rowman and Littlefield, 2002).

——. *Globalization, Spirituality, and Justice: Navigating the Path to Peace* (Maryknoll, NY: Orbis, 2007).

Guild, Elspeth. *Security and Migration in the 21st Century* (Cambridge: Polity Press, 2009).

Hagan, Jacqueline Maria. *Migration Miracle: Faith, Hope and Meaning on the Undocumented Journey* (Cambridge, M.A.: Harvard University Press, 2008).

Hanciles, Jehu. *Beyond Christendom: Globalization, African Migration and the Transformation of the West* (New York: Orbis, 2008).

Hardwick, Susan Wiley. *Russian Refuge: Religion, Migration and Settlement on the North American Pacific Rim* (Chicago, IL: University of Chicago Press, 1993).

Haywood, John. *The Great Migrations: From the Earliest Humans to the Age of Globalization* (London: Quercus, 2009).

Heyer, Kristin. *Kinship Across Borders: A Christian Ethic of Immigration* (Washington, DC: Georgetown University Press, 2012).

Heyward, Carter. *The Redemption of God: A Theology of Mutual Relation* (New York: University Press of America, 1982).

Hick, John. *God and the Universe of Faiths: Essays in the Philosophy of Religion* (London: Macmillan Press, 1973).

Hill, Brennan. *The Ongoing Renewal of Catholicism* (Winnona, MN: St. Mary's Press, 2008).

Hollifield, James and Caroline Brettell. eds. *Migration Theory: Talking Across Disciplines* (New York: Routledge, 2000).

Hondagneu-Sotelo, Pierette. *God's Heart Has No Borders: How Religious Activists Are Working for Immigrant Rights* (Berkeley, CA: University of California Press, 2008).

International Organization for Migration. *World Migration Report 2010: The Future of Migration: Building Capacities for Change* (Geneva: IOM, 2010).

———. *World Migration Report 2011: Communicating Effectively About Migration* (Geneva: IOM, 2011).

Isherwood, Lisa and Dorothea McEwan. *Introducing Feminist Theology* (Sheffield: Sheffield Academic Press, 2001).

Jenkins, Philip. *The Next Christendom: The Coming of Global Christianity* (Oxford: Oxford University Press, 2003).

Johnson, Paul. *Diaspora Conversions: Black Carib Religion and the Recovery of Africa* (Berkeley, CA: University of California Press, 2007).

Joselit, Jenna Weissman. *A Parade of Faiths: Immigration and American Religion* (New York: Oxford University Press, 2007).

Kelly, Anthony. *Eschatology and Hope* (Maryknoll, NY: Orbis, 2006).

Kerwin, Donald and Jill Marie Gerschutz. *And You Welcomed Me: Migration and Catholic Social Teaching* (Lanham, MD: Lexington Books, 2009).

Kivisto, Peter and Thomas Faist. *Beyond a Border: The Causes and Consequences of Contemporary Immigration* (Thousand Oaks, CA: Pine Forge Press, 2010).

Klassen, Chris. ed. *Feminist Spirituality: The Next Generation* (Lanham, MD: Lexington, 2009).

Kneebone, Susan. ed. *Refugees, Asylum Seekers and the Rule of Law: Comparative Perspectives* (Cambridge, MA: Cambridge University Press, 2009).

Koenig, John. *New Testament Hospitality: Partnership with Strangers as Promise and Mission* (Philadelphia, PA: Fortress Press, 1985).

Kristeva, Julia. *Strangers to Ourselves*, Trans. Leon S. Roudiez (New York: Columbia University Press, 1991).

Kuschel, Karl-Josef. *Laughter. A Theological Reflection*, Trans. John Bowden (London, SCM Press, 1994).

Lee, Jung Young. *Marginality: The Key to Multicultural Theology* (Minneapolis, MN: Fortress Press, 1995).

Levitt, Peggy. *The Transnational Villagers* (Berkley, CA: University of California Press, 2001).

Lewis, Donald. ed. *Christianity Reborn: The Global Expansion of Evangelicalism in the Twentieth Century* (Grand Rapids, MI: Eerdmans, 2004).

Lorentzen, Lois Ann et al., eds. *Religion at the Corner of Bliss and Nirvana: Politics, Identity and Faith in New Migrant Communities* (Durham, NC: Duke University Press, 2009).

Louis, William Roger. *The British Empire in the Middle East, 1945–1951: Arab Nationalism, the United States and Postwar Imperialism* (New York: Oxford University Press, 1984).

Macquarrie, John. *Paths in Spirituality* (New York: Harper and Row, 1972).

Maimbo, Samuel Munzele et al., *Migrant Labor Remittances in South Asia* (Washington, DC: The World Bank, 2005).

Marcel, Gabriel. *Homo Viator: Introduction to a Metaphysic of Hope*, trans., E. Crauford (New York: Harper and Row, 1966).

Mares, Peter. *Borderline* (Sydney: University of New South Wales Press, 2002).

Massaro, Thomas. *Living Justice: Catholic Social Teaching in Action* (Lanham, MD: Rowman and Littlefield, 2012).

May, Melanie. *A Body Knows: Theopoetics of Death and Resurrection* (New York: Continuum, 1995).

Mayotte, Judy. *Disposable People: The Plight of Refugees* (Maryknoll, NY: Orbis Books, 1992).

McBrien, Richard. *Catholicism* (New York: Harper Collins, 1994).

Mercado, Leonardo. *Filipino Popular Devotions: The Interior Dialogue Between Traditional Religion and Christianity* (Manila, Phils: Logos, 2000).

Min, Anselm, *Dialectic of Salvation: Issues in Theology of Liberation* (Albany, NY: State University of New York Press, 1989).

Mission for Filipino Migrant Workers. *Filipino Workers: Off to Distant Shores*, (Hong Kong: MFMW, 1983).

Ogletree, Thomas. *Hospitality to the Stranger: Dimensions of Moral Understanding* (Philadelphia: Fortress Press, 1985).

Olupona, Jacob and Regina Gemignani. *African Immigrant Religions in America* (New York: New York University Press, 2007).

Ormerod, Neil and Shane Clifton. *Globalization and the Mission of the Church* (New York: T & T Clark, 2010).

Papastergiadis, Nikos. *The Turbulence of Migration: Globalization, Deterritorialization, and Hybridity* (Cambridge: Polity Press, 2000).

Parrenas, Rhacel Salazar. *Servants of Globalization: Women, Migration and Domestic Work* (Stanford, CA: Stanford University Press, 2001).

Pickering, Sharon. *Women, Borders and Violence: Current Issues in Asylum, Forced Migration and Trafficking* (New York: Springer, 2010).

Plaskow, Judith and Carol Christ, eds. *Weaving the Visions: New Patterns in Feminist Spirituality* (New York: Harper One, 1989).

Pohl, Christine. *Making Room: Recovering Hospitality as a Christian Tradition* (Grand Rapids, MI: Wm B. Eerdmans Publishing Company, 1999).

Pistone, Michele and John Hoeffner. *Stepping Out of the Brain Drain: Applying Catholic Social Teaching in a New Era of Migration* (Lanham, MD: Lexington Books, 2007).

Portier, William. *Tradition and Incarnation* (New York: Paulist Press, 1993).

Rawls, John. *Political Liberalism* (New York, NY: Columbia University Press, 1993).

Riley, Maria. *Trouble and Beauty: Women Encounter Catholic Social Teaching* (Washington D.C.: Center for Concern, 1992).

Robertson, Roland. *Globalization: Social Theory and Global Culture* (London: Sage Publications, 1992).

Ruether, Rosemary Radford. *Christianity and Social Systems: Historical Constructions and Ethical Challenges* (Lanham, MD: Rowman and Littlefield, 2009).

—— and Eugene Bianchi. *From Machismo to Mutuality: Essays on Sexism and Woman-Man Liberation* (Mahwah, NJ: Paulist Press, 1976).

Russell, Letty. *Household of Freedom: Authority in Feminist Theology* (Philadelphia: The Westminster Press, 1987).

——. *Just Hospitality: God's Welcome in a World of Difference* (Louisville, KY: WJK Press, 2009).

Salgado, Sebastião. *Migrations: Humanity in Transition* (New York: Aperture, 2000).

Sassen, Sasskia. *Globalization and its Discontents* (New York: Columbia University Press, 1998).

Schreiter, Robert J. *The New Catholicity: Theology Between the Global and the Local* (Maryknoll, NY: Orbis Books, 1997).

Schüssler-Fiorenza, Elisabeth. *Discipleship of Equals: A Critical Feminist Ekklesia-Logy of Liberation* (New York: Crossroad, 1993).

Scott, James. *Domination and the Arts of Resistance* (New Haven, CT: Yale University, 1990).

——. *Weapons of the Weak: Everyday Forms of Peasant Resistance* (New Haven, CT: Yale University Press, 1995).

Sheldrake, Philip. *Spirituality and History* (New York: Crossroad, 1992).

Shorter, Aylward. *Toward a Theology of Inculturation* (Eugene, OR: Wipf and Stock, 2006).

Snyder, Sussana. *Asylum-Seeking, Migration and Church* (Burlington, VT: Ashgate, 2012).

Sobrino, Jon. *Spirituality of Liberation: Toward Political Holiness* (Maryknoll, NY: Orbis, 1988).

——. *Jesus the Liberator: A Historical-Theological Reading of Jesus of Nazareth* (New York: Orbis, 1993).

——. *The Principle of Mercy: Taking the Crucified People from the Cross* (Maryknoll, NY: Orbis Books, 1994).

——. *Witnesses of the Kingdom: The Martyrs of El Salvador and the Crucified Peoples* (Maryknoll, NY: Orbis, 2003).

Soerens, Matthew and Jenny Hwang. *Welcoming the Stranger: Justice, Compassion and Truth in the Immigration Debate* (Downer's Grove, IL: Intervarsity Press, 2009).

Solimano, Andrés. *International Migration in the Age of Crisis and Globalization: Historical and Recent Experiences* (Cambridge: Cambridge University Press, 2010).

Spencer, Linbert. *Building a Multi-ethnic Church* (London: SPCK, 2007).

Stewart, Columba. *Prayer and Community: The Benedictine Tradition* (Maryknoll, NY: Orbis, 1998).

Swidler, Leonard. *After the Abslolute: The Dialogical Future of Religious Reflection* (Minneapolis: Fortress Press, 1990).

Tenaganita. *The Revolving Door: Modern Day Slavery Refugees* (Kuala Lumpur, Malaysia: Tenaganita, 2008).

ter Haar, Gerrie. *Halfway to Paradise: African Christians in Europe* (Cardiff: Cardiff Academic Press, 1998).

Tunstall, Kate, ed. *Displacement, Asylum, Migration: Oxford Amnesty Lectures* (Oxford: Oxford University Press, 2006).

Tweed, Thomas and Stephen Prothero. *Asian Religions in America: A Documentary History* (New York: Oxford University Press, 1998).

United Nations Department of Economic and Social Affairs. *International Migration 2009* (New York, NY: UN, 2009).

United Nations. *The Millennium Development Goals Report 2012* (New York, NY: United Nations, 2012).

Vertovec, Steven and Ceri Peach. eds. *Islam in Europe: The Politics of Religion and Community* (London: Palgrave, 1997).

Volf, Miroslav. *Exclusion and Embrace: A Theological Exploration of Identity, Otherness and Reconciliation* (Nashville, TN: Abingdon Press, 1996).

Vuola, Elina. *Limits of Liberation: Feminist Theology and the Ethics of Poverty and Reproduction* (New York: Sheffield Academic Press, 2002).

Weintraub, Sidney and Sergio Diaz-Briquets. *Migration, Remittances, and Small Business Development: Mexico and Carribean Basin Countries* (Boulder, CO: Westview Press, 1991).

Welch, Sharon. *A Feminist Ethic of Risk* (Minneapolis, MN: Fortress Press, 2000).

Williams, Delores. *Sisters in the Wilderness: The Challenge of Womanist God-Talk* (Maryknoll, NY: Orbis, 1993).

Wilson, John P. and Boris Drozdek. eds. *Broken Spirits: The Treatment of Traumatized Asylum Seekers, Refugees and War and Torture Victims* (London: Routledge, 2004).

World Council of Churches. *A Moment to Choose: Risking to Be With Uprooted People* (Geneva: WCC, 1996).

ARTICLES IN BOOKS AND JOURNALS

Abella, Manolo and Lin Lean Lim. "The Movement of People in Asia: Internal, Intra-regional and International Migration," in Christian Conference of Asia, *Uprooted People in Asia* (Hong Kong: CCA, 1995): 11–36.

Aldrich, Lou S.J. "A Critical Evaluation of the Migrant Workers' Situation in Taiwan in Light of the Catholic Social Tradition," in *Faith on the*

Move: Toward a Theology of Migration in Asia, ed. Fabio Baggio and Agnes Brazal (Manila, Phils.: Ateneo de Manila University Press, 2008): 49–67.

Amoah, Elizabeth. "A Living Spirituality Today," in *Spirituality of the Third World*, ed. K.C. Abraham and Bernadette Mbuy-Beya (Maryknoll, NY: Orbis Books, 1994): 50–54.

Anghie, Tony and Wayne McCormack. "The Rights of Aliens: Legal Regimes and Historical Perspectives," in *Migration in the 21st Century*, ed. Thomas N. Maloney and Kim Korinek (London: Routledge, 2011): 23–53.

Anõnuevo, Mai Dizon. "Revisiting Migrant Women's Lives: Stories of Struggles, Failures, and Successes," in *Coming Home: Women, Migration and Reintegration*, ed. Estrella Dizon-Anõnuevo and Augustus T. Anõnuevo (Quezon City, Philippines: Balikbayani Foundation and the ATIKHA Overseas Workers and Communities Initiative, Inc., 2002): 17–29.

Antone, Hope S. "Asian Women and the Globalization of Labor," *The Journal of Theologies and Cultures in Asia* Vol. 2 (2003): 97–111.

Appleby, Kevin. "The Role of the Catholic Church in Immigrant Integration," *The Review of Faith and International Affairs* Vol. 9, No. 1 (Spring 2011): 67–70.

Aquino, Maria Pilar. "The Feminist Option for Poor and Oppressed in the Context of Globalization," in *The Option for the Poor in Christian Theology*, ed. Daniel Groody (Notre Dame, IN: University of Notre Dame Press, 2007): 191–215.

Armitage, Janet S. and Rhonda E. Dugan. "Marginalized Experiences of Hispanic Females in Youth-Based Religious Groups," *Journal for the Scientific Study of Religion* Vol. 45, No. 2 (2006): 217–231.

Ashley, Wayne. "The Stations of the Cross: Christ, Politics and Processions on New York City's Lower East Side" in *Gods of the City: Religion and the American Urban Landscape*, ed. Robert Orsi (Bloomington, IN: Indiana University Press, 1999): 341–366.

Asis, Maruja. "Caring for the World: Filipino Domestic Workers Gone Global," in *Asian Women as Transnational Domestic Workers*, ed. Shirlena Huang, Brenda S. Yeoh and Noor Abdul Rahman (Singapore: Marshall Cavendish, 2005): 21–53.

——. "Philippines," *Asian and Pacific Migration Journal* Vol. 17, Nos. 3–4 (2008): 349–378.

Athukoraia, Premachnadra. "The Use of Migrant Remittances in Development: Lessons from the Asian Experience," *Journal of International Development* Vol. 4, No. 5 (1992): 511–529.

Atkinson, Joseph. "Family as Domestic Church: Developmental Trajectory, Legitimacy and Problems of Appropriation," *Theological Studies* Vol. 66, No. 3 (September 2005): 592–604.

Baggio, Fabio. "Diversity in Trinitarian Communion: Pointers Toward a Theology of Migrations," in *Migration in a Global World*, ed. Solange Lefebvre and Luis Carlos Susin, Concilium 2008/5 (London: SCM Press): 74–85.

—— "The Migrant Ministry: A Constant Concern for the Catholic Church," *Asian Christian Review* Vol. 4, No. 2 (Winter 2010): 47–69.

Battistella, Graziano. "Irregular Migration: Issues from the Asian Experience," in Pontifical Council for the Pastoral Care of Migrants and Itinerant People, *Migration at the Threshold of the Third Millennium: Proceedings of the IV World Congress on the Pastoral Care of Migrants and Refugees*, Vatican, 5–10 October 1998: 144–166.

——. "The Human Rights of Migrants: A Pastoral Challenge," in *Migration, Religious Experience and Globalization*, ed. Gioacchino Campese and Pietro Ciallella (New York: Center for Migration Studies, 2003): 76–102.

——. "Migration and Human Dignity," in *A Promised Land, A Perilous Journey:Theological Perspectives on Migration*, ed. Daniel Groody and Gioacchino Campese (Notre Dame, IN: University of Notre Dame Press, 2008): 177–191.

——. "The Poor in Motion: Reflections on Unauthorized Migration," *Asian Christian Review* Vol. 4, No. 2 (Winter 2010): 70–81.

Bedford-Strohm, Heinrich. "Responding to the Challenges of Migration and Flight from a Perspective of Theological Ethics," in Churches' Commission for Migrants in Europe, *Theological Reflections on Migration: A CCME Reader* (Brussels: CCME, 2008): 38–46.

Bevans, Stephen. "Mission *among* Migrants, Mission *of* Migrants," in *A Promised Land, A Perilous Journey: Theological Perspectives On Migration*, ed. Daniel Groody and Gioacchino Campese (Notre Dame, IN: University of Notre Dame Press, 2008): 89–106.

Bidegain, Ana María. "Living a Trans-national Spirituality: Latin American Catholic Families in Miami," in *Migration in a Global World*, ed. Solange Lefebvre and Luis Carlos Susin, Concilium 2008/5 (London: SCM Press): 95–107.

Blume, Michael S.V.D. "Migration and the Social Doctrine of the Church," in *Migration, Religious Experience and Globalization*, ed. Gioacchino Campese and Pietro Ciallella (New York: Center for Migration Studies, 2003): 62–75.

Bouma-Prediger, Steven. "Environmental Racism," in *Handbook of U.S. Theologies of Liberation*, ed. Miguel de la Torre (St. Louis, MO: Chalice Press, 2004): 281–287.

Brennan, Frank. "Human Rights as a Challenge to National Policies that Exclude Refugees: Two Case Studies from Southeast Asia," in *Driven from Home: Protecting the Rights if Forced Migrants*, ed. David Hollenbach (Washington, D.C.: Georgetown University Press, 2010): 97–114.

Brubaker, Pamela. "Reforming Global Economic Policies," in *Justice in a Global Economy: Strategies for Home, Community and World*, ed. Pamela K. Brubaker, Rebecca Todd Peters and Laura A. Stivers (Louisville, KY: WJK Press, 2006): 127–139.

Bundang, Rachel. "May You Storm Heaven with Your Prayers: Devotions to Mary and Jesus in Filipino-American Catholic Life," in *Off the Menu: Asian and Asian North American Women's Religion and Theology*, ed. Rita Nakashima Brock et al. (Louisville: WJK Press, 2007): 87–105.

Cahill, Lisa. "Justice, Gender, and the Market," in *Outside the Market No Salvation*, ed. Dietmar Mieth and Marciano Vidal, Concilium 1997/2 (London: SCM Press): 133–142.

——. "Family and Catholic Social Teaching," in *Change in Official Catholic Moral Teaching: Readings in Moral Theology No. 13*, ed. Charles E. Curran (New York: Paulist, 2003): 253–268.

——. "Marriage: Developments in Catholic Theology and Ethics," *Theological Studies* Vol. 64, No. 1 (March 2003): 78–105.

—— "Commentary on *Familiaris Consortio*," in *Modern Catholic Social Teaching: Commentaries and Interpretations*, ed. Kenneth Himes (Washington, DC: Georgetown University Press, 2005): 363–388.

Campese, Gioacchino. "¿*Cuantos Mas*?: The Crucified Peoples at the U.S. Mexico Border," in *A Promised Land, A Perilous Journey: Theological Perspectives On Migration*, ed. Daniel Groody and Gioacchino Campese (Notre Dame, IN: University of Notre Dame Press, 2008): 271–298.

——. "The Irruption of Migrants: Theology of Migration in the 21st Century," *Theological Studies* Vol. 73, No. 1 (March 2012): 3–32.

Chai, Karen. "Competing for the Second Generation: English-Language Ministry at a Korean Protestant Church," in *Gatherings in Diaspora: Religious Communities and the New Immigration*, ed. R. Stephen Warner and Judith Wittner (Philadelphia, PA: Temple University Press, 1998): 295–331.

Chang, Man Wai and Yvonne Darlington. " 'Astronaut Wives: Perceptions of Changes in Family Roles," *Asian and Pacific Migration Journal* Vol. 17, No. 1 (2008): 61–77.

Cheng, Shu-Ju Ada. "Migrant Women Domestic Workers in Hong Kong, Singapore, and Taiwan: A Comparative Analysis," in *Asian Women in Migration*, ed. Graziano Battistela and Anthony Paganoni (Quezon City, Philippines: SMC, 1996): 109–122.

Chikane, Frank. "Spirituality of the Third World: Conversion and Commitment," in *Spirituality of the Third World*, ed. K.C. Abraham and Bernadette Mbuy-Beya (Maryknoll, NY: Orbis Books, 1994): 173–181.

Coleman, John A. S.J. "Making the Connections: Globalization and Catholic Social Thought," in *Globalization and Catholic Social Thought: Present Crisis, Future Hope*, ed. John A. Coleman, S.J. and William F. Ryan, S.J. (Ottawa: Novalis, 2005): 9–27.

Cooper, Catherine R. and Rebecca Burciaga. "Pathways to College, to the Professoriate, and to a Green Card: Linking Research, Policy, and Practice on Immigrant Latino Youth," in *Migration in the 21st Century: Rights, Outcomes and Policy*, ed. Thomas N. Maloney and Kim Korinek (London: Routledge, 2011): 177–191.

Copeland, M. Shawn. "Interaction of Racism, Sexism and Classism in Women's Exploitation," in *Women, Work, and Poverty*, ed. Elisabeth Schüssler Fiorenza and Anne Carr, Concilium 194 (London: SCM Press, 1987): 19–27.

Crusemann, Frank. " 'You Know the Heart of the Stranger' (Exodus 23:9): A Recollection of the Torah in the Face of New Nationalism and Xenophobia," in *Migrants and Refugees*, ed. Dietmar Mieth and Lisa Sowle Cahill, Concilium 1993/4 (London: SCM Press): 95–109.

Cruz, Gemma Tulud. "Weapons of the Weak: Cultural Forms of Resistance and their Implications for Missionary Theology and Practice," in *Mission and Culture: The Louis J. Luzbetak Lectures*, ed. Stephen Bevans (Maryknoll, NY: Orbis, 2012): 249–273.

Danesi, P. Giacomo. "Towards a Theology of Migration," in World Council of Churches, *Church and Migration: WCC Fifth Assembly Dossier No. 13* (Geneva: WCC Migration Secretariat, 1981): 10–41.

Davalos, Karen Mary. "The Real Way of Praying: The *Via Crucis*, Mexicano Sacred Space, and the Architecture of Domination," in *Horizons of the Sacred: Mexican Traditions in U.S. Catholicism*, ed. Timothy Matovina and Gary Riebe-Estrella (Ithaca, NY: Cornell University Press, 2002): 41–68.

De Anda, Neomi. "Border Cuentos: Sources for Reflections on Migration," *New Theology Review* Vol. 20, No. 3 (August 2007): 24–35.

Douglas, Thomas J. "Changing Religious Practices Among Cambodian Immigrants in Long Beach and Seattle," in *Immigrant Faiths: Transforming Religious Life in America*, ed. Karen Leonard et al. (Lanham, MD: Altamira Press, 2005): 123–144.

Ebaugh, Helen Rose and Janet Saltzman Chafetz. "Introduction," in *Religion and the New Immigrants: Continuities and Adaptations in Immigrant Congregations*, ed. Helen Rose Ebaugh and Janet Saltman Chafetz (Walnut Creek, CA: Altamira Press, 2000): 3–16.

——. "Reproducing Ethnicity," in *Religion and the New Immigrants: Continuities and Adaptations in Immigrant Congregations*, ed. Helen Rose Ebaugh and Janet Saltman Chafetz (Walnut Creek, CA: Altamira Press, 2000): 80–99.

Egan, Robert. "The Mystical and the Prophetic: Dimensions of Christian Existence," *The Way* (Supplement, 2002): 92–106.

Ellacuria, Ignacio. "The Crucified People," in *Mysterium Liberationis: Fundamental Concepts of Liberation Theology*, ed. Ignacio Ellacuria and Jon Sobrino (Maryknoll, NY: Orbis, 1993): 580–603.

Elizondo, Virgilio. "Popular Religion as Support of Identity based on the Mexican-American Experience in the U.S.A.," in *Spirituality of the Third World*, ed. K.C. Abraham and Bernadette Mbuy-Beya (New York: Orbis, 1994): 55–63.

——. "Living Faith: Resistance and Survival," in *Mestizo Worship: A Pastoral Approach to Liturgical Ministry*, ed. Virgilio P. Elizondo and Timothy Matovina (Collegeville, MN: Liturgical Press, 1998): 5–21.

——. " 'Transformation of Borders': Border Separation or New Identity," in *Theology: Expanding the Borders*, ed. Maria Pilar Aquino and Roberto S. Goizueta (Mystic, CT: Twenty-Third Publications, 1998): 22–39.

Emmer, Pieter. "'We are Here Because You were There': European Colonialism and Intercontinental Migration," in *Migrants and Refugees*, ed. Dietmar Mieth and Lisa Sowle Cahill, Concilium 1993/4 (London: SCM Press): 42–51.

Engh, Michael S.J. "Companion to Immigrants: Devotion to Our Lady of Guadalupe among Mexicans in the Los Angeles Area, 1900–1940," *Journal of Hispanic/Latino Theology* Vol. 5, No. 1 (1997): 37–47.

Espin, Orlando. "Popular Religion as an Epistemology (of Suffering)," *Journal of Hispanic/Latino Theology* Vol. 2, No. 2 (1994): 55–78.

Fernandez-Kelly, Patricia. "Facts and Fictions of Unauthorized Immigration to the US," in *Migration in the 21st Century: Rights, Outcomes and Policy*, ed. Thomas N. Maloney and Kim Korinek (London: Routledge, 2011): 192–201.

Fiorenza, Elisabeth Schüssler. "The Endless Day: Introduction," in *Women, Work, and Poverty*, ed. Elisabeth Schüssler Fiorenza and Anne Carr, Concilium 194 (London: SCM Press, 1987): xvii–xxiii.

Fiorenza, Francis Schüssler. "Redemption," in *The New Dictionary of Theology*, ed. Joseph A. Komonchak, Mary Collins and Dermot A Lane (Dublin: Gill and Macmillan, 1987): 836–851.

Firer-Hinze, Christine. "Bridge Discourse on Wage Justice: Roman Catholic and Feminist Perspectives on the Family Living Wage," in *Feminist Ethics and the Catholic Moral Tradition*, ed. Charles Curran, Margaret Farley and Richard McCormick (New York: Paulist, 1996): 511–540.

Fletcher, Jeanine Hill. "Religious Pluralism in an Era of Globalization: The Making of Modern Religious Identity," *Theological Studies* Vol. 69, No. 8 (June 2008): 394–411.

Foroutan, Yaghoob. "Migration and Gender Roles: The Typical Work Pattern of the MENA Women," *International Migration Review* Vol. 43, No. 4 (Winter 2009): 974–992.

Francis, Mark C.S.V. "Hispanic Liturgy in the U.S.: Toward a New Inculturation," *Journal of Hispanic/Latino Theology* Vol. 8, No. 2 (2000): 33–54.

Fredericks, James. "The Catholic Church and the Other Religious Paths: Rejecting Nothing That Is True and Holy," *Theological Studies* Vol. 64, No. 2 (June 2003): 225–254.

Gebara, Ivone. "A Cry for Life from Latin America," in *Spirituality of the Third World*, ed. K.C. Abraham and Bernadette Mbuy-Beya (Maryknoll, NY: Orbis Books, 1994): 109–118.

George, Sheba. "Caroling with the Keralites: The Negotiation of Gendered Space in an Indian Immigrant Church," in *Gatherings in Diaspora: Religious Communities and the New Immigration*, ed. R. Stephen Warner and Judith Wittner (Philadelphia, PA: Temple University Press, 1998): 265–294.

Go, Stella. "International Labor Migration and the Filipino Family: Examining the Social Dimensions," *Asian Migrant* Vol. 14, No. 4 (Oct.–Dec. 2001): 103–109.

Goizueta, Roberto. "Reflecting on America as a Single Entity: Catholicism and U.S. Latinos," in *Many Faces, One Church: Cultural Diversity and the American Catholic Experience*, ed. Peter Phan and Diana Hayes (Lanham, MD: Sheed and Ward, 2004):69–82.

Gómez, Raul R. "Beyond *Sarapes* and *Maracas*: Liturgical Theology in a Hispanic/Latino Context," *Journal of Hispanic Theology* Vol. 8, No. 2 (2000): 55–71.

Gonzales-Butron, Maria Arcelia. "The Effects of Free-market Globalization on Women's Lives," in *Globalization and its Victims*, ed. Jon Sobrino and Felix Wilfred. Concilium 2001/5 (London: SCM Press): 43–50.

Gonzalez, Joaquin Jay. "Americanizing Philippine Churches and Filipinizing American Congregations," in *Religion at the Corner of Bliss and Nirvana: Politics, Identity and Faith in New Migrant Communities*, ed. Lois Ann Lorentzen et al. (Durham, NC: Duke University Press, 2009):141–165.

Gonzalez, Justo. "Hispanic Worship: An Introduction," in *Alabadle!Hispanic Christian Worship*, ed. Justo L. Gonzalez (Nashville: Abingdon Press, 1996): 9–28.

Graham, Elaine. "Gender," in *An A-Z of Feminist Theology*, ed. Lisa Isherwood and Dorothea McEwan (Sheffield: Sheffield Academic Press, 1996): 78–80.

Greinacher, Norbert and Norbert Mette. "Editorial," in *Popular Religion*, ed. Norbert Greinacher and Norbert Mette, Concilium 186 (London: T &T Clark, 1986): ix–xi.

Groody, Daniel. "Fruit of the Vine and Work of Human Hands: Immigration and the Eucharist," in *A Promised Land, A Perilous Journey: Theological Perspectives on Migration*, ed. Daniel Groody and Gioacchino Campese (Notre Dame, IN: University of Notre Dame Press, 2008): 299–315.

——. "Dying to Live: The Undocumented Immigrant and the Paschal Mystery," in *Migration in a Global World*, ed. Solange Lefebvre and Luiz Carlos Susin Concilium 2008/5 (London: SCM Press): 108–117.

——. "Crossing the Divide: Foundations of a Theology of Migration and Refugees," *Theological Studies* Vol. 70, No. 3 (September 2009): 638–677.

——. "Jesus and the Undocumented Immigrant: A Spiritual Geography of a Crucified People," *Theological Studies* Vol. 70, No. 2 (June 2009): 298–316.

Gudorf, Christine. "Encountering the Other: The Modern Papacy on Women," in *Change in Official Catholic Moral Teaching: Readings in Moral Theology No. 13*, ed. Charles E. Curran (New York: Paulist, 2003): 269–284.

Gutierrez, Gustavo. "Memory and Prophecy," in *The Option for the Poor in Christian Theology*, ed. Daniel G. Groody (Notre Dame, IN: University of Notre Dame Press, 2007): 17–38.

——. "Poverty, Migration, and the Option for the Poor," in *A Promised Land, A Perilous Journey: Theological Perspectives on Migration*, ed. Daniel Groody and Gioacchino Campese (Notre Dame, IN: University of Notre Dame Press, 2008): 76–86.

Hagan, Jacqueline Maria. "The Church vs. the State: Borders, Migrants, and Human Rights," in *Religion and Social Justice for Immigrants* ed. Pierrette Hondagneu-Sotelo (New Brunswick, NJ: Rutgers University Press, 2007): 96–101.

——. "Faith for the Journey: Religion as a Resource for Migrants," in *A Promised Land, A Perilous Journey: Theological Perspectives On Migration*, ed. Daniel Groody and Gioacchino Campese (Notre Dame, IN: University of Notre Dame Press, 2008): 3–19.

Hanciles, Jehu J. "Migration and Mission: Some Implications for the Twenty-first Century Church," *International Bulletin of Missionary Research* Vol. 27, No. 4 (October 2003):146–53.

Hanlon Rubio, Julie. "The Dual Vocation of Christian Parents," *Theological Studies* Vol. 63, No. 4 (December 2002): 786–812.

Harvey, William S. "British and Indian Scientists in Boston Considering Returning to their Home Countries," *Population, Space and Place* Vol. 15 (2009): 1–16.

Hayes, Patrick. "Massachusetts Miracles: Controlling Catholic Cures in Boston, 1929–1930," in *Saints and Their Cults in the Atlantic World*, ed. Margaret Cormack (Columbia, SC: University of South Carolina Press, 2007): 111–127.

Heaney-Hunter, Joanne. "Domestic Church: Guiding Beliefs and Daily Practices," in *Christian Marriage: Contemporary Theological and Pastoral Perspectives*, ed. Michael G. Lawler and William P. Roberts (Collegeville: Liturgical Press, 1996): 59–78.

Henau, Ernest. "Popular Religiosity and Christian Faith," in *Popular Religion*, ed. Norbert Greinacher and Norbert Mette, Concilium 186 (London: T &T Clark, 1986): 71–81.

Heyer, Kristin "Social Sin and Immigration: Good Fences Make Bad Neighbors," *Theological Studies* Vol. 71, No. 2 (June 2010): 410–436.

——. "Reframing Displacement and Membership: Ethics of Migration," *Theological Studies* Vol. 73, No. 1 (March 2012): 188–206.

Hilkert, Mary Catherine. "The Option for the Poor in the Context of Globalization: A Feminist Vision," in *The Option for the Poor in Christian Theology*, ed. Daniel Groody (Notre Dame, IN: University of Notre Dame Press, 2007): 228–237.

Himes, Kenneth O.F.M. "Introduction," in *Modern Catholic Social Teaching: Commentaries and Interpretations*, ed. Kenneth O.F.M. Himes (Washington, D.C.: Georgetown University Press, 2004): 1–6.

——. "Globalization with a Human Face: Catholic Social Teaching and Globalization," *Theological Studies* Vol. 69, No.2 (June 2008): 269–289.

—— and James Coriden. "The Indissolubility of Marriage: Reasons To Reconsider," *Theological Studies* Vol. 65, No. 3 (September 2004): 453–499.

Hoang, Linh. "Crossing and Dwelling: Hospitality in a Theology of Migration," *Asian Christian Review* Vol. 4, No. 2 (Winter 2010): 82–97.

Hondagneu-Sotelo, Pierette and Ernestine Avila. "'I'm Here, But I'm There': The Meaning of Latina Transnational Motherhood," *Gender and Society*, Vol. 11, No. 5 (1997): 548–571.

Hoover, Robin. "The Story of Humane Borders," in *A Promised Land, A Perilous Journey: Theological Perspectives On Migration*, ed. Daniel Groody and Gioacchino Campese (Notre Dame, IN: University of Notre Dame Press, 2008): 160–173.

Huguet, Jerold W. "Towards a Migration Information System in Asia: Statistics and the Public Discourse on International Migration," *Asian and Pacific Migration Journal*, Vol. 17, Nos. 3–4 (2008): 231–255.

Húwelmeier, Gertrud. "Female Believers on the Move: Vietnamese Pentecostal Networks in Germany" in *Gender, Religion and Migration: Pathways to Integration*, ed. Glenda Tibe Bonifacio and Vivienne SM. Angeles (Lanham, MD: Lexington Books, 2010): 115–131.

Isasi-Diaz, Ada Maria. "A Hispanic Garden in a Foreign Land," in *Inheriting Our Mothers' Gardens*, ed. Letty Russell et al. (Philadelphia: Westminster Press, 1988): 91–106.

———. "Solidarity: Love of Neighbor in the 21st Century," in *Lift Every Voice: Constructing Christian Theologies from the Underside*, ed. Susan Brooks Thislethwaite and Mary Potter Engel (Maryknoll, NY: Orbis Books, 2004): 30–39.

Jachimowicz, Maia and Deborah W. Meyers. "Executive Summary," in *Women Immigrants in the United States Conference Proceedings*, ed. Philippa Strum and Danielle Tarantolo (Washington, DC: Woodrow Wilson International Center for Scholars, 2002): 1–6.

Jacob, Simon and Pallavi Thakur. "Jyothi Hindu Temple: One Religion, Many Practices," in *Religion and the New Immigrants: Continuities and Adaptations in Immigrant Congregations*, ed. Helen Rose Ebaugh and Janet Saltman Chafetz (Walnut Creek, CA: Altamira Press, 2000): 151–162.

Joh, W. Anne. "Relating to Household Labor Justly," in *Justice in a Global Economy: Strategies for Home, Community and the World*, ed. Pamela K. Brubaker, Rebecca Todd Peters and Laura Stivers (Louisville, KY: Westminster John Knox Press, 2006): 29–39.

Johnson, Todd and Gina Bellofatto. "Migration, Religious Diasporas, and Religious Diversity: A Global Survey," *Mission Studies* Vol. 29, No. 1 (July 2012): 3–22.

Kanapathy, Vijayakumari. "Malaysia," *Asian and Pacific Migration Journal* Vol. 17, No. 3–4 (2008): 335–347.

Ketelers, Johann. "Migrants To and From Asia, And Their Families: Responses To New Challenges in Advocacy," in *The Migrant Family in Asia: Reaching Out and Touching Them*, ed. Anthony Rogers, FSC (Manila, Phils: Office for Human Development, 2007): 121–132.

Kratz, Bridget. "Libertarianism and Catholic Social Teaching on Immigration," *Journal of Markets and Morality* Vol. 15, No. 1 (Spring 2012): 21–36.

Kroeger, James M.M. "The Faith-Culture Dialogue in Asia: Ten FABC Insights on Inculturation," *East Asian Pastoral Review* Vol. 45, No. 3 (2008): 239–260.

——. "Living Faith in a Strange Land: Migration and Interreligious Dialogue," in *Faith on the Move: Toward a Theology of Migration in Asia*, ed. Fabio Baggio and Agnes Brazal (Manila, Phils.: Ateneo de Manila University Press, 2008): 219– 251.

Kuschel, Karl-Josef. "The Destructive and Liberating Power of Laughter: Anthropological and Theological Aspects," *Concilium* Vol. 4 (2000): 114–121.

Kwok, Pui-Lan. "Feminist Theology as Intercultural Discourse," in *The Cambridge Companion to Feminist Theology*, ed. Susan Frank Parsons (Cambridge: Cambridge University Press, 2002): 23–39.

Lacocque, A. "The Stranger in the Old Testament," in *World Council of Churches and Migration: WCC Fifth Assembly Dossier No. 13* (Geneva: WCC Migration Secretariat, 1981): 49–59.

Lancee, Bram. "The Economic Returns of Immigrants' Bonding and Bridging Social Capital: The Case of the Netherlands," *International Migration Review* Vol. 44, No. 1 (Spring 2010): 202–226.

LaRousse, William M.M. "Migration and Mission," in *Faith on the Move: Toward a Theology of Migration in Asia*, ed. Fabio Baggio and Agnes Brazal (Manila, Phils.: Ateneo de Manila University Press, 2008): 155–176.

Lasalle-Klein, Robert. "A Postcolonial Christ," in *Thinking of Christ: Proclamation, Explanation, Meaning*, ed. Tatha Wiley (New York: Continuum, 2003): 135–153.

Leddy, Mary Jo. "When the Stranger Summons: Spiritual and Theological Considerations for Ministry," *New Theology Review* Vol. 20, No. 3 (August 2007): 5–14.

Llanos, Christopher S.J. "Refugees or Economic Migrants: Catholic Thought on the Moral Roots of the Distinction" in *Driven from Home: Protecting the Rights of Forced Migrants*, ed. David Hollenbach, S.J. (Washington, D.C.: Georgetown University Press, 2010): 249–269.

Loughry, Maryanne. "The Experience of Displacement by Conflict: The Plight of Iraqi Refugees," *Driven from Home: Protecting the Rights of Forced Migrants*, ed. David Hollenbach, S.J. (Washington, D.C.: Georgetown University Press, 2010): 169–183.

Lussi, Carmem. "Human Mobility as a Theological Consideration" in *Migration in a Global World*, ed. Solange Lefebvre and Luis Carlos Susin, Concilium 2008/5 (London: SCM Press): 49–60.

Machado, Daisy. "The Unnamed Woman: Justice, Feminists, and the Undocumented Woman," in *Religion and Justice: A Reader in Latina Feminist Theology*, ed. Maria Pilar Aquino et.al. (Austin, TX: University of Texas, 2002): 161–176.

——. "Promoting Solidarity with Migrants," in *Justice in a Global Economy: Strategies for Home, Community and the World*, ed. Pamela K. Brubaker,

Rebecca Todd Peters and Laura Stivers (Louisville, KY: Westminster John Knox Press, 2006):115–126.

Maldonado, Luis. "Popular Religion: Its Dimensions, Levels and Types," in *Popular Religion*, ed. Norbert Greinacher and Norbert Mette, Concilium 186 (London: T &T Clark, 1986): 3–11.

Marchetto, Agostino. "The Migrant Family: Challenges Today and the Way Forward for the Church," in *The Migrant Family in Asia: Reaching Out and Touching Them*, ed. Anthony Rogers, FSC (Manila, Phils: Office for Human Development, 2007): 13–27.

Marquardt, Marie Friedman. "Structural and Cultural Hybrids: Religious Congregational Life and Public Participation of Mexicans in the New South," in *Immigrant Faiths: Transforming Religious Life in America*, ed. Karen Leonard et al. (Lanham, MD: Altamira Press, 2005): 189–218.

Marrujo, Olivia Ruiz. "Immigrants at Risk, Immigrants as Risk: Two Paradigms of Globalization," in *Migration, Religious Experience and Globalization*, ed. Gioacchino Campese and Pietro Ciallella (New York: Center for Migration Studies, 2003): 17–28.

——. "The Gender of Risk: Sexual Violence against Undocumented Women," in *A Promised Land, A Perilous Journey: Theological Perspectives On Migration*, ed. Daniel Groody and Gioacchino Campese (Notre Dame, IN: University of Notre Dame Press, 2008): 225–239.

Matovina, Timothy. "Marriage Celebrations in Mexican-American Communities," in *Mestizo Worship: A Pastoral Approach to Liturgical Ministry*, ed.Virgilio P. Elizondo and Timothy Matovina (Collegeville, MN: Liturgical Press, 1998): 93–102.

McAlister, Elizabeth. "The Madonna of 115th Street Revisited: Vodou and Haitian Catholicism in the Age of Trasnationalism," in *Gatherings in Diaspora: Religious Communities and the New Immigration*, ed. R. Stephen Warner and Judith Wittner (Philadelphia, PA: Temple University Press, 1998): 123–160.

McCann, Dennis. "Catholic Social Teaching in an Era of Economic Globalization," *Business Ethics Quarterly* Vol. 7, No. 2 (1997): 57–70.

McKay, Deidre. "Filipinas in Canada: Deskilling as a Push toward Marriage," in *Wife or Worker: Asian Women and Migration*, ed. Nicola Piper and Mina Roces (Lanham, MD: Rowman and Littlefield, 2003): 23–52.

——. "Success Stories?: Filipina Migrant Domestic Workers in Canada," in *Asian Women as Transnational Domestic Workers*, ed. Shirlena Huang, Brenda S. Yeoh and Noor Abdul Rahman (Singapore: Marshall Cavendish, 2005): 305–340.

Menjivar, Cecilia. "Serving Christ in the Borderlands: Faith Workers Respond to Border Violence," in *Religion and Social Justice for Immigrants*, ed. Pierrette Hondagneu-Sotelo (New Brunswick, NJ: Rutgers University Press, 2007): 110–115.

Min, Anselm. "Migration and Christian Hope," in *Faith on the Move: Towards a Theology of Migration in Asia*, ed. Fabio Baggio and Agnes Brazal (Quezon City, Phils: Ateneo de Manila University Press, 2008): 177–202.

Min, Pyong Gap. "The Structure and Social Functions of Korean Immigrant Churches in the United States," *International Migration Review* Vol. 27 (1992): 1370–1394.

———. "Religion and Maintenance of Ethnicity among Immigrants: A Comparison of Indian Hindus and Korean Protestants," in *Immigrant Faiths: Transforming Religious Life in America*, ed. Karen Leonard et al. (Lanham, MD: Altamira Press, 2005): 99–122.

———. "Severe Underrepresentation of Women in Church Leadership in the Korean Immigrant Community in the United States," *Journal for the Scientific Study of Religion* Vol. 47, No. 2 (2008): 225–241.

Moghadam, Valentine. "Gender Aspects of Employment and Unemployment in a Global Perspective," in *Global Employment: An International Investigation into the Future of Work*, ed. Mihaly Simai, Valentine M. Moghadam, and Arvo Kuddo (London and Tokyo: Zed Books and UNU Press, 1995): 111–139.

Morokvasic, Mirjana. "Birds of Passage are also Women," *International Migration Review* Vol. 18, No. 4 (Winter 1984): 886–907.

Müller, Dennis. "A Homeland for Transients: Towards and Ethic of Migrations," in *Migrants and Refugees*, ed. Dietmar Mieth and Lisa Sowle Cahill, Concilium 1993/4 (London: SCM Press): 130–147.

Nakamatsu, Tomoku. "International Marriage though Introduction Agencies: Social and Legal Realities of 'Asian' Wives of Japanese Men," in *Wife or Worker: Asian Women and Migration*, ed. Nicola Piper and Mina Roces (Lanham, MD: Rowman and Littlefield, 2003): 181–202.

Nakasone, Ronald and Susan Sered. "Ritual Transformations in Okinawan Immigrant Communities," in *Immigrant Faiths: Transforming Religious Life in America*, ed. Karen Leonard et al. (Lanham, MD: Altamira Press, 2005): 79–98.

Nava, Alex. "God in the Desert: Searching for the Divine in the Midst of Death," in *A Promised Land, A Perilous Journey: Theological Perspectives On Migration*, ed. Daniel Groody and Gioacchino Campese (Notre Dame, IN: University of Notre Dame Press, 2008): 62–75.

Neil, Bronwen and Pauline Allen. "Displaced Peoples: Reflections from Late Antiquity on a Contemporary Crisis," *Pacifica* Vol. 24 (February 2011): 29–42.

Nguyen, vanThanh SVD. "Asia in Motion: A Biblical Reflection on Migration," *Asian Christian Review* Vol. 4, No. 2 (Winter 2010): 18–31.

Nowrojee, Binaifer. "Sexual Violence, Gender Roles and Displacement" in *Refugee Rights: Ethics, Advocacy, and Africa*, ed. David Hollenbach (Washington, DC: Georgetown University Press, 2008): 125–136.

Okure, Teresa. "Africa: A Refugee Camp Experience," in *Migrants and Refugees*, ed. Dietmar Mieth and Lisa Sowle Cahill, Concilium 1993/4 (London: SCM Press): 12–21.

O'Neill, William S.J. and William C. Spohn. "Rights of Passage: The Ethics of Immigration and Refugee Policy," *Theological Studies* Vol. 59, No. 1 (1998): 84–106.

Opiniano, Jeremiah. "Social Capital and the Development Potential of Migration in Barangay Sta. Rosa," in *Coming Home: Women, Migration and Reintegration*, ed. Estrella Dizon- Anonuevo and Augustus T. Anonuevo (Manila, Phils: ATIKHA, 2002):152–168.

Osaki, Keiko. "Economic Interactions of Migrants and their Household of Origin: Are Women More Reliable Supporters," *Asian and Pacific Migration Journal* Vol. 8, No. 4 (1999): 447–471.

Packers, Corinne, Vivien Runnels and Ronald Labonté. "Does the Migration of Health Workers Bring Benefits to the Countries They Leave Behind?" in *The International Migration of Health Workers*, ed. Rebecca S. Shah (London: Palgrave, 2010): 44–61.

Painadath, Sebastian S.J. "Federation of Asian Bishops' Conferences' Theology of Dialogue," in *Dialogue?: A Resource Manual for Catholics in Asia*, ed. Edmund Chia (Bangkok: Federation of Asian Bishops' Conferences, 2001): 102–105.

Parreñas, Rhacel Salazar. "The Gender Paradox in the Transnational Families of Filipino Migrant Women," *Asian and Pacific Migration Journal* Vol. 14, No. 3 (2005): 243–268.

Parker, Cristian. "Popular Religion and Protest Against Oppression: The Chilean Example," in *Popular Religion*, ed. Norbert Greinacher and Norbert Mette, Concilium 186 (London: T &T Clark, 1986): 28–35.

Pasquier, Michael. "Our Lady of Prompt Succor: The Search for an American Marian Cult in New Orleans," in *Saints and Their Cults in the Atlantic World*, ed. Margaret Cormack (Columbia, SC: University of South Carolina Press, 2007): 128–149.

Pecklers, Keith S.J. "The Liturgical Year and Popular Piety," in *Directory on Popular Piety and the Liturgy: A Commentary*, ed. Peter Phan (Collegeville, MN: Liturgical Press, 2002): 77–100.

Phan, Peter. "Multiple Religious Belonging: Opportunities and Challenges for Theology and Church," *Theological Studies* Vol. 64, No. 3 (September 2003): 495–519.

——. "Where We Come From, Where We Are, and Where We Are Going: Asian and Pacific Catholics in the United States," *American Catholic Studies* Vol. 118, No. 3 (2007): 1–26.

Pohl, Christine. "Responding to Strangers: Insights from the Christian Tradition," *Studies in Christian Ethics* Vol. 19, No. 1 (2006): 81–101.

Portes, Alejandro. "Immigration Theory for a New Century: Some Problems and Opportunities," in *The Handbook of International Migration: The American Experience*, ed. Charles Hirschman, Philip Kasinitz, and Josh deWind (New York: Russell Sage Foundation, 1999): 21–33.

Portes, Alejandro et al. "Bridging the Gap: Transnational and Ethnic Organizations in the Political Incorporation of Immigrants in the United States," in *Migration in the 21st Century: Rights, Outcomes and Policy*, ed. Thomas N. Maloney and Kim Korinek (London: Routledge, 2011): 126–157.

Principe, Walter. "Towards Defining Spirituality," *Studies in Religion* Vol. 12, No. 2 (1983): 127–141.

Purcell, Mike. "Christ the Stranger: The Ethical Originality of Homelessness," in *Migration in a Global World*, ed. Solange Lefebvre and Luis Carlos Susin, Concilium 2008/5 (London: SCM Press): 61–73.

Richard, Pablo. "A Theology of Life: Rebuilding Hope from the Perspective of the South," in *Spirituality of the Third World*, ed. K.C. Abraham and Bernadette Mbuy-Beya (Maryknoll, NY: Orbis Books, 1994): 92–108.

Richman, Karen. "The Protestant Ethic and the Dis-Spirit of Vodou," in *Immigrant Faiths: Transforming Religious Life in America*, ed. Karen Leonard et al. (Lanham, MD: Altamira Press, 2005): 165–187.

Riley, Maria. "Reception of Catholic Social Teaching among Christian Feminists," in *Rerum Novarum: One Hundred Years of Catholic Social Teaching*, ed. John Coleman and Gregory Baum, Concilium 1991/5 (London: SCM Press): 105–118.

——. "Feminist Analysis: A Missing Perspective," in *John Paul II and Moral Theology: Readings in Moral Theology No. 10*, ed. Charles Curran and Richard McCormick (New York: Paulist Press, 1998): 276–290.

Rivera Pagan, Luis. "Xenophobia or Xenophilia: Towards a Theology of Migration," *The Ecumenical Review* Vol. 64, No. 4 (December 2012): 575–589.

Robb, Carol S. "Principles for a Woman-Friendly Economy," *Journal of Feminist Studies in Religion* Vol. 9, No. 1–2 (Spring/Fall 1993): 147–160.

Rodriguez, Jeanette. "Devotion to Our Lady of Guadalupe Among Mexican-Americans," in *Many Faces, One Church: Cultural Diversity and the American Catholic Experience*, ed. Peter Phan and Diana Hayes (Lanham, MD: Rowman and Littlefield, 2004): 83–97.

Rodriguez, Jose David. "The Parable of the Affirmative Action Employer," *Apuntes* Vol. 15, No. 5 (1988): 418–424.

Rodríguez, Néstor P. "The Social Construction of the US-Mexico Border," in *Immigrants Out! The New Nativism and the Anti-Immigrant Impulse in the United States*, ed. Juan F. Perea, (New York: New York University Press, 1997): 223–243.

Rogers, Anthony FSC. "Towards Globalising Solidarity Through Faith Encounters In Asia," in *The Migrant Family in Asia: Reaching Out and Touching Them*, ed. Anthony Rogers, FSC (Manila: Office for Human Development, 2007): 68–71.

Ruiz, Jean Pierre. "The Bible and People on the Move: Another Look at Matthew's Parable of the Day Laborers," *New Theology Review* Vol. 20, No. 3 (August 2007): 15–23.

Salzmann, Todd and Michael Lawler. "Catholic Sexual Ethics: Complementarity and the Truly Human," *Theological Studies* Vol. 67, No. 3 (September 2006): 625–652.

Sanks, T. Howland. "Globalization and the Church's Social Mission," *Theological Studies* Vol. 60, No. 4 (December 1999): 625–651.

Schneiders, Sandra. "The Study of Christian Spirituality," *Christian Spirituality Bulletin* Vol. 1, No. 1 (1998): 3–12.

Schotsmans, Paul. "Ethnocentricity and Racism: Does Christianity have a Share in the Responsibility," in *Migrants and Refugees*, ed. Dietmar Mieth and Lisa Sowle Cahill, Concilium 1993/4 (London: SCM Press): 87–94.

Schreiter, Robert. "Globalization, Postmodernity and the New Catholicity," in *For All People: Global Theologies in Contexts*, ed. Else Marie Wiberg Pedersen, Holger Law and Peter Lodberg (Grand Rapids, MI: Eerdmans, 2002): 13–31.

——."Catholicity as Framework for Addressing Migration," in *Migration in a Global World*, ed. Solange Lefebvre and Luis Carlos Susin, Concilium 2008/5 (London: SCM Press): 32–46.

Sciorra, Joseph. "We Go Where the Italians Live: Religious Processions as Ethnic and Territorial Markers in a Multi-Ethnic Brooklyn Neighborhood," in *Gods of the City: Religion and the American Urban Landscape*, ed. Robert Orsi (Bloomington, IN: Indiana University Press, 1999): 310–339.

Scullion, Dianne. "Gender Perspectives on Child Trafficking: A Case Study of Child Domestic Workers," in *Gender and Migration in 21st Century Europe*, ed. Helen Stalford, Samantha Currie and Samantha Velucci (Surrey: Ashgate, 2009): 45–60.

Sheldrake, Philip. "Christian Spirituality as a Way of Living Publicly: A Dialectic of the Mystical and Prophetic," *Spiritus: A Journal of Christian Spirituality* Vol. 3, No. 1 (2003): 19–37.

Sigler, Danielle Brune. "Daddy Grace: An Immigrant's Story," in *Immigrant Faiths: Transforming Religious Life in America*, ed. Karen Leonard et al. (Lanham, MD: Altamira Press, 2005): 67–78.

Sim, Amy. "Introduction: Women, Mobilities, Immobilities and Empowerment," *Asian and Pacific Migration Journal* Vol. 18, No.1 (2009): 1–15.

——. "Women Versus the State: Organizing Resistance and Contesting Exploitation in Indonesian Labor Migration to Hong Kong," *Asian and Pacific Migration Journal* Vol. 18, No.1 (2009): 47–75.

Sorensen, Ninna Nyberg and Luis Guarnizo. "Transnational Family Life Across the Atlantic: The Experience of Colombian and Dominican Migrants in Europe," in *Living Across Worlds: Diaspora, Development and Transnational Engagement*, ed. Ninna Nyberg Sorensen (Geneva: IOM, 2008): 151–176.

Spencer, Aida Besancon. "God the Stranger: An Intercultural Hispanic American Perspective" in *The Global God: Multicultural and Evangelical Views of God*, ed. Aida B. Spencer and William David Spencer (Grand Rapids, Michigan: Bridge Point Books, 1998): 89–103.

——. "Being a Stranger in a Time of Xenophobia," *Theology Today* Vol. 54 (April 1997–January 1998): 464–469.

Ströher, Rev. Marga Janete. "People Are Made To Shine – Not To Suffer," in World Council of Churches, *The Prophetic Mission of Churches in Response to Forced Displacement of Peoples*, Report of a Global Ecumenical Consultation, Addis Ababa, November 6–11, 1995 (Geneva: World Council of Churches, 1996): 44–52.

Sullivan, Kathleen. "St. Mary's Catholic Church: Celebrating Domestic Religion," in *Religion and the New Immigrants: Continuities and Adaptations in Immigrant Congregations*, ed. Helen Rose Ebaugh and Janet Saltman Chafetz (Walnut Creek, CA: Altamira Press, 2000): 125–140.

——. "St. Catherine's Catholic Church: One Church, Parallel Congregations," in *Religion and the New Immigrants: Continuities and Adaptations in Immigrant Congregations*, ed. Helen Rose Ebaugh and Janet Saltman Chafetz (Walnut Creek, CA: Altamira Press, 2000): 255–289.

Suzuki, Nobue. "Gendered Surveillance and Sexual Violence in Filipino Premigration Experiences to Japan," in *Gender Politics in the Asia Pacific Region*, ed. Brenda S. Yeoh, P. Teo and S. Huang (London and New York: Routledge, 2002): 99–116.

Tanaka, Kei. "Japanese Picture Marriage and the Image of Immigrant Women in Early Twentieth-century California," *The Japanese Journal of American Studies* No. 15 (2004): 115–138.

Tellez, Eliseo Jr. "An Overview of Filipino Migrant Workers in Hong Kong," in Christian Conference of Asia, *Serving One Another: The Report of the Consultation on the Mission and Ministry to Filipino Migrant Workers in Hong Kong*, April 28–May 1, 1991 Kowloon, Hong Kong (Kowloon, H.K.: CCA Urban Rural Mission, 1991): 75–83.

Tibe-Bonifacio, Glenda and Vivienne SM.Angeles. "Building Communities through Faith: Filipino Catholics in Philadelphia and Alberta," in *Gender, Religion and Migration: Pathways to Integration*, ed. Glenda Tibe Bonifacio and Vivienne SM. Angeles (Lanham, MD: Lexington Books, 2010): 257–273.

Tomasi, Silvano. "The World-wide Context of Migration: The Example of Asia," in *Migrants and Refugees*, ed. Norbert Greinacher, Concilium 1993/4 (London: SCM Press): 3–11.

——. "The Prophetic Mission of the Churches: Theological Perspectives," in *The Prophetic Mission of the Churches in Response to Forced Displacement of Peoples*, Report of a Global Ecumenical Consultation, Addis Ababa, November 6–11, 1995 (Geneva: World Council of Churches, 1996): 36–43.

——. "Migration and Catholicism in a Global Context," in *Migration in a Global World*, ed. Solange Lefevbre and Luiz Carlos Susin, Concilium 2008/5 (London: SCM Press): 13–21.

——. "Human Rights as a Framework for Advocacy on Behalf of the Displaced: The Approach of the Catholic Church," in *Driven from Home: Protecting the Rights of Forced Migrants*, ed. David Hollenbach, S.J. (Washington, D.C.: Georgetown University Press, 2010): 55–69.

Tweed, Thomas. "Identity and Authority at a Cuban Shrine in Miami: *Santería*, Catholicism, and Struggles for Religious Identity," *Journal of Hispanic/Latino Theology* Vol. 4, No. 1 (1996): 27–48.

Tyner, James. "The Web-Based Recruitment of Female Foreign Domestic Workers in Asia," *Singapore Journal of Tropical Geography* Vol. 20, No. 2 (1999): 193–209.

Uteng, Tanu Priya. "Gendered Mobility: A Case Study of Non-Western Immigrant Women in Norway," in *Ethics of Mobilities*, ed. Sigurd Bergmann and Tore Sager (Hampshire: Ashgate, 2008): 73–101.

Valerio, Rosanna Luz F. "Pagtitimpi at Panggigigil: Sex and the Migrant Woman," in *Coming Home: Women, Migration and Reintegration*, ed. Estrella Dizon-Anōnuevo and Augustus T. Anōnuevo (Quezon City, Philippines: Balikbayani Foundation and the ATIKHA Overseas Workers and Communities Initiative, Inc., 2002): 60–69.

Valtonen, Kathleen. "East Meets North: The Finnish-Vietnamese Community," *Asian and Pacific Migration Review* Vol. 5, No. 4 (1996): 471–489.

van Tubergen, Frank. "Religious Affiliation and Attendance Among Immigrants in Eight Western Countries: Individual and Contextual Effects," *Journal for the Scientific Study of Religion* Vol. 45, No. 1 (2006): 1–22.

Villalba, May-an. "Migrant Workers Challenge Globalization," *In God's Image* Vol. 19, No. 1 (2000): 30–34.

Walligo, John Mary. "A Call for Prophetic Action," in *Catholic Theological Ethics in the World Church: The Plenary Papers from the First Cross-cultural Conference on Catholic Theological Ethics*, ed. James F. Keenan, S.J. (New York: Continuum, 2007): 253–261.

Wellmeier, Nancy J. "Santa Eulalia's People in Exile: Maya Religion, Culture and Identity in Los Angeles," in *Gatherings in Diaspora: Religious Communities and the New Immigration*, ed. R. Stephen Warner and Judith Wittner (Philadelphia, PA: Temple University Press, 1998): 97–122.

Wilfred, Felix. "Towards a Better Understanding of Asian Theology," *Vidyajyoti Journal of Theological Reflection* Vol. 62, No. 12 (1998): 890–915.

Yang, Fenggang. "Chinese Gospel Church: The Sinization of Christianity," in *Religion and the New Immigrants: Continuities and Adaptations in Immigrant Congregations*, ed. Helen Rose Ebaugh and Janet Chafetz (Walnut Creek, CA: Altamira Press, 2000): 89–107.

—— and Helen Rose Ebaugh. "Religion and Ethnicity Among New Immigrants: The Impact of Majority/Minority Status in Home and Host Countries," *Journal for the Scientific Study of Religion* Vol. 40, No. 3 (2001): 367–378.

——. "Transformations in New Immigrant Religions and Their Global Implications," *American Sociological Review* Vol. 66, No. 2 (April 2001): 269–288.

Yang, Jenny. "A Christian Perspective on Immigrant Integration," *The Review of Faith and International Affairs* Vol. 9, No. 1 (Spring 2011): 77–83.

Yeoh, Brenda S.A., Elspeth Graham and Paul J. Boyle. "Migrations and Family Relations in the Asia-Pacific Region," *Asian and Pacific Migration Journal* Vol. 11, No. 1 (2002): 1–11.

Youngs, Gillian. "Breaking patriarchal bonds: Demythologizing the public/private," in *Gender and Global Structuring: Sightings, Sites, and Resistances*, ed. Marianne H. Marchand and Anne Sisson Runyan (London: Routledge, 2003): 44–58.

Yun Chai, Alice. "Women's history in public: 'picture brides' of Hawaii," *Women's Studies Quarterly* Vol. 16, Nos. 1–2 (Spring-Summer 1988): 51 62.

Zappone, Katherine E. "Women's 'Special Nature': A Different Horizon for Theological Anthropology" in *The Special Nature of Women?*, ed. Anne Carr and Elisabeth Schüssler Fiorenza, Concilium 1991/6 (London: SCM Press): 87–97.

"Case Studies: Migrant Workers and the Fishermen's Service Center, Presbyterian Church of Taiwan," in Christian Conference of Asia, *Uprooted People in Asia* (Hong Kong: CCA, 1995): 131–134.

ARTICLES IN NEWSPAPER, MAGAZINE, INTERNET AND UNPUBLISHED PAPERS AND DISSERTATIONS

Adam, David. "50M Environmental Refugees by the End of Decade, UN Warns," <http://www.guardian.co.uk/environment/2005/oct/12/naturaldisasters.climatechange1> accessed January 24, 2013.

Amnesty International. "Refugee Women in Chad Face High Levels of Rape Despite UN Presence," <http://www.unhcr.org/refworld/docid/4ac48301le.html> accessed August 30, 2012.

Angeles, Vivienne SM. " "From Catholic to Muslim: Changing Perceptions of Gender Roles in the Balik-Islam Movement in the Philippines." Paper presented at the European Southeast Asian Studies Conference (EUROSEAS), L'Orientale, University of Naples, Italy, September 12, 2007.

Aning, Jerome. "Filipino Woman Runs for Seat in South Korean Parliament," <http://globalnation.inquirer.net/31289/filipino-woman-runs-for-seat-on-south-korean-parliament> accessed August 1, 2012.

——. "Pinoys, Asians Protest Low HK Wage for Maids," <http://services.inquirer.net/print/print.php?article_id=20090907-223983> accessed June 16, 2012.

Archibold, Randal C. "Arizona Enacts Stringent Law on Immigration," <http://www.nytimes.com/2010/04/24/us/politics/24immig.html> accessed July 22, 2012.

"Asian and Pacific U.S. Catholics Will Celebrate Heritage, Tenth Anniversary of Bishops' Pastoral Statement *Harmony in Faith*" <http://www.usccb.org/comm/archives/2011/11-090.shtml> accessed August 11, 2012.

Associated Press. "Immigrant Beaten to Death in Pennsylvania," <http://www.msnbc.msn.com/id/25739051/> accessed July 6, 2012.

"Atin-Atin Lamang," *TNT Hong Kong* Vol. 1, No. 3: 23.

Burr, Thomas. "Utah's Wester Attends White House Immigration Meeting," <http://www.sltrib.com/csp/cms/sites/sltrib/pages/printerfriendly.csp?id=51658822> accessed May 27, 2011.

Cahill, Petra. "From Congo to New York: A Refugee's Story of Redemption," <http://www.msnbc.msn.com/id/43382766/ns/us_news-life> accessed June 19, 2011.

Canlas, Jomar. "Riyadh Nabs 14 OFWs for Practicing Religion," *The Manila Times* (October 7, 2010): 3.

Capdevilla, Gustavo. "IOM Report: Filipinas, Russians Trafficked for US Military Bases in Korea," *OFW Journalism Consortium Eleventh News Packet* (November 13, 2002): 15.

Caruso, Julia. "Immigration Battle Looms on the Horizon," <http://immigrationworksusa.org/uploaded/file/10-10_National_Journal_-_Immigration_battle_looms_on_the_horizon.pdf> accessed May 26, 2011.

Castles, Stephen. *The Myth of the Controllability of Difference: Labour Migration, Transnational Communities and State Strategies in East Asia.* See <http://www.unesco.org/most/apmrcast.htm> accessed June 16, 2012.

Cerojano, Teresa. "Asia Women's Jobs Vulnerable Despite Recovery," <http://services.inquirer.net/print/print.php?article_id=20110429–333633> accessed April 30, 2011.

Chia, Edmund. "Dialogue with Religions of Asia: Challenges from Within," <http://www.sedos.org/english/within_chia.html> accessed May 24, 2011.

Cowell, Alan and Elisabetta Povoledo. "UN Urges Ships to Help Migrants in Mediterranean," <http://www.nytimes.com/2011/05/10/world/africa/10migrants.html?_r=0> accessed November 18, 2012.

Cummins, John S. *From Alien to American: Acceptance Through Citizenship* (1998) <http://old.usccb.org/comm/archives/1998/98-101a.shtml> accessed March 28, 2012.

Fandl, Kevin J. "Trading Mexicans: Immigration Reform and International Trade" (October 16, 2008) <http://ssrn.com/abstract=1285479> accessed April 3, 2012.

"Filipino Migrant Workers in Hong Kong," *Asian Migrant* Vol. 7, No. 1 (January-March 1994): 6–7.Goodwin, Liz. "Muslim Americans Still Find Acceptance Elusive in the Wake of Bin Laden's Death," <http://news.yahoo.com/s/yblog_thelookout/20110511/us_yblog_thelookout/muslim-americans-still-find-acceptance-elusive-in-the-wake-of-bin-ladens-death> accessed August 12, 2012.

Grant, David. "Deportations of Illegal Immigrants in 2012 Reach New US Record," <http://www.csmonitor.com/USA/2012/1224/Deportations-of-illegal-immigrants-in-2012-reach-new-US-record> accessed January 23, 2013.

Gromisch, Elizabeth Stannard. "Refugees and the Risk of Rape," <http://www.thewip.net/contributors/2009/07/refugees_and_the_risk_of_rape.html> accessed August 28, 2012.

Hawwa, Sithi. "Religious Conversion of Filipina Domestic Helpers in Hong Kong," *ISIM Newsletter* 4 (1999): 10.

Hornick, Ed. "Nebraska City's Controversial Immigration Rule Passes," <http://edition.cnn.com/2010/POLITICS/06/22/fremont. immigration.ballot/> accessed September 20, 2012.

Hsu, Spencer. "Border Deaths are Increasing,"<http://www.washington post.com/wp-dyn/content/article/2009/09/29/AR2009092903212. html> accessed August 20, 2012.

Hume, Tim. "Photographer Captures 'New Slaves' of the Gulf," <http:// edition.cnn.com/2011/11/11/world/meast/emirates-workers-art/ index.html> accessed July 3, 2012.

"Immigrants turn to the sea to enter US illegally," <http://www.cbsnews. com/2100-201_162-6807922.html> accessed September 21, 2012.Jones, Maggie. "Postville, Iowa Is Up for Grabs," <http://www.nytimes.com/ 2012/07/15/magazine/postville-iowa-is-up-for-grabs.html?pagewanted= all> accessed August 18, 2013.

Jordan, Pav. "Mexican Farmers See Death Sentence in NAFTA," <http://www.commondreams.org/headlines02/1228-07.htm> accessed January 24, 2013.

K. Susan. "More Gripes from Husbands of OFWs," <http://globalnation. inquirer.net/27225/more-gripes-from-husbands-of-ofws> accessed August 4, 2012.

——. "On OFW Family Problems: Readers Talk Back," <http:// globalnation.inquirer.net/27831/on-ofw-family-problems-readers-talk-back> accessed August 11, 2012.

——. "The Tragic Sagas of BSAs in Taiwan," <http://globalnation.inquirer. net/25033/the-tragic-sagas-of-bsas-in-taiwan> accessed February 5, 2012.

Kelly, Graham and John Hooper. "Grim Toll of African Refugee Mounts on Spanish Beaches," <http://www.guardian.co.uk/world/2008/jul/ 13/spain > accessed November 20, 2012.

Kelly, Joe and James Massola. "Government Reveals Rioting, Mass Breakout of Detainees," <http://www.theaustralian.com.au/news/ nation/government-reveals-rioting-mass-breakouts-of-detainees/ story-e6frg6nf-1226021185013> accessed July 21, 2012.

Kwon, Jin Sook. *Contemplating Connection: A Feminist Pastoral Theology of Connection for Korean Christian Immigrant Parent-Child Relationships*, Unpublished Ph.D dissertation, Claremont School of Theology, September 2011.

Lee, Simon and Fox Hu. "Hong Kong Maids Lose Final Appeal for Residence Rights," <http://www.bloomberg.com/news/2013-03-25/ hong-kong-court-rejects-residency-appeal-by-domestic-helper.html> accessed August 20, 2013.

Lichtarowicz, Ania. "Hunger Index Shows One Billion Without Enough Food," <http://www.bbc.co.uk/news/science-environment-11503845> accessed January 21, 2013.

Martin, Michelle. "Posada Draws Attention to Immigration Reform," <http://ncronline.org/news/immigration-and-church/posada-draws-attention-immigration-reform> accessed April 3, 2012.

"Maternity Benefits for Maids Opposed" *Philippine Daily Inquirer* (July 4, 1997): 3.Medina, Jennifer. "Arriving as Pregnant Tourists, Leaving with American Babies," <http://www.nytimes.com/2011/03/29/us/29babies.html> accessed June 30, 2012.

Monteiro, Rita. "Global Mom: Migrant Mom," <http://www.national catholicreporter.org/globalpers/gp050703.htm> accessed August 19, 2012.

Mulong, E. "Mothers Once Again," *TNT Hong Kong* Vol. 6, No. 4 (June–July 2000): 4–5.

——."When Children Become Parent Carers," *TNT Hong Kong* Vol. 7, No. 1 (February–March 2001): 9.

Nanko Fernandez, Carmen. "Preference for the Young," *Vital Theology* Vol. 4, No. 2–3 (April/May 2007): 13.

Parker, Ashley and Jonathan Martin. "Senate, 68 to 32, Passes Overhaul for Immigration," <http://www.nytimes.com/2013/06/28/us/politics/immigration-bill-clears-final-hurdle-to-senate-approval.html?pagewanted=all&_r=0> accessed August 18, 2013.

Pew Research Center's Forum on Religion and Public Life. "Faith on the Move: The Religious Affiliation of International Migrants," <http://www.pewforum.org/Geography/Religious-Migration-exec.aspx> accessed November 29, 2012.

Pisa, Nick. "Italy Declares State of Emergency over Influx of 5,000 Tunisian Immigrants," <http://www.telegraph.co.uk/news/worldnews/europe/italy/8321427/Italy-declares-state-of-emergency-over-influx-of-5000-Tunisian-immigrants.html> accessed July 23, 2012.

Preston, Julia. "Obama to Push Immigration Bill as One Priority," <http://www.nytimes.com/2009/04/09/us/politics/09immig.html> accessed August 26, 2012.

Ratha, Dilip, Sanket Mohapatra and Ani Silwal. "World Bank: Migration and Development Brief No. 10," <http://siteresources.worldbank.org/INTPROSPECTS/Resources/334934-1110315015165/Migration&DevelopmentBrief10.pdf > accessed January 9, 2013.

Reuters. "GAO Study Links Arizona Wildfires to Illegal Immigrants," <http://usnews.msnbc.msn.com/_news/2011/11/22/8955730-gao-study-links-arizona-wildfires-to-illegal-immigrants> accessed November 23, 2012.

Rimmer, Rev. Chad M. "Prospects for Ecumenism in the 21st Century: Towards an Ecumenical Theology of the Wilderness," <http://www.oikoumene.org/en/programmes/the-wcc-and-the-ecumenical-movement-in-the-21st-century/relationships-with-member-churches/60th-anniversary/contest/essay-towards-an-ecumenical-theology-of-the-wilderness.html> accessed November 28, 2012.

Ringen, Patricia. "Parenting Tips for Overseas Working Moms," <http://globalnation.inquirer.net/11589/parenting-tips-for-overseas-working-moms> accessed October 19, 2012.

Roderick, Daffyd. "Making the Poor Even Poorer," <http://www.time.com/time/magazine/article/0,9171,189810,00.html> accessed August 28, 2012.

Ruffins, Ebonne. "Rescuing Girls from Sex Slavery," <http://www.cnn.com/2010/LIVING/04/29/cnnheroes.koirala.nepal/index.html> accessed August 30, 2012.

Sahagun, Louis. "A Mother's Plight Revives the Sanctuary Movement," *Los Angeles Times* June 2, 2007, B2.

Spandl, Sister Stephanie. "One Family Under God: A Theological Reflection on Serving our Immigrant Brothers and Sisters as Christian Social Workers," <http://www.nacsw.org/Publications/Proceedings2008/SpandlSOne.pdf> accessed January 28, 2013.

"Special Report on Migration," *The Economist* (January 5, 2008): 3–16.

St. John, Warren. "The World Comes to Georgia, and an Old Church Adapts," <http://www.nytimes.com> accessed August 3, 2012.

The Evangelical Free Church of America. *A Stranger at Our Gates: A Christian Perspective on Immigration*, Resolution adopted at a General Conference, 1996 The Evangelical Free Church of America <http://www.gum.org/download/EvangelicalFree-GeneralConferenceonImmigration-1996.pdf> accessed December 5, 2012.

The Pew Forum on Religion and Public Life. "Public Remains Conflicted over Islam," <http://www.pewforum.org/Muslim/Public-Remains-Conflicted-Over-Islam.aspx> accessed August 14, 2012.

United for Foreign Domestic Workers' Rights. *Saya Migran: A Domestic Worker's Guide to Understanding and Asserting Our Rights* (Hong Kong: UFDWR, 2007). Available at <http://ufdwrs.blogspot.com.au/2009/06/saya-migran-comics.html> accessed August 3, 2012.

United Nations. *The Millennium Development Goals Report 2012* (New York, NY: United Nations, 2012).

United Nations Department of Economic and Social Affairs. "International Migrants by Age," *Population Facts* No. 2010/6 <http://www.un.org/esa/population/publications/popfacts/popfacts_2010-6.pdf> accessed July 23, 2012.

UNHCR. "Asylum Levels and Trends in Industrialized Countries, First Half 2012," <http://www.unhcr.org/507c000e9.html> accessed January 24, 2013.

USCCB. "A Resolution by the National Conference of Catholic Bishops," <http://www.usccb.org/mrs/reform.shtml> accessed October 26, 2012.

——. "Asian and Pacific U.S. Catholics Will Celebrate Heritage, Tenth Anniversary of Bishops' Pastoral Statement *Harmony in Faith*"<http://www.usccb.org/comm/archives/2011/11-090.shtml> accessed August 11, 2012.

———. *Popular Devotional Practices: Basic Questions and Answers* <http://www.nccbuscc.org/bishops/devprac.shtml> accessed September 9, 2012.

Uy, Jocelyn. "Quiapo Faithful Abroad can Hear Mass Online," <http://technology.inquirer.net/6205/quiapo-faithful-abroad-can-hear-mass-online> accessed November 18, 2012.

Uy, Veronica. "International Labor Organization: 40M Illegal Migrants Prop up Economies," <http://newsinfo.inquirer.net/topstories/topstories/view/20081027-168750/40M-illegal-migrants-prop-up-economies> accessed June 26, 2012.

Vuorinen, Pihla. "Family in Transition: Transnational Family Ties and Identity Negotiation" <http://www.erm.ee/pdf/pro15/pihla.pdf> accessed August 1, 2012.

Index